PETE ROSE: MY STORY

Books by Roger Kahn

JOE AND MARILYN *(1986)*

GOOD ENOUGH TO DREAM *(1985)*

THE SEVENTH GAME *(1982)*

BUT NOT TO KEEP *(1978)*

A SEASON IN THE SUN *(1977)*

HOW THE WEATHER WAS *(1973)*

THE BOYS OF SUMMER *(1972)*

THE BATTLE FOR MORNINGSIDE HEIGHTS *(1970)*

THE PASSIONATE PEOPLE *(1968)*

PETE ROSE: MY STORY

Pete Rose and Roger Kahn

Macmillan Publishing Company
New York
Collier Macmillan Publishers
London

Macmillan Publishing Company
866 Third Avenue, New York, NY 10022
Collier Macmillan Canada, Inc.

Library of Congress Cataloging-in-Publication Data
Rose, Pete, 1941–
    Pete Rose : my story / Pete Rose and Roger Kahn.
      p. cm.
    ISBN 0-02-560611-5
    1. Rose, Pete, 1941– . 2. Baseball players—United States—
Biography. 3. Cincinnati Reds (Baseball team) I. Kahn, Roger.
II. Title.
GV865.R65A3 1989   89-13166 CIP
796.357′092—dc20
[B]

Macmillan books are available at special discounts for bulk purchases
for sales promotions, premiums, fund-raising, or educational use.
For details, contact:

                    Special Sales Director
                    Macmillan Publishing Company
                    866 Third Avenue
                    New York, NY 10022

DESIGNED BY ERICH HOBBING

10 9 8 7 6 5 4 3 2 1

Printed in the United States of America

For Harry Francis Rose of Cincinnati,
and Gordon Jacques Kahn of Brooklyn,
who, had they met, might have talked a little baseball.

—PETE AND ROGER

Contents

An Editorial Word   ix

Author's Note   xi

A Word of Thanks   xiii

Preface   xv

1   A Hall-of-Fame Promise   1

2   To Reach the Unreachable Star   21

3   Beginnings   39

4   Boyhoods   55

5   Up from the Minors   85

6   A Rose Grows in Cincinnati   103

7   The Thrill of the (Plastic) Grass   139

8   No Longer a Red   179

9   Almost a Centerfold   209

10   The Gambler   231

11   Fathers and Sons   271

Index   291

Photo Credits   299

An Editorial Word

I'm grateful for the cooperation given to me by Pete Rose, his business and professional associates.

Pete spoke to me with absolute candor on a great variety of subjects, many extremely personal. With Pete's approval, Reuven J. Katz made available to me documents relating to many of the most intimate aspects of the ballplayer's life.

In turn, I have agreed to consider carefully Pete's and Mr. Katz's views on what material was appropriate for this book.

Final editorial authority remained with me.

—ROGER KAHN

Author's Note

Research for this book began in 1986. No one anticipated then the events of spring and summer 1989, disorder, grief and cataclysm.

Macmillan has provided me, and indeed Pete Rose, with a bounty of editing judgment and support in the persons of William Rosen, the publisher; Rick Wolff, the senior editor; and my old friend Edward T. "Ned" Chase, one of the first editors who recognized, in the 1970s, that *The Boys of Summer* was likely to become what it indeed became in many opinions: *the* classic baseball book; *the* classic baseball best seller.

It was our collective decision not to tear this work apart when Rose was suspended from baseball. This book is a chronology of events, I would hope more than that as well, and the 1989 debacle is, in addition to everything else, a part of that chronology. In looking back, I see what could be read as foreshadowing.

What were the gamblers up to in the summer of 1869 when the peerless Red Stockings played a much-discussed and hotly rumored game against the Haymakers of Troy, New York? The contemporary account furnished by the *Cin-*

cinnati Gazette, available at certain libraries, is, as the historians like to say, "current as today."

William Staubitz, journalist and sheriff, provided vivid accounts of gambling in and around Cincinnati in more recent times, when Pete was growing up. Listening to Big Bill Staubitz I did not mean to hazard the lit'r'y art of foreshadowing. Let Hardy be Hardy. I meant to practice reporting. The reporting now seems, at least to me and my editorial allies, foreshadowing. That is, I believe, worthy of note.

I hope this book can be read as a history, as a life story. I could have thrown up an attention-grabbing first chapter but nobody thought it would be a good idea to begin a book, years in the making, with a *Playboy* interview, a *Sports Illustrated* cover story. If anyone had, they would have needed to find another writer.

On the other side, Rose and his advisors and I have agreed that I will not write a legal brief for the defense, an apologia. I know better than most that Pete, like myself, is no paragon. I believe, with all my heart, that he deserves better than he has gotten.

—ROGER KAHN
Croton-on-Hudson, N.Y.
September 1, 1989

A Word of Thanks

I should like to thank the following for assistance, advice or both:

George "Sparky" Anderson, Gerald Astor, Andrew Attaway, Willard Bailey, Buddy Bell, Sheldon "Chief" Bender, Bill Bergesch, Eddie Biles, Damaso Blanco, Vida Blue, Congressman Sherwood Boehlert, Steve Boros, Ralph Boyle, Jon Braude, Marty Brennaman, Dave Bristol, Jeanine Bucek, Don Buford, Fran Carter, Ron Cey, Peter Clark, Davey Concepcion, Congressman Silvio O. Conte, Roger Craig, Kal Daniels, Eric Davis, Bill Deane, George Diaz, Dock Ellis, John Erardi, Edward Falcone, John Felske, Jim Ferguson, Steve Garvey, Bill Giles, Barry Golson, Alan Green, Ralph Griesser, Danny Gumz, Joe Gumz, Phyllis Halliday, Pat Harmon, Walt Harmon, Paul Heacock, Don Heffner, Tommy Helms, Orel Hershiser, Dorrel "Whitey" Herzog, Charles Hickey, Greg Hoard, Erich Hobbing, Terry Kennedy, Hal Lanier, Barry Larkin, Earl Lawson, Bill Lee, Camillo Lo Giudice, Davey Lopes, Bill McDonald, Candy Maldonado, Gene Michael, Zoe Moffitt, Jim Murray, LaVerne Rose Noeth, Paul "Pappy" Nohr, Joe Nuxhall, Ron Oester, The Honorable Thomas P. "Tip" O'Neill, Jr., Dave Parker, Gabe Paul, Tony Perez, Gaylord Perry, Vada Pinson,

Lora Porter, Frank Robinson, George Rohrer, Carol Rose, David Rose, Jackie Rose, Pete Rose, Jr., Al Rosen, Alan Roth, Chris Sabo, Carl Scheele, Mike Schmidt, Caryl Rose Schnebelt, Marge Schott, Vin Scully, Phil Seghi, Art Shamsky, Dick Sisler, Jayson Stark, William "Big Bill" Staubitz, Samantha Stevenson, Chuck Tanner, Bob Trumpy, Gary Van Allen, Johnny Vander Meer, Peter Wessley, Joel Youngblood, Jim Zarchin.

Mike Shannon, editor of *Spitball*, a magazine devoted to baseball fiction and poetry, abandoned his muses for a time and contributed by working, interviewing, and researching. Susan Kilgour drew out distaff subjects, including LaVerne Rose Noeth, and typed the manuscript. If I've overlooked anyone, my apologies. Although all these people contributed, responsibility for any errors is my own.

Gerard F. McCauley, my literary agent, provided invaluable support through what became a marathon run, with one helluva bell-lap sprint at the end.

Katharine Colt Johnson, my bride, brought insights from her professional discipline, psychology, and cherished gifts of patience, kindness, and love.

—R.K.

Preface

The genesis of this book was a telephone call from Nancy Sarnoff many summers ago, asking if I would like to work on a book with her client, Pete Rose. Ms. Sarnoff is a merchandising person, suitably attractive and persuasive, but quite beyond her siren sounds, the idea of bunking in with the ballplayer who had created the most remarkable career of his era proved irresistible. And not only to myself.

I probed a bit to see what I might do, and soon my phone began ringing once again. This time the callers were other writers who had heard about the project through the wind tunnels of gossip that stir both baseball and publishing. These writers to the man said that if I didn't want to work with Rose, they most certainly did, and if I declined, would I nudge the adventure their way. Among the callers were friends, acquaintances, and strangers, journalists, novelists, and a college English professor. All were polite, poised, but slightly breathless. Such is one touch of the impact of Peter Edward Rose.

We knew each other a bit personally and more by reputation. Pete was a wonder of sport, indeed American society, grand master of bat and ball, good cheer, and discipline and competitive fire. He was also pretty close to a genius at

charming the armies of the press. He was long since the hero
of a hundred magazine articles and just about the perfect
television talk-show guest. Indeed, after Rose surpassed Ty
Cobb's record for hits over a career, the entire "Donahue"
show moved from its home base to Cincinnati just to have a
lively hour with Pete. He is also important enough so that
after the notorious 1988 umpire-bumping incident, he drew
an editorial of reproach from that guardian of fair play and
evenhanded policies, *The New York Times.* ("Mr. Rose has
committed a serious offense. As a virtual living legend of
baseball, he has a special duty to behave responsibly.") Further, when he was himself suspended from organized baseball, his exit press conference was televised, live, on coast-to-
coast television.

Now here is a curious thing. The Virtual Living Legend is
quick and funny and insightful, but his preferred style is to
work in short bursts and within the frame of a modest vocab-
ulary. If he put his mind to it, I believe he could master
polysyllables with dispatch, but Rose has spent his working
life on fields where, appropriately and traditionally, talk is
direct. Caught on the roller coaster of a pennant race, year
after year, baseball men generally save abstractions and
meditation for their retirement years.

"A book," a wonderful essayist once wrote, "ought to have
some excuse for being written. Too often this is kept a mys-
tery from the reader." Were Rose and I going to deliver a
work that would simply be a continuation of Rose's earlier
collaborations, diaries, and the like, which were fine as far as
they went but did not really try to go very far? Or would we
strive in some way we did not yet understand to set down the
bar of music that is the man?

We agreed to try the second, and more difficult, course,
and we talked many times about how to proceed. "You're the
writer," Pete would say, and of course I was. Pete was the
ballplayer, the talker, the manager, the humorist, the adven-

turer, cracking huge line drives at the age of forty-five, bashing fastballs that made younger men flinch.

"Then why don't we do it as it is?" I said. "You'll talk some and we'll set that down. I'll do my research, write some, and we'll set that down as well. Combine the two and we'll have, I hope, a real book."

"Real book?" Pete said.

I began to explain and what I said was fine with Pete. He likes matters finalized, decisions. He understood what I was suggesting and then said, " 'Scuse me, Rog. I gotta go hit."

That, then, is what we have done. Rose speaks with candor about his wondrous life in baseball and equally so about more personal matters, ranging from a sad, strained divorce to a tremendously publicized paternity suit to his recent suspension from the game he loves.

Everything of value Pete Rose said appears on the following pages as Pete Rose said it. The voice you hear is his; the emotions, the words, the tone. But we have not limited ourselves to tape-recording conversations.

Others interplay prominently in his life: his brother, his teammates, his rivals, his mother, and Rose's personal hero, his late father. One also wants a sense of Rose's place, Cincinnati, the site of the first professional baseball team, and a city with an extraordinary history. The history helped shape the boyhood that made the man. To interweave these elements I use another voice, my own.

Thus the two of us contribute, without my having to put facts or words into Rose's gullet and without Rose having to pretend that he has suddenly become interviewer, researcher, and author, all at once, all by himself. He appears, we hope, not as a mythic figure, or a public-relations creation, but as he really is, both human and heroic.

Although this is somewhat different from the standard form of celebrity books, neither Pete nor I think that this is startling. What we offer is what we agreed to offer long ago, after Nancy Sarnoff and I talked and all those other writers began calling me.

An honest collaboration.

ROGER KAHN

He's right. He's the writer. But I don't think he could do much with a major league fastball on the fists.

PETE ROSE

PETE ROSE: MY STORY

1

A Hall-of-Fame Promise

CINCINNATI, 1986

"Hey, Rog. I'll never lie to you."

The ballplayer had made his pronouncement. He would talk about the sweet times, that incredible run of base hits and headfirst slides, rocketing line drives and hard-eyed one-line jokes, that reach back generations to his youth, in what now seems to have been the middle ages of baseball. And he would talk about harder times, divorce, and being banished from his native town, and even, since he insists on honesty, about a paternity suit that fell like shrapnel in the middle stages of his glorious career. And of course, he would talk about his suspension from the game, but that would come much later.

Sportswriters call his face craggy. In happier times, a few, grappling toward poetry (and characteristically finding only hyperbole) suggest that its likeness should be blasted into Mount Rushmore, there to gaze stonily, alongside presidents,

1

above the heads and baseball caps of tourists. Washington, Jefferson, and Rose.

"Hey, Pete, I'll never lie to you."

He nodded, but only slightly, either unimpressed by an advertisement for myself or unwilling to give away a smile. We were discussing his own integrity, not mine. The sportswriters talk about his openness and it is true that he has been answering almost all their questions, with decent candor, day after day, game after game, for more than a quarter of a century, from Kennedy through Bush. Decent candor, but not suicidal. He is neither a simple nor a one-dimensional man.

"Actually," he said, "I only read two books in my whole life and that includes *The Official Pete Rose Scrapbook.* That's not a book—it's a bunch of pictures. I done the captions." Now a smile turned the craggy face into Huckleberry Finn. "I want you to know the truth while we're working here together. I've written more damn books than I've read." (The final score seems to be about 14–2.)

"Pete," I said, "you're lying."

He blinked. His broad mouth went thin-lipped and the corners turned down in the suggestion of a pugnacious sneer. But he said nothing. He loves to talk, but understands the impacts of silence.

"You graduated from high school," I said, picking up my thread.

"Took me five years."

"Yes, but you graduated, Western Hills High, you say. So you *must* have read more than two books."

He stood up behind the desk in his manager's office, which is walled with pale green cement block. The sneer gave way to one of his trademark looks: a boyish, radiant, dancing grin. "Uh-uh. Not books. I got by high school reading *chapters.*"

Now Pete Rose and I laughed together as he said without smugness, "You see. I'll always tell you the truth."

                    *   *   *

He is, quite properly, a hero of these American times, a hero without pretensions, pomposity, or artifice, but one who is sure of his place and the worth of his accomplishments. He lives in a great rambling contemporary house in Indian Hill, a confidently prosperous suburb on the east side of Cincinnati, Ohio, that is a world away from the river town on the west side where he grew up in more settled times. The house stands among five acres and walking the grounds you find a pool and a handsome stone stable where Pete Rose, the old blue-collar kid, the long-ago river rat, keeps horses. They are quarter horses, four in all, taut and muscled, out of the American Southwest. They are said to sprint a quarter-mile more swiftly than any other breed. For fun, he sometimes rides one of his animals bareback, at appalling speed, over the rolling land he has worked so hard to come by.

He is fascinated by horses and by their successors, motor cars. His favorite vehicle, at least for the time being, is a red-and-gold beast, personally designed for him by Mario Andretti, the great race driver, on the chassis of a growling Porsche. He loves games, he likes the taste of risk, and one day he began to let the car out flat on an empty stretch of road. The acceleration is almost piercing, throwing you back in your seat, the way a jet fighter buffets you on takeoff. And then the sight of the countryside flashing by, faster, ever faster, creating flashes of color, excitement, and a touch of fear. When he performed this superstart, he watched the road but I could tell, pressed backward as I was, that I was drawing an occasional glance. Ol' Pete was casing me for panic.

But I like fast cars and even auto racing and he slowed at length, perhaps dismayed or perhaps with a certain masked approval.

"I know you don't drink," I said, answering an unasked question, "and I know you have major league reflexes, so I wasn't particularly alarmed."

"Plus," Rose said, "I maintain my cars the way they're supposed to be maintained, so every part works like it should."

We wound among upland meadows, the car clinging to the blacktop Ohio road, Rose driving with great concentration and an economy of motion, no flailing, no waggling out of lane. "How fast can this beast go?" I asked.

"Not with these tires," Rose said, "but with racing tires, it'll do something like 220."

"That must be handy in downtown Cincinnati."

The easy sarcasm struck him as criticism. He likes needling, the back-and-forth banter of ballplayers that surely must be as old as baseball. But criticism, particularly of his life-style, is something else. "Hey, Rog," he said, as he whipped the gold-red Porsche beside a thin green clutch of pin oaks. "It's *my* money."

Traveling with him, running with him, riding with him, you come away feeling you have just gone to the most rousing summer camp ever invented. Take his tennis game, for example, a sport he plays with great joy and enthusiasm, without threatening the memory of Bill Tilden. He runs and flails and chatters away in sheer happiness at competition. He *works* at baseball. He *plays* tennis. There is none of the heavy cathedral silence of professional tennis on a court with Rose, no barking at line calls, no tantrums. A weak second serve floats up in a doubles match and Pete cries at the opposing netman, "Comin' right at ya nose."

The netman, who happened to be myself, managed to put away Pete's smash with a reflex volley. "Damn," Rose said, "how come you didn't hit like that in the first set, when you were playing on my side?" A hard look, then a laugh. We're having *fun*.

Another soft shot. Rose rushes up toward net, shouting,

almost laughing one more time: "I got me an angle." He settles the point with a hard, slanting forehand, and nods and shakes a fist and readies himself to play (and talk) some more.

These passions, fast cars, horses, tennis, and even gin rummy, are similar, but secondary to, the passion of his life, which is, of course, professional baseball. It is baseball, not the others, that has brought him millions of dollars, his house, his car, his fame. It is in baseball that he has been able to display his particular blend of gifts, coordination, intelligence, courage, before an enormous and generally adoring public.

Rose bargains his baseball contracts hard. Sheldon "Chief" Bender, an experienced hand in the Cincinnati Reds' front office, remembers that Rose was "always a hard [man to] sign. It would be one thing after another," Bender said, "even before free agency began and sometimes it could drive you a little nuts, but once he signed, and of course he always did, he put all the contract stuff behind him and he went to work. I never knew any ballplayer, and I go back a ways, who worked harder with what he had than Pete Rose."

He bargained hard and he worked hard, by which I mean he practiced for hours, clutching ground balls before games, simulating game situations during batting practice, and once in a while, when his hitting dissatisfied him, imposing extra batting practice on himself, after a game. Few ballplayers— now in these halcyon million-dollar-salary days, or even long ago when athletes were undersalaried glorified field hands— have ever done that. After a game you're tired. Aches run through your body like electric needles and, if you haven't hit well, you feel annoyed. You want to get away from the ballpark, the scene of your embarrassment, where you took the collar, 0-for-4, today. But Pete Rose would stay at the ballpark and fight through the twinges because, above all things, he didn't want to go 0-for-4 tomorrow.

He does not affect false modesty. One afternoon in the pale green office, he said, "I'm the best hitter you've ever known."

I blinked. I knew—and Pete knows I knew—Ted Williams and Stan Musial.

He stared through the blink. "And I play the hardest of anyone you've known. Who've you seen play the game as hard as me?" I thought, Jackie Robinson, for one. But I said nothing. Silence, one learns, can cut several ways.

"And I'm just about the best promotion man that's ever been in baseball." A final blink as I remembered Casey Stengel and all his glorious obfuscating soliloquies that captured generations of journalists and with them the Congress and most of the population of the United States.

And yet here is Pete Rose, chunky, strong, and indefatigable, with more base hits than Williams or Musial, more hustle than the Happy Hooker, and, during at least two episodes of tremendous drama and emotion, as good a friend as the American press has found since that anonymous character called Deep Throat crawled out of the plumbing and began to tattle on Watergate.

Rose grinned. I wondered if he wanted me to challenge his assertions, but before I spoke he said, mildly, "At least that's what I think."

Does Pete Rose, the ballplayer, really regard himself as the best batter, the hardest player, the finest promotion man major league baseball has seen in fifty years? The question is less formidable than it sounds. When he says such things he means them at the moment that he speaks. When he says such things he is also giving himself a pep talk, reinforcing his positive attitude, keeping his self-image up there on Rushmore, a sensible thing for a ballplayer to do. But after he contemplates a bit, if you want to debate, Rose isn't inclined to argue. *You* think Williams hit better, Robinson played as hard, Stengel promoted baseball with more genius.

All right, it's a democracy. Opinions are as free as South Dakota air. Pete's ego is healthy, but not overblown.

"Look, I got the hits," he said of his total of 4,256, "and when I was chasing Ty Cobb, I had to do a couple of press conferences every day and every writer will tell you I handled them okay, more than okay, and I'm going into the Hall of Fame. I know all that. I'd have to be dumber than I am *not* to know all that. So what am I gonna tell you, I got a little lucky and that's how come I hit in forty-four straight games and went 5-for-5 ten times and broke Cobb's record when I hit 4,192? It wouldn't make sense saying a career like that is just luck and you'd have to be dumber than *you* are to believe that it was.

"One thing that gets me sore is when I hear that somebody's said, the trouble with Pete Rose is that he's an egomaniac. Hell, I talk about my career, and why not? People have been asking me about my career since the days when John Kennedy was president, even before. What am I supposed to do, *not* talk about my career? If I shut up like that, the writers would say I wasn't an egomaniac. I was a clam."

He shook his head, momentarily frustrated. "Egomaniac! Has there ever been a better team player than me?"

A purist might call that an oxymoron: I'm not an egomaniac and I'm the best of all team players. But Rose has his own logic which runs a powerful course. He began as a second baseman and then, across the seasons, he agreed to switch to right field, left field, third base, and finally first base until he became the only athlete since the dawn of time to have played more than 500 major league games at five—count 'em; five it is—different positions. "When I agreed to leave left field, George Foster [who is black] took over," Rose says. "When I switched off first, Dan Driessen [also black] got the job. I tell you one of the few things I hate is racial prejudice— hate it!—so don't take me wrong when I say I done more for black employment than the NAACP."

Just sitting with him, surrounded by all that hyperactivity, leaves you breathless. His face changes, his mood shifts, and he can in one instant return to school days, twisting a towel into the shape of a saxophone and pretending to play a forgotten fifties rock song, and in the next moment grow stern and even careworn as he considers a pennant race, say 1987, that is turning sour for his Cincinnati Reds.

He is very quick, very incisive, and, under a shell of tempered iron, extremely kind.

"I'm not a sentimental person," says hard-nosed, hard-sliding Peter Edward Rose. "I don't spend all that much time thinking about the past, 'cept once in a while at special times I think about my dad, who died on December 9, 1970, and was the greatest influence on my life. And sometimes I even think he was the only influence in my life. Some kinda guy, my dad. We'll talk about him. But I'm pretty much a here-and-now fella. Always have been."

"I like to have fun. I have fun around baseball and I have fun playing tennis and I have fun with the writers, too, and maybe even make it fun for them." A good example cropped up after stories of Dwight Gooden's frightful struggles with the Tampa police led the young and possibly tormented pitcher into court and, subsequently, a felony conviction. Gooden had attended a basketball game with friends in Tampa and when police later stopped his Mercedes a dangerous, ugly brawl exploded.

"What about Gooden?" someone asked Rose in March of 1987.

"Bring him over here," Pete said. "I'll take him. He can play for me. I'll even chauffeur him to and from basketball games."

Certainly Rose works at baseball but what dominates and what he consciously works at maintaining is a sense of fun. One spring training eons ago, in his boyish crew-cut days,

Rose drew a walk and sprinted to first base, as would become his custom. Mickey Mantle and Whitey Ford, a pair of droll and laid-back Yankees, watched from the dugout. A burble of scorn broke through. "Hey," Ford yelled, "look at Charlie Hustle."

Thus was a nickname born. It has stayed with Rose for a quarter century. "I wouldn't say I mind it," Rose remarked. "I've sure gotten good mileage out of it, if you count up all those columns of ink. But it isn't exactly right. I want to get what I'm saying now precise. Hustle may be just a little downgrading, like I don't have a lot of skills, you know? I do have outstanding skills—who's had better hand-to-eye coordination?—and I got the most out of them, sure, but not so much with hustle as with enthusiasm. All these years, from the first pro game in Geneva, New York, in 1960 until today, I haven't lost one damn bit of enthusiasm for baseball. That's why I've been able to work so hard. So maybe we need a new nickname. What do you say? Eddie Enthusiasm. Probably never catch on like Charlie Hustle."

His face was gentle as he spoke but one never quite forgets that other aspect: challenging, almost combative. Elements of defiance color his life. He told a reporter, he actually said, in staid Germanic Cincinnati, Ohio, hometown to the Reds, to generations of conservative Republicans named Taft, and to the buttoned-down company that manufactures Ivory soap, that what he really liked, what he relished, were fast horses, fast life, and a young wife. "And I got all three."

The Reds let him go after the 1978 season—a year in which he batted safely in forty-four consecutive games—dispatching Cincinnati's native son to Philadelphia (where he would hit .331 in 1979 and lead the Phillies into the World Series in 1980 and 1983). As we shall see, the Reds' motives for this blockheaded move still stir ardent debates among the brauhauses in the Rhineland city. No one can be certain—the Reds' official story is that Rose and his attorney simply demanded too much money—but Pete with his quick tongue and street-smart instincts has a working theory.

"The divorce from my first wife, Karolyn, got a little rough. I told the writers, what else could I have said, that it was *all* my fault, 100 percent my fault. But I think—I can't be positive—the Reds management didn't like the divorce stuff in the papers. And that's the bottom line why they got rid of me."

"Musta been good to come back," I said.

"Was it good to come back?" Rose said. "And break Cobb's record? And have 'em name a street after me? Hell, I come back from a trip and I'm driving to the park and there it is, this huge green-and-white sign, Pete Rose Way. In my own hometown. A street named after me. Right near Riverfront. Did that feel good? Hey, damn right."

He has a nice, fast humor, often teasing, never self-mocking, sometimes caustic, never cruel. His latest employer, a chunky, driving, stocky woman born in 1928, one Marge Schott, is ardently in love with her Cincinnati Reds, but equally passionate about her massive hound, a Saint Bernard called Schottzie. (Without picking on the dog, which almost everyone else has done, I suggest a more suitable name would be Baskerville.) In a recent Cincinnati media guide, Mrs. Schott made sure that Schottzie was given both a photo—she put a Reds cap on the dog!—and a twelve-line profile, which read in part:

> Schottzie joined the Reds in December, 1984, when her mistress became general partner, and made an immediate impact at the press conference by sitting on the foot of Manager Pete Rose. . . .

Rose's relationship with the dog improved to tolerable, at least in public. Privately he complained, "I was over at Marge's house one day trying to explain why we needed more pitching, and how we might get it without busting our salary frame, and the dog comes over and puts its big head on my lap and starts drooling through these enormous teeth, onto my crotch. The feeling wasn't great."

Such comments discomfit Reuven J. Katz, Rose's longtime attorney, fan, and friend. Katz has always felt that getting along with the present Cincinnati management started by getting along with the Saint Bernard, even when it slavers. Lawyers think like that; often they are right. But one day, when Katz was away, Rose told me with great enthusiasm how he was going to buy a baby lion for Tyler Rose, his younger son, a rugged, stocky imp, then going on two.

"I was out to this place where they bred this lion cub and they had the cub's daddy chained to a tree. I went up to take a look. I got too close, 'cuz when the daddy stuck out his paw he knocked me backward fifteen feet. But won't that be great, having a lion cub for my kid to play with. I'm gonna call the cub Seibu because over in Japan, where I been a few times, they got a pro ball club called the Seibu Lions. A lion cub for my kid to play with up on Indian Hill. I didn't have no lion cub when I was growing up. My dad was just a bank teller with a big family. We couldn't afford one."

"How poor was your family?" I said.

"We weren't rich, but we weren't so poor my sisters had to be made in Japan. Ha-ha. Anyway this lion cub doesn't look like a cat. It's got real thick legs and it's kinda wobbly on them right now, but you can tell real quick this isn't no cat. It's a lion."

"Pete," I said, "what are you going to do with the lion when it grows up?"

"Oh," he said, "it can eat Marge's dog."

When I relayed this to Counsellor Katz—a mistake—during the fifth inning of a game that the Reds were playing badly, Katz winced. As long as Katz had to negotiate with Schott, he didn't want to do it against a background of even faint hostility. But Pete is Pete—he *likes* barbed jokes—and Marge is Marge. Indeed, after she purchased a controlling interest in the Reds on December 21, 1984, thus saving Cincinnati baseball from possible extinction, she said with candor and a certain wit of her own: "With Pete's mouth and my mouth, I don't know how we're going to handle all this."

Although a pennant eluded them both, the answer had to be passably well. The Reds that Rose and later Schott inherited were coming off successive last-place finishes and there was fairly serious talk of moving the team out of Cincinnati, home of the very first professional ball club on earth, to Louisville or New Orleans or Columbus. (Under Rose, the team finished second every season until 1989, the year of the Giamatti-Dowd debacle. Schott said little on the record, but twice during the Rose investigation she had to be hospitalized for stress-related ailments.)

Pete said once, you could look it up in the *Cincinnati Post* or the *Enquirer,* that he never intended to manage. He also said once, and you can look that up as well, that he would never be able to break Ty Cobb's revered record of 4,191 major league hits because he would not be able to play long enough under the demanding conditions of contemporary baseball.

"People like to ask me," Rose said, "if I was always planning to be a manager and do I model myself after one of the ten major league managers I played for, say, maybe Sparky Anderson? The answer to both questions is no; the only person I try to model myself after is my father. But what I did, what I've always done and I learned from my dad, is try to play the game as though you were managing. I study the pitchers and I study the pitching rotations. I don't believe

I'm all that good a hitter against a pitcher the first time I see him. I want to know what he throws. I need to study that. They can tell you Orel Hershiser has a fine curve, which he does, but I need to see the windup, the delivery, the spin, the actual break of the ball. And when does he like to throw the curve? First pitch? Will he throw it when he's behind in the count? What about his fastball and his slider? If you figure out all the combinations—the order of pitches, the different speeds, the location, all the rest—batting can get to sound very complicated, like you need a degree in statistics to be a hitter. If you did, I wouldn't be where I am. I was pretty good at arithmetic when I put my mind to it at Western Hills High, but that algebra! That fucking algebra. Would somebody mind telling me what algebra was supposed to be about?"

"English major, Pete. I majored in English. You're on your own."

He gave me a little grinning nod. "I also study the rotations of the pitchers and I always have. If we're playing the Houston Astros [when Nolan Ryan was still there in 1986], it helps me, and it helps my players who want to be helped, to know that Nolie goes against us Tuesday night. That helps even a full week in advance. Ol' Nolie. He's so old, he's just six years younger than me, but he still throws hard, throws good power stuff, which is amazing for a guy with all his years.

"He likes to throw that hard one near the letters, and when it closes with the plate the ball sails clear up and out of the damn strike zone. The pitch looks good coming in, you really think you see it, but the pitch turns out to be a ball. If you swing at it, just like a softball riser, you'll miss it or at best hit under it. Pop fly. You have to tell yourself in the batter's box this is Ol' Nolie Ryan throwing that hard sucker pitch. You have to keep that burning in your mind. Then you have the sense to lay off it.

"How does it help knowing on a Wednesday afternoon

that you hit against Ryan the following Tuesday night? It keeps a part of your mind going, keeps you fully aware. Baseball isn't like football, which I love, where they give you six days to prepare for your next game. You get one day, part of a day, really, and if it's a double-header and you're playing both ends, you have about twenty minutes. So what you have to do is keep a feel for a flow. Next few days may be the Dodgers, with Valenzuela and Hershiser, two very different pitchers, but just around the corner comes Houston, Ryan and Scott. Know where you are, like when you're driving a car, and know what's coming around the corner. If you let yourself, if you're not afraid to work your body, work your mind, you can always do more than one thing, concentrate on more than one thing at a time. Or so I believe.

"While we've been working on this book, you remember, damn right you remember, we played three hands of gin rummy while we were running the tape recorder and talking. I won all three hands, too, although I don't know if you'll let me get that into the book. What the hell's the title gonna be anyway?"

"Gin Rummy with the Rich and Famous. Keep talking, Pete."

"You might be an all right writer but you don't play gin in my league. Or baseball neither, I'd bet, if I was a betting man, which I am, but only within reason, not the rent money."

Pete continues: "Have some fun. Hey, a good title for the book would be *Having Fun,* right? No, wrong. It isn't right. You're not smiling. You should always be trying to have some fun and if you're not having fun, do something else, go somewhere else. They say you only live once, but listen to this, buddy, because I mean it:

"If you do it right, once is enough."

We were playing yet another hand of gin in the green

windowless office, the tape silently recording the setting
down of cards.

"What do you say, Rog? What's the name of this game?
Ginsy, Rog, and that's no drink. That's what I got in my hand.
Ha-ha.

"Maybe you didn't shuffle the cards real good."

"Enough with the damn cards," I said. "I have a question
for the book."

Rose waited.

"If you could tell every child who dreams of playing in the
major leagues a single thing that would help his dream come
true, what would that be?"

The swagger drained from Pete. "You're gonna laugh."

"No way."

"He won't laugh," Tommy Helms said.

"Okay," Rose said, "when you play the game, offense or
defense, always watch the ball."

"I'm not laughing, but some Little League coach might.
He'd say that's ridiculously simple."

"Well, then, maybe so is baseball," Rose said. "Because
most of the time you're doing one of two things. On defense
you're moving toward the ball. How the hell else are you
gonna catch it? On offense you're moving away from the ball.
You're not exactly looking to get tagged out. How are you
going to do either of these things worth a damn if you aren't
always watching the ball?"

"Not to mention hitting," I said.

"I didn't mention it," Rose said, "because I wasn't looking
to insult your intelligence."

Summer camp. The days are camping days with Rose. One
feels transported back to times when we were in our youth
and sinew and every sunrise carried the promise of adventure. But camp, stripped of the mists of memory, with senti-

mentality torn away, had days and nights of pain. So indeed does time with Rose.

He bought the tiny lion, Seibu, for his tow-headed little Tyler, but Seibu never got to devour Mrs. Schott's dog. The Reds made a brief trip—inconsequential in a divisional race the Astros would win going away—and Rose and his second wife, Carol, left Tyler and Seibu in the care of a young baby-sitter.

The sitter took Tyler off shopping and a neighbor's large dog—*not* Mrs. Schott's Schottzie—bounded onto the Roses' property, attracted perhaps by the soprano howls tawny, redolent Seibu uttered as he wobbled about his pen.

And then the neighbor's dog ate Rose's lion cub.

Jumped the cub, killed it with a snarl, and in the end left nothing but a tuft of tail.

"That really happened?" I said to Rose.

"It really happened," he said in a lifeless voice.

"What are you going to do?"

"What can I do? Carol and I took apart the pen. We just got rid of everything that might remind Tyler of his baby lion that got killed. That's all we can do. It happened a few days ago. The baby-sitter is still crying."

Two other poignant moments were rather closer to sport. On August 13, 1986, Rose went 5-for-5 against the San Francisco Giants. He cracked out four of the hits, including a double, typical whistling Rose line drives. One was a bloop, or as players say today, a flare. All right—5-for-5 at the age of forty-five. When Rose thunked his fifth hit into left-center field, Mrs. Al Rosen, wife of the president of the San Francisco Giants, stood up and cheered. That night's achievement seemed, at least to me and Rita Rosen, to define more than baseball. Rose was a man beating back time.

He was subdued in his office. A reporter said, "Would you happen to know, Pete, how many times you've gone 5-for-5?"

His voice, sometimes barking, sometimes boyish, sounded hoarse with weariness.

"That would be ten," Rose said.

"Uh, would you know about the National League record?"

"I got it now, if I'm not mistaken," Rose said. "The old record was nine. Belonged to Max Carey."

"Major league record?"

"Again, if I'm not mistaken, that would be Cobb." He was recovering. A touch of joviality brightened his face. "You guys remember Cobb," he said. "Supposed to have been a mean guy, but he got a lot of hits."

Greg Hoard, a lean, sandy-haired reporter for the *Enquirer*, usually does soft-voiced interviews. Now he burst forth with an ebullient cry of "Pete, what does this mean to you?"

The joviality vanished. Rose met Hoard's blue eyes. "A slightly larger stone on my grave," said the most enduring ballplayer of our time.

As one of the smallest cities in the major leagues (population: 385,409), Cincinnati guards its baseball pride with certain traditions. For as long as anyone can remember, the Reds have opened their season on an April Monday, one day before other National League teams begin, as a formal acknowledgement of baseball's roots. The Cincinnati Red Stockings of 1869 won fifty-seven games, tied one, and lost none at all as the country's first wholly professional team.

Another local custom was an occasional game called the Businessman's Special, which proceeded from the geography of the place. Cincinnati is a river town hard by the Ohio and, except at rush hours, you can traverse it in about ten minutes. The Businessman's Special started at 12:35 and after Riverfront Stadium was opened downtown on June 30, 1970, a man could leave his office at 12:15, take in a ball game, and usually walk back to work in less time than it takes to make a dinner date with a shy secretary.

Women's Liberation struck first in New York but swiftly swept into the provinces, including southern Ohio. The Businessman's Special was renamed the Luncheon Special in 1979, the better to attract female junior executives in the service of Procter & Gamble.

On Monday, August 18, 1986, in a Luncheon Special, the Reds defeated the last-place San Diego Padres, 5–2. There was no sense of triumph in beating the Padres, everyone was doing it, and their manager was waiting to be fired. And feminism had hardly packed the ballpark. The crowd, including yuppie females, numbered under 18,000, many preoccupied or hung over. They didn't make much noise.

"Well, our damn work day is over pretty early," Rose said. The last reporter had left. It was 3:05. "Watcha wanna do?"

"How about we go to an art museum?" I said.

"How about the track? There's a little place near here, Latonia Downs [now Turfway]. Pretty fair horses. You come with me, you sit in a box over the finish line. It's glassed in. Nobody bothers us. We read *The Racing Form* and get to watch the horses."

Off we hurtled in the red-and-gold rocket to a special Pete Rose parking slot. We jogged up a back stairway, into the glassed-in box, and Pete studied the *Form* as though it were Ron Darling. People kept bringing us sodas and iced teas.

Rose liked a gray horse that ran fifth. Then he liked a bay that won.

"Hey, Rog."

My call to attention.

"Peter."

"You know what I'd really like to do?" He was wearing sneakers and a warm-up suit over a T-shirt. "I'd like to come here every morning, first put on a necktie and bring binoculars, and be a breeder. I know horses. I'd *love* to be a breeder."

"Are you all right?" I was referring to money. I knew his income to the penny for ten years but I also knew that his well-publicized divorce and the ill-begotten, infamous paternity suit had been extremely expensive.

"I am all right," he said. The warm-up suit was the color of silver. Far below, in the lake at Latonia Downs, two swans split the water in white nobility. "Well, wait, you know it's a complicated thing being Pete Rose and I got a lawyer, an accountant, and a coupla agents. So I better correct that. I *think* I'm all right. At least Reuven Katz tells me that I am."

"So do it, Pete," I said. "You don't have to keep managing and traveling and pumping up young players. You've passed Cobb. That's enough. More than enough. You want to go breed horses, go breed horses. Breed one for me."

The granite street-smart look returned.

"Rog?"

"Yes."

"In order to go be a breeder of horses, you can't have money that you count. That's not enough. You get my drift, ol' buddy?"

"Not yet."

"Look," spoke Peter Edward Rose, "I already got money that you count. But to be a breeder of horses, you can't only have that. You gotta have money that you weigh."

2

To Reach
the Unreachable Star

CINCINNATI, 1987

Tyrus Raymond Cobb. The name rings with antique Roman grandeur and, perhaps, the hint of a bloody and sulphurous lord raging through Wales. (There is, in fact, a figure in Roman history named Tyrrhus, but he was a shepherd, not a warrior, in such ancient times that he seems about as mythic as he is real.)

By most accounts, the Tyrus Cobb of the twentieth century was a man so full of fury, so brimming with bile, that some describe him as psychotic. Perhaps so. Assuredly he was mean, vindictive, paranoid, and in later years consistently drunk.

Near the end of his life—he died on July 17, 1961—Cobb was riding in a car beside a prolific California writer named Al Stump, who had been engaged to set down an authorized biography.

"Have you got enough to finish?" Cobb asked.

"More than enough." (In fact the book, which Cobb approved, was somewhat bland, but Stump later composed a memoir written in blood.)

"Give 'em the word then," Ty Cobb told Al Stump. "I had to fight all my life to survive. They were all against me . . . tried every dirty trick to cut me down. But I beat the bastards and left them in the ditch."

By this time Cobb had reached the age of seventy-four. He was long since a Hall of Famer, secure at a summit of baseball history, and through tough contract bargaining and cold-eyed investing, he had amassed a personal fortune of $10 million. But Ty Cobb, that magnificent competitive ballplayer, would never, in this world, know a season of mellow mists.

Stories tumble down in a clattering slide of rock and metal. Before games Cobb was said to have sat in the dugout, sharpening his spikes with a file, where all the other teams could see. Unless you want to bleed, Cobb was saying, you'd better believe that the baselines belong to me. He once punched a roommate he found soaking in a tub. "Cobb," he announced, when quiet returned, "bathes first." He stepped in a patch of wet asphalt on the way to a ballpark, and responded by assaulting the workman who had been peacefully patching the road.

Arguments persisted whether Cobb was the greatest ballplayer of his time. Early in his major league career, which spanned twenty-four years, some preferred Pittsburgh's great-fisted shortstop, John Peter "Honus" Wagner, nicknamed the Flying Dutchman. Later Yankee legions gathered behind that mighty flagon on stilts, Babe Ruth. But on one point there is no serious argument. Tyrus Raymond Cobb was the roughest son of a bitch who ever played the game.

In the last years, as he traveled about seeking treatment for cancer, Cobb always carried a brown bag which, he told Stump, contained "a million dollars in negotiable securities."

All right. Don't leave home without security, particularly when you're feeling sick. But, as Cobb would say, you've got to watch the bastards. On top of the securities lay the Prussians' favorite pistol, a Luger, fully loaded.

Cobb's fury—some surely was innate—exploded after an August night in 1905 when his mother fired a shotgun and blew off his father's head. William Herschel Cobb of Royston, Georgia, was an editor, a state senator, and a scholar. He was also, he suspected, being cuckolded by his wife, Amanda Chitwood Cobb. He left the house one evening, by horse and buggy, then doubled back, hoping or fearing to catch his wife with a lover. In the dark Amanda noticed a figure climbing into her bedroom window. She was frightened; she didn't recognize her husband, or so the story is told. Mistaking William for an intruder, Amanda Cobb fired a shotgun and shot her husband dead.

Drunk or sober, Cobb himself never told this story in detail. He would mention, "My father had his head blown off by a member of my own family and I've never gotten over it." Then, without identifying his mother as the killer, he would move swiftly away from the particulars of that nightmare evening.

What Cobb did say—and Pete Rose says the same thing—was, "My father was a great man." Then Cobb would add in an oddly menacing way: "He was the only man who ever made me do his bidding."

Requiescat. Let the dead bury the dead. Ty Cobb hammered out 4,191 major league hits, a record that virtually everyone, including Peter Edward Rose, believed would last as long as baseball.

"Mr. Rose," a young reporter asked not long ago, "what do you think Ty Cobb would hit today?"

Cobb's lifetime batting average was .367. Rose thought briefly and said, "Oh, about .333."

"That's all?" the reporter said.

"That's all," Rose said, "but that's not bad considering that Cobb's been dead for twenty-five years."

"I don't know just when I first heard about Ty Cobb," Rose says. "I'm good at dates and numbers, things like that. My own first hit: April 4, 1963, a triple off Bob Friend at Crosley Field. Four thousand one hundred and ninety-two? Well, I guess you know that. If you didn't, we wouldn't be working together on this book, am I correct?

"Remembering when I first heard Cobb's name, it must have been from Dad. To be truthful, I don't recall just when. Probably I was little. Probably I didn't appreciate how important the man's name was. And not just probably, I guarantee this, you could bet money on it and win, I didn't have any idea how important the name Cobb would end up being in my life.

"Even before I got close to the record, way before I thought I'd ever be able to break it, I did hear quite a bit about the man. There used to be a broadcaster of the Reds games when I first came up, named Waite Hoyt. He came from Brooklyn, like you, Rog, but maybe he could play the game a little better. He pitched in the majors for twenty years.

"Waite was a great story-teller and an outstanding man. I know he had trouble with his drinking for a time. Then he joined Alcoholics Anonymous and he never drank again. In fact he became one of those people they have in A.A. who are always on call to help somebody else fighting the booze. Like if it was three in the morning and an alcoholic was fighting to stay clean and felt he needed a drink, right then, at three, he'd call Hoyt. And Waite would get dressed and go over and calm the other person and stay right with him until that urge to drink was beaten. So even aside from his ball playing and his broadcasting, Waite was an outstanding person. A contributing person. He should be re-membered.

"Waite liked to sit in the dugout and tell us about the old times and the big stars he played with. The stories about Babe Ruth were always funny. Babe Ruth was not the strict-est-trained guy in the history of baseball, if I'm not mistaken. And the ones about Cobb were mean. Mean stories. Let me tell you two things about that.

"I don't like to hear about baseball books that are full of mean stories. You take that Jim Bouton who wrote *Ball Four.* I been told there are a lot of mean stories in there about Mickey Mantle, Roger Maris—and I know that the publishers say you got to have controversy because controversy sells books. Well, I'll bet you today that Jim Bouton is sorry that he wrote *Ball Four* twenty years ago."

I broke in. "He isn't. His second wife is a psychologist, a beautiful psychologist. He's moved away from baseball with a whole new set of interests. He certainly seems happy and he's proud of *Ball Four.*"

"Yeah? Well, is he proud he never gets invited back to an old-timers' game in Yankee Stadium or anywhere else? I guarantee you he isn't proud of that."

I conceded that Mr. Rose had a point.

"So to be honest, I could be wrong, but I don't believe I'm that controversial a guy. What's so controversial about me?"

"Your divorce," I said. "Your paternity suit."

"Maybe, but I'm not the first person who ever got divorced and I'm not the first ballplayer to get named in a paternity suit. We're gonna talk about them things, too, but straight and honest."

He was following a thread and didn't want to lose it. "I was talking about 'mean.' Some people look at me, they see the way my face is when I'm determined—you can't be smiling *all* the time—and they figure that I'm mean. Pete Rose is

mean. Now let me ask you. Did you ever see me turn down
a little kid who wanted an autograph?"

I never had.

"I'm competitive. I'm enthusiastic. I play hard. But mean?
That ain't me."

I mentioned two famous plays. In the 1970 All-Star Game,
at Riverfront Stadium, Rose ran over an American League
catcher named Ray Fosse. Rose scored the run and Fosse was
never again as physically sound as he had been. Three years
later at Shea Stadium, Rose slid hard into second base and the
New York Mets' skinny shortstop Derrel "Bud" Harrelson.
He dumped Harrelson, who came up swinging and spitting.
A brief bout ensued, matching cruiserweight Pete Rose
against (to hear New York fans tell it) an amiable midget.

People uttered sour comments on each incident. Why
crash into the opposing catcher during an All-Star game
which, when you snip through the hype and hoopla, is only
an exhibition, as opposed to a championship game? "I only
play baseball one way," Rose says. "The way my father taught
me. I play hurt, I play tired, I play hard as hell. Don't tell me
it's an exhibition or it's spring training. Don't tell me to take
it easy between the lines. That's not me. That's not my dad.
If I play a charity softball game, for nothing, not a dime, I go
all out."

But to the critics . . . can there ever be a superstar without
critics hopping in his footpaths? No, there cannot be. So some
bad words on Pete held that he had broken up a catcher in
an exhibition game and then, to show the mighty New York
media how tough he was, he had picked a fight with an
unarmed pigmy.

"Both times I made the right play. I wasn't trying to hurt
anybody and I wasn't trying to get hurt myself. There was
nothing mean, and there was nothing sissy. Play the game.

"Cobb must have been a very different feller from me, but
I just wouldn't feel right spreading mean stories myself about

such a great ballplayer. Besides, there's one thing away from baseball that I have very much in common with Ty Cobb.

"We both thought the world of our fathers."

It can be said that Rose's epochal quarter-century pursuit of Cobb began on that April day in 1963, so long ago that few Americans had heard of Vietnam, when Pete lined a triple to right-center field against the right-handed Pittsburgh pitcher named Bob Friend. (It might also be said that the pursuit began on the western edge of Cincinnati on scruffy little diamonds where children played at baseball in the 1940s. Pete has always been pursuing *something;* if not Cobb specifically, then excellence.)

But the major league turns at bat, against the most wicked fastballs and sliders on earth, from hit number 1 to hit number 4,192, take the chronicler, as they took Rose, on a Homeric journey, past perils and prejudices and even through a banishment until at last we see Ulysses coming home in a baseball reenactment of mankind's oldest story of the voyage from desolation to light.

By 1979, Rose was through in Cincinnati. The contract bickering of earlier seasons expanded into trench warfare and Rose, with Reuven Katz working his side, was ready to fight to be paid what he thought he was worth. The season just ended, 1978, was memorable in the Reds' and Rose's history because Pete batted safely in forty-four consecutive games. That tied a National League record, and left him in the end only twelve behind the all-time record, which was posted on a Cooperstown fence by that strangely sour baseball deity, Joseph Paul DiMaggio.

Stymied in Cincinnati, Katz shopped Pete, marketed him like a Procter & Gamble soap flake, and Rose signed with the Philadelphia Phillies for $805,000, which was more than twice what the Reds had offered.

Rose moved to Philadelphia, where he would remain through the season of 1983. He was thirty-six when he left his

native town and certain baseball men suggested quietly, not
directly to the press, that he was losing bat speed. We read
more about a pitcher's velocity than a hitter's bat speed, but
both are parts of the same equation. Major league baseball
proceeds from two elements of the superswift: pitch speed
and bat speed. Put more simply, the stories argued that Rose,
the hitter, was slowing down. No source has ever gone public
but a good guess takes us to the Cincinnati front office people
who let Rose go.

In 1983—he was forty-two—he had an off year, and the
Phils released him. No less a baseball figure than William
Giles, the dynamic and enthusiastic president of the Phillies,
told Katz privately, "We hate to lose Pete, but I want to be
frank. His bat speed is slowing down."

"So that was twice I had to hear about that," Katz recalls,
"but we were able to get a contract from Montreal for the
season of 1984. And at $500,000. Not bad for a forty-three-
year-old singles hitter who had no bat speed."

It is a point of high professionalism with Pete Rose that a
big-league ballplayer should not complain. "I never complained," he says. "I was so damn happy, a skinny little kid
from Anderson Ferry playing in the major leagues, that there
wasn't a single thing to complain about. But a lot of ballplayers do complain and as a manager I've got to deal with
that.

"They say it's hot in Riverfront Stadium. I tell 'em, bring
your own weather.

"They say the ball hops too high off the infield in Houston.
I tell 'em, bring your own turf.

"They say it's windy in San Francisco. I tell 'em, bring your
own dome."

Rose does not, with rare exceptions, complain to the press
or the sportscasters or—*ever*—to fans who have paid to see
him play and manage. But he is a native American, an American original, and once in a while with friends and confidants

he indulges in an implicative First Amendment right. That is the right peaceably to bitch.

As an Ohio Valley native, he grew up across a bright span of hot, humid summers. If Rose could bring his own weather to a ballpark, his preference would be fair and warm. As well as his five seasons in Philadelphia worked, his stretch in Montreal went badly. He was able to bat only .259 in ninety-five games. In Canada he did set a National League record for career doubles—one of the nineteen major records that he would establish—but this old, vibrant, craggy infielder-outfielder didn't blend into Manager Bill Virdon's plans for the Expos, as a team emphasizing youth and speed. "I spent some time on the bench," he says, "and whenever I've got to do that, I try to contribute. But the truth is that sitting on the bench back then was not something I enjoyed anywhere near the way I enjoyed playing. There's a lot of little kid in every good major league player. Roy Campanella said that. Probably true about him and I guess it's true about me. Anyway, what little kid who knew how to play ever wanted to spend the games getting splinters in his backside? Not this particular kid, anyway."

In August of 1984, Reuven Katz went off with his wife Catherine for a weekend of rest at a friend's home near Old Forge, New York, among the tree-pillared Adirondack Mountains. After an evening of good talk, the Katzes retired to a guest house where they were startled at 12:30 A.M. by a knock at the door.

"Phone call for you, Reuven. It's Pete Rose up in Montreal."

"I don't know and he won't tell me," Katz says, "how he found out where I was, let alone the phone number. But I knew if he had gone to all that trouble and was calling at that late an hour, the news was probably not going to be good. In all likelihood, not a happy call."

Katz donned slippers, wrapped himself in a robe, and pro-

ceeded toward the main house through Adirondack dark.
When he picked up the phone, he heard Pete Rose say, "Get
me out of here!"

Katz's style suggests that he has all matters before him
under control even when, as in this case, he did not. He
assured Rose that he would certainly get him out of Montreal, provided he were given enough time for morning to
arrive and twenty-six major league general managers to
awaken.

Katz concedes that he suddenly knew the precise meaning
of "angst."

"Here was Pete, obviously unhappy, obviously not a hot
twenty-two-year-old prospect, and—this is important—playing part-time ball in an off season for a salary of $500,000 a
year."

While Rose was finding a measure of grief in territory that
more naturally belonged to *Les Habitants*, the Reds were
finding their own disasters in the river city where professional baseball began. The famous Big Red Machine blazed
gloriously in 1975, with 108 victories and a thrilling World
Series triumph over the Boston Red Sox. To me, at least, the
Machine ran most remarkably the following October, when
they swept away the Yankees, blew past Thurman Munson,
Catfish Hunter, and the rest of George Steinbrenner's af-
fluent hirelings, four games to none in a Series that quite
simply was a mismatch. (Some suggested the Yankees should
have been required to pay their way in.)

The Reds and notably Rose played with a style of simply
heroic arrogance. The Yankees' lead-off hitter was a skittery
left-handed batsman named John Milton Rivers, called
Mickey, whose forte was slapping hard drives through the
left side of the infield, or once in a while dropping a bunt.
Rose moved up so close to home plate that he could have
counted Rivers's nostril hairs had he been so inclined, and
suddenly we beheld an unusual tableau. There stood Rivers

wiggling at home plate, trying to position himself to hit the ball over third. Right before him crouched third baseman Rose, poised, ready, and totally without fear.

Perhaps Rivers feared that if he connected solidly he might have killed Pete Rose with a line drive. Perhaps the appearance of this squat, defiant infielder in his face simply unnerved him. Whatever, Rose's combination of courage and gamesmanship effectively took the bat out of Rivers's hands. The outfielder hit only .167 during the 1976 Series.

Then, across the next few seasons, the Cincinnati management proceeded to dismantle what was certainly the finest of all Cincinnati teams. Tony Perez was dispatched to Montreal at the end of 1976. Rose was shipped by riverboat to Philadelphia for the 1979 season. George "Sparky" Anderson, the manager who had won four pennants in nine years, was fired after 1978. And, as someone wrote at that time, "The Big Red Machine very quickly became the little red train that couldn't."

In both 1982 and 1983, the Cincinnati Reds finished last. Home attendance, which had once exceeded 2.6 million, slid downward by more than one half. This created a crisis beyond the diamond for the team from River City. To survive financially would they have to be moved, perhaps to New Orleans? Would the birth site of professional baseball lose its franchise?

This was the background against which Reuven Katz telephoned Robert Howsam, who replaced Dick Wagner as president of the Reds in 1983. Katz was marketing a part-time player, who was performing undistinguishedly for Montreal, whom even the Seattle inepts didn't want. And he was trying to make a sale to a losing team that may have been running out of money.

Bob Howsam brightened the conversation by saying he had some interest in Rose and that he certainly recognized Rose as an important man in Cincinnati baseball history.

Presently, he conceded that he was not pleased with Manager Vern Rapp, who couldn't get the club to win and appeared to be growing ever more angry. After one loss, Rapp reached such a furied pitch that he kicked over buffet tables in the clubhouse, ruining a colorful spread of food. ("If you think about that," Rose says, "it doesn't make real good sense. Win or lose, the players got to eat.")

Howsam said he might be willing to try Rose as a manager, even though Rose had no previous experience. ("Yeah," Rose says, "but I always played like a manager. I kept my head in every part of every game I ever played.")

The bad news, Howsam said, was that the Reds couldn't afford to pick up Rose's salary of $500,000. The figure, not negotiable, would have to be $225,000. Even worse news was that Howsam wanted Rose to manage but absolutely did not want him as a player.

"Why not?" Katz said.

"He can't hit any more," pronounced Howsam, a generally sound baseball man.

"I'm not gonna tell you that this made for an easy decision," Rose said, "but I made it right away. There aren't many things I back away from. If they wouldn't let me play back home in Cincinnati, then I was damned if I was going to manage. I'd hang in at Montreal and take my chances, as a free agent it looked like, the following year. But I *wanted* to come home, and be with the Reds when they won a pennant. I wanted to come home like a kid who forgot his school lunch somewhere and is standing in the yard smelling his mother's cooking through a window. No. More than that. I wanted to come home more than that. Forty-three or not, I *knew* I still could hit. I wasn't ready to stop. I wouldn't stop. But who wanted me? A tight time. Cobb? I knew every hit Cobb had and every hit I had. I may not be a college graduate—I ain't—but I can count."

The bargaining proceeded tensely, until at length Bob

Howsam conceded. For the rest of the year, at least, the Reds would yield on one point. They couldn't do much worse than they were doing. All right. All right. They'd let Ol' Pete play a few more games.

A final problem persisted. The Major League Baseball Players Association has rules in its overall contract with the club owners. No player's salary may be reduced more than 20 percent in a single cut. Howsam stuck to his *sine qua non:* $225,000 or zero. Rose applied for a dispensation and his union, which has no history of flexibility, understood at once and agreed.

On August 16, 1984, the Reds announced that Peter the Prodigal was coming home. Fans painted signs, in Cincinnati Red: "YOU'RE BACK WHERE YOU BELONG."

The next day Ol' Pete walked into the lime-green office at Riverfront Stadium and put on a Cincinnati uniform for the first time in six years. When Rose had last worn one, back in 1978, he told reporters that he knew about Ty Cobb's famous record of 4,191 hits, but that he really had no chance to reach it "because I won't be able to play that long." Now in Cincinnati, he pulled on his white uniform shirt, with the big red number 14 on the back. He was playing longer than he had dreamed he could.

In the early evening of August 17, Pete stood in the batter's box against a Chicago righthander named Dick Ruthven. It was his first time up. There was one man on base. Rose took a strike and a ball. He likes to see "what the other feller's throwing." Then he lined a whistling shot to center field. Pete chugged round first and he chugged toward second, and when Bob Dernier threw the ball away, he kept chugging until he leaped into that marvelous headfirst slide that has split the air of so many summer nights. He dirtied his uniform but he came up safe at third. (The hit was officially ruled a single and a two-base error.)

Peter Edward Franchise was back home.

*   *   *

"It was something coming home," Rose says. "I don't get too sentimental, but it was something. And the negotiations to get me were also something. At one point I called Bob Howsam myself and told him I thought I could help as a player, and that I was willing to fill in and pinch-hit. As a manager I wasn't going to insist that I had to play every day because of Cobb or anything else. I told him I wanted to play because I could help the team. That took some talking. A lot of talking. We were on the phone for two hours. I should have called Howsam collect.

"But I guess not. You don't want to nickel-and-dime away the important things. And I got the job."

Rose had batted .259 for Montreal. For the balance of 1984 as player-manager of the Reds, he hit .365, not a bad major league number for a forty-three-year-old who has lost his bat speed. He would be back with the Reds in 1985 and when that season began, he stood ninety-five hits short of the unreachable record.

"Baseball is peaks and valleys," Rose says. "You don't want to let yourself feel too high when you're on a peak, because then you're gonna feel too damn low when the valley comes. You try to keep your emotions as even as you can, although if you have any sense you recognize that it's an emotional game.

"There were two peaks ahead of me for '85. I couldn't help knowing they were there. The first was the team peak, a pennant, and that really is the first peak in the major leagues. Has to be. The team comes first. We finished fifth in '84 but I honestly thought with a few good moves we could win the division in '85. We didn't. The Dodgers did, but we came in second. That's as high as we went because that particular team didn't beat the Dodgers head-to-head. You've got to do that, beat the other contender one-on-one. We didn't and we finished where we belonged.

"The second peak I had ahead of me was personal. On opening day—Monday, April 8, at Riverfront—I needed ninety-five hits to break Cobb's record. That was when they played the National Anthem. When the game ended—we won it 4–1—I needed ninety-three. I doubled in the fifth and batted in two runs and I singled in the second and knocked in another. I got my hits and we won the game. I hadn't seen a nicer major league opener since 1963 when I was a rookie and most of the old Reds wouldn't talk to me. That was the way things were."

The 1985 Cincinnati Reds held first place for all of two days before a defeat by Bill Gullickson, then with Montreal, dropped them into second. They moved back into the lead for six days later in April. Then they lost to Houston, 8–3. The team would not occupy first place again. Eventually they finished five-and-a-half games behind Los Angeles and the Dodgers' amiable, formerly pear-shaped manager, Tom Lasorda, who annoys certain Cincinnati fans so much that they carry signs into Riverfront Stadium denouncing "The Blue Tub of Goo."

So there was not much of a pennant race in Cincinnati, but 1985 may have been the most exciting of all baseball seasons in River City. Rose closed on Cobb slowly, persistently, bravely. By July 1, when he disturbed a commanding four-hitter worked by the Dodgers' Orel Hershiser IV with a sharp single, Rose stood only thirty-nine hits behind Cobb. By August 1, he was twenty-five hits back.

"That's about when the media began their pursuit. I was pursuing Cobb and the media was pursuing me. I almost always enjoy talking to the media. I like going back and forth with reporters. I like throwing them a good one-liner when I can think of one. Being with media, to tell the truth, gives me a chance to be as witty as I know how to be. Besides, long ago Sparky Anderson told me, 'When a reporter comes in with questions, don't go giving him any uncivil-

ized answers. That man has a job to do. It's part of *your* job
to help him do it.'

"In the standard major league contract, you have to promise that you'll promote the game. This isn't always enforced.
My good friend Lefty [the pitcher Steve Carlton] would talk
to writers all about his collection of fermented juices. Wine.
Lefty had a great collection of the grape and he'd rap about
that with anybody who would listen. So it isn't true he
wouldn't talk to the press.

"But not about baseball. He wouldn't say a word about his
pitching. I guess he figured he spoke with his left arm.

"I had one like Lefty last year. John Denny. A born-again
Christian, he said he was. Born again and born again and
born again. He said the media was corrupt because—he really said this—the media had convinced the world that America was not a Christian country.

"Hey, I'm a manager not a philosopher and I sure as hell
can't be a dictator. That wouldn't work with today's players.
So I listened to Lefty Carlton about the Chablis and I heard
out Denny on his friend God and his enemy the press. After
Denny had an up-and-down year in 1986, and got charged
with assault by one writer, we released him. Contract or no,
these fellers, Lefty and Denny, wouldn't talk to the writers.
Well, I talk to the writers every day, and for as long as they
need to hear me.

"Anyway now I'm closing in on Cobb in 1985 and the
media is closing in on me. A fellow named Rick Reilly from
Sports Illustrated wanted to talk to me 'in depth.' All right.
I'll go as deep as I can, but he's doing a magazine story, not
a book. Now he says he's got to talk to my wife Carol and my
ex-wife Karolyn. That's simply thrilling, setting up the two
ladies, both named Mrs. Rose, so he could compare notes. But
I went along with it. Leslie Stahl, who has that nice blow-
dried hair, wanted me for the CBS show "Face the Nation."
Somebody else and somebody else and somebody else. I even

let a couple of fellers from NBC stay up at my house in Indian Hill. They said they wanted to see how I live.

"Pressure? Hell, getting up in the morning on a bad day is pressure. It's also attention. Dave Parker, our fine right fielder, said that players on my team actually enjoyed all the media. Every day's like the World Series, some of them said.

"As for me, I got to a point that season where I knew I was going to break the record. All I had to do was what I always done: See the ball, hit the ball, and it would come. See the ball, hit the ball, and don't get hurt. I'm pretty good at all three.

"All right. The total number of media covering me went higher and higher. It finally got up to four hundred and it's September 11, 1985. Another press conference. Someone asks where I get my strength from. One of my commercials—I been doing about ten—is for Wheaties, the breakfast cereal. They advertise 'Great out of the Box.' I don't say anything but I unbutton my jersey. All the reporters see my T-shirt that says 'Wheaties, Great out of the Box.' That broke them up.

"I have a good batting practice, hitting the ball hard. At 7:48 a small plane flies over Riverfront trailing a streamer. It read: 'Latonia [one of his favorite racetracks] is betting on Pete.' The crowd, 47,237, goes nuts. I'm actually feeling fairly calm.

"At 7:50 our left-handed starter, Tom Browning, gets the San Diego Padres out in order. At 7:57, we come to bat and Eddie Milner pops out against Eric Show. I follow, carrying my black Mizuno bat, Kentucky lumber milled in Japan. The crowd stands up and starts making noise. I take Show's first pitch. Fastball high. I foul one back and take another ball. The digital clocks say that it is 8:01. See the ball. Hit the ball. The baseball is what I'm watching. Show throws and I line the hit, the big one, number 4,192, bouncing into the turf in left-center field.

"Man. Fireworks light up the sky. I round first, clap hands with Tommy Helms, my coach. Steve Garvey of the Padres grins and says, 'Thanks for the memories.' I shake his hand and he runs off the field. Garry Templeton, the shortstop, tosses over the ball as a memento. Some official takes the ball for safekeeping. Up above, a Goodyear blimp hovers with blinking lights that say: 'Pete Rose, 4,192.' Someone drives out a new red Corvette with a license plate, 'PR 4192.'

"And the people! They kept cheering and whistling and stomping. Almost all the other players leave the field. It's *my* moment. Some other official takes away first base, the base I touched for 4,192.

"And the people! They stand and cheer and cheer. Seven minutes. Now I got no ball, no glove, no bat, no *base*. For the first time in my life I don't know what to do on a ballfield.

"I look up. I'm not a very religious person, but I see clear in the sky, my dad, Harry Francis Rose, and Ty Cobb.

"Ty Cobb was in the second row. Dad was in the first.

"That's when I went. I started crying and Tommy Helms, the coach, put an arm around me and motioned for my son, Petey, the bat boy. I hugged my son and then I cried real hard.

"I think I know why. With Dad in the sky and Petey in my arms, you had three generations of Rose men together, in spite of time, in spite of change, in spite of death.

"So that's what it was that made me cry."

3

Beginnings

ANDERSON FERRY, OHIO, LONG AGO

... my father's father's father who hit a ball with a stick while he was camped outside Vicksburg in June of 1863, and maybe my son's son's son, for baseball is continuous like nothing else among American things, an endless game of repeated summers, joining the long generations of all the fathers and all the sons.

—DONALD HALL

Almost always the beginnings are the same. The weather has lightened just a shade, but a hard breeze slants across the field. Winter has passed, but its afterbite persists, summoning up memories of short, confining days. In the North with its enervating snowstorms, or in the South where days bring bleak and windy rains, winter restricts a boy to quarters. It leaves him housebound, pacing, restless, caged.

Spring enters on silent feet. Jailbreak! The boy rummages through what gear he can find, an old black mitt that slowly leaks away its lifeblood, dry strands of crackly straw. A bat

39

scarred by those glorious moments when the boy cracked the wood hard against a baseball. The ball itself, lumpy as an insomniac's pillow and, after long use, just about as soft.

"Come on. Let's go."

No time for winter dreaming, fantasies of new gloves that still smell of fresh leather, new gloves to caress and shape and rub with neat's-foot oil.

"Come on and we can hit a few around."

The ringing of a joyous bell. The boy springs up, with glove and bat and ball, and follows his father's quick-paced walk, cantering, trying to contain the excitement within him, bursting like spring.

"We'll loosen up, then you can hit a few. We want to make sure you find a comfortable stance. Short stride. Quick hands. Try to hit the ball about eight inches in front of home plate. Think you can do that?"

"Yep." Can the boy do that? He has been waiting for nothing else, dreaming of nothing else through all the winter schooldays. Slowly and carefully, feeling their muscles loosen, the father and son begin to throw.

Slowly, carefully, and lovingly as well. The old ritual—"continuous like nothing else among American things"—has been renewed. Man and boy have survived another winter. In their America, at least, April is not the cruelest month.

"Where were you born?" I asked Peter Edward Rose, in the office where, with his friend and boss, Bill Bergesch, he was laboring to create another Red Machine.

"The hospital across from the University of Cincinnati. What the hell's the name of it? Deaconess. Yeah. That's it. Deaconess Hospital is where I came into the world. I got a good memory but I'm not gonna tell you I remember being born. My mom, LaVerne—everybody calls her Rosie—had four kids, my brother David and my sisters Jackie and Caryl, and all the births were simple, and all of us were born kinda big. Every one of us started out at more than nine pounds.

"I think I was born in the morning. The morning of April 14, 1941. That's the same date when Abe Lincoln was shot and it's also the same day the Titanic went down."

"So before you came along, April 14 was a day of disasters."

Rose grinned. "On the eve of the fourteenth, I think it was, the Titanic went down, so there were still some people swimming out there on my birthday is all I could tell you. But for real, April 14 has worked out to be a neat birthday. Every so often, when I was a kid, April 14 would be Easter Sunday. So it was like the ladies put on their best dresses and wore spring flowers on my birthday. Not bad, if you like to look at ladies in pretty dresses, wearing flowers, which I do. And later, when I made the major leagues, April 14 was sometimes opening day. So sometimes, when we were still playing the 154-game season, they'd celebrate my birthday by opening the baseball season. That wasn't bad, either, if you enjoy playing ball, which I always have and believe I will until the day that I die.

"Up in the late stages of my career, maybe I'd be on the road on April 14, and then the announcer would tell the crowd it was my birthday. By then I was well known, and I'd get a hand. Another not-bad deal, am I right? How'd you like to have 45,000 people standing up and wishing *you* a happy birthday.

"You got to say that for a ballplayer, April is just about the best month to be born. Every year, every April, a brand new season starts, so if you're a ballplayer, every April you get to be born again. I'm not talking about religion here. I'm not what you'd call a real religious guy. I'm talking about the ballfield, the place where I belong. That's where I get born all over again, every year, every April 14.

"Maybe that's what keeps me young."

*   *   *

The boyhood was shaped by sports, dominated by sports, illuminated by sports. Rose has thought about that as much as he cares to; he is profound and complex, but he does not chew his innards and verbalize like a character in one of those James Joyce novels he has not read. In essence, he is an existential man. "You know why I played sports so much when I was a kid?" he says. "Because there was nothing else to do."

As though it were as simple as that. Of course, there were other things to do in Anderson Ferry, hard by the Ohio River, that heartland flow that sweeps and curls and sometimes floods down its arcing reach, 1,306 miles, third-longest river in the lower forty-eight, after the Mississippi and the Columbia, bending its way from Pittsburgh, where the Allegheny and the Monongahela come together as its source, etching a valley that runs among six states until the river at last finds its way safe into the Mississippi basin at Cairo, Illinois, discharging 258,000 cubic feet of water every second.

There were books to read, musical instruments to play, histories to learn, paintings to create, and even jigsaw puzzles to assemble, except there weren't really, in the sprawling frame house at 4404 Braddock Avenue, where Pete Rose grew up. "You know what we had?" Pete says. "A little television set, a big wooden box with a tiny round screen, seven-inch picture I think it was, and I remember when I was a kid watching the Cleveland Browns. Otto Graham. Marion Motley. Dante Lavelli. A great team. A championship team. But how much could you see on a seven-inch round screen with a picture that was full of snow?" (Now that he has moved from the western edge of Cincinnati to Indian Hill, now that he has become the most famous baseball man on earth, Rose watches television via a satellite dish, no snow, on a projection screen so large that you sense in his vast living room that you have stumbled into a free drive-in movie theater.)

The old Braddock Avenue house, where Pete's sister Jackie

lived until 1986, was set in steep terrain only a few hundred yards from the Ohio River. "My grandmother," Pete says, "used to talk about the floods she'd seen, the river coming up maybe twenty feet over its banks. It never got to reach our house, but you always knew the river was out there."

The dominant figure in the old house long ago, and in Pete's life to this day, was Harry Francis Rose, also called Pete, a rugged, handsome character, who served long years as a bank teller, who was not above a rapid game of craps in some quiet side street, and who lived for his family and for sports. "I'll tell you about my dad," Rose says. "He played semipro football until he was forty-four years old. You know how rugged semipro football is. It's just as rough as the National Football League, and you don't have the good equipment, the fancy shoulder pads and stuff, and you don't have the good trainers and good doctors. Even when the equipment improved, my dad would never wear a face mask. He said it messed up peripheral vision when he was running with the ball. He played for a lot of different teams. The best known was called the Cincinnati Bengals, same as the N.F.L. team today. One day when he was forty, he kicked off at Boldface Field, which is where I did a lot of growing up, and somebody hit him with a helluva block and fractured his hip. My dad went down, but he kept crawling, broken hip and all, and made the tackle. That's the kind of guy my father was."

Did old Pete *really* make a tackle after he had suffered a hip fracture? Pete says he did, believes he did, and that should be enough. Sons' memories of fathers surely are sacred.

Sometimes, as we worked together, Pete would ask about the progress of this book. "You got my father in there?"

"Yes, I do."

"How about Reuven Katz? He in there? He's been real important to me. Carol, my wife? The kids? Fred Hutchinson, my first major league manager, hell of a guy. They in there?"

"They will be, Pete."

"And my dad . . ." The voice is questioning, almost a supplication. "My dad's *got* to be in the book."

At one point I asked Pete to comment on the influences that various managers had worked on his sense of the game.

"None of them influenced me," he said, a statement that was somewhat surprising. Rose greatly admires Fred Hutchinson, not merely for the way he ran the Reds but for the courage with which Hutch faced the lung cancer that killed him in 1964 at the age of forty-five. Rose also likes George "Sparky" Anderson and on other occasions cited some of Anderson's counsel on dealing with the press. But this day he was making another point, which he overstated, lest there be any possibility that I miss it. "There's only one person that's *really* influenced me," Rose said, "and that was my dad."

Harry Francis Rose was born in Cincinnati on January 20, 1912, and died, after ascending the steep steps of his front porch, on December 9, 1970. One of Pete's most vivid memories springs from the day that he was told his father was dead. His father had seemed indomitable, as enduring as earth and sky.

Pete remembers driving to a barber shop and, as he sat getting his brown hair cut, hearing the telephone ring. The barber took the call and the man's face suddenly grew serious. He hung up, returned to his customer in the chair and said directly, "Pete. Your father died."

Rose felt an agony of shock and horror. "My father?" he said to the barber. "You must mean my mother."

The sudden death of rugged Harry Rose, at fifty-eight, still spreads aftershocks among the survivors of his Midwestern clan. LaVerne Noeth, Pete's mother, divides her time between a retirement community in Tampa, Florida, and Cincinnati. "The truth is," she says, "I'm proud of all my children, not just Pete. But it isn't really the same as it was when my first husband was alive." She is a short, energetic senior citizen. "Why, once I called Pete up for Reds tickets and he forgot to call me back and I had to pay my own way into a Reds game that my own son was managing! That wouldn't have happened if my first husband was alive."

"If she says I forgot to call back," Rose remarks, "then I guess I forgot to call her back, or I didn't get the message. Didn't you ever forget to call *your* mother back?"

"We're close," says David Rose, Pete's younger brother, "but we're not as close as we were when Dad was alive. One thing Dad always did was treat us the same, even though Pete was older. We were just the same to him. He loved his kids."

Pete's own comment on his father's death is unadorned. "There's nothing wrong with crying when there's something to cry about and when Dad died so sudden, I musta cried for three days."

Cincinnati would be surpassed in size by at least a half dozen Midwestern cities during the twentieth century. It is, in effect, the smallest city represented in the major leagues and for the Reds to succeed in our high-rolling times when ball clubs very quickly lose (or make) fortunes, the team has to draw from a wide area beyond its corporate limits: Indiana, southern Ohio, West Virginia, and Kentucky. When that happens, as it did with the Red Machines of the 1970s, or simply with an interesting club, like the one Rose managed in 1987, attendance exceeds two million people, or more than five times the number of souls living in Cincinnati proper.

Some time ago, near the batting cage amid the mountainous cement grandstands and faded plastic grass of Riverfront Stadium, Rose said to a visiting towel boy, a young man performing menial chores: "Welcome to the baseball capital of the world."

Rose has a nice manner with anonymous young people, when he is not being plagued for autographs or being studied by the jeaned and sneakered legions of the press.

The boy turned to me. "Is Cincinnati really the baseball capital of the world?"

"The first professional game was played here," I said.

"He's right," Rose said. Rose threw a glance at the gray hairs in my beard. "Roger knows that because he covered it."

The young man blinked. I had other things to do, and passed up an easy chance—"In the first professional game ever played, Pete Rose went 2-for-4."

Early baseball, evolving from the English games of rounders and cricket, was an amateur sport, which as several have pointed out, was a way of maintaining caste, of limiting the game to people who had spare time and money; in the old-fashioned term, the upper crust. William Howard Taft is said to have weighed 354 pounds when he was president of the United States. As a rich boy in Cincinnati he was nicknamed "Big Lub." In young and relatively less corpulent years, Big Lub Taft is said to have been a powerful hitter for a sandlot team representing the Mount Auburn district.

The word "amateurism" derives from the Latin verb *amare,* to love, and suggests someone who plays a sport (or a viola, for that matter) solely for the love of playing. An amateur takes no wages, no expenses, no bronze Cadillac Seville from the alumni boosters association after a hard-running sophomore season. To the amateur, love is not for sale.

From time to time, a slick magazine story appears announcing, shrill and mournful: Amateurism Dead in America. No, it is not. I know a surgeon who plays viola in a quartet, draws no fee, and has to pay for everything including the resin on his bow. On a more complicated level, Pete and I have known ladies whose love was no more for sale than it was for rent. When Rose and I locked in the fierce embrace

of tennis, before an audience of one person, a club reception-
ist answering the telephone, we were playing amateur sport.
Ivan Lendl, the professional, might well have laughed, but as
Rose said, "Fun. We were just havin' a little fun." We love to
play. We're tennis amateurs.

However, major sport, the stuff of newspaper headlines
and essays in *The Sporting News,* has become strictly professional, a rooted business full of unfortunate jargon such as
"the bottom line." That is so whether the athletes are
proudly professional, like the Cincinnati Reds, or deviously
so, like running backs at U.C.L.A. In baseball, basketball, golf,
hockey, tennis, and even footracing, both amateurism and
pseudo-amateurism have been swept away before a great
green tide of professionalism. Cash.

Among all our team sports, the green tide first came rolling up to baseball, crashing beyond the banks of the Ohio.
Most historians agree that the Civil War was significant in
expanding baseball from a set of upper-class amateur out-
ings to the broadly based professional sport it would become. During off hours at the camps behind the front, sol-
diers played ball, officers mixing with enlisted men to create
winning teams. Some roughnecks turned out to be good fastball hitters. Caste persists in America to this spring, but the
objective in baseball is to win, whether the means are cork-
ing a bat, scuffing a ball, or sharing uniform colors with sadis-
tic rowdies. The late John Lardner put this point nicely in
doggerel:

> *Right or wrong is all the same*
> *When baby needs new shoes.*
> *It isn't how you play the game,*
> *It's whether you win or lose.*

The Cincinnati Base Ball Club was founded on July 23,
1866, in the law offices of Tilden, Sherman, and Moulton, and

quickly made an agreement with the Union Cricket Grounds to use the cricket site as its home field. The Cincinnati club, outfitted with and nicknamed the Red Stockings, flowered swiftly, and as this first professional baseball team blossomed, amateurism began to wither. By 1868, the Red Stockings engaged four players on salary, including the famous center fielder Harry Wright, who abandoned his earlier career as a jeweler to represent the Red Stockings. Wright was paid $1,200 for the season.

During the winter of 1868–69 amateurism fled. The Red Stockings decided to recruit and pay the best ballplayers they could find. A lawyer named Aaron B. Champion became president and appointed Harry Wright as his manager. Then, scouting out ball-playing hatters, piano-makers, insurance men, and marble cutters from as far off as New Hampshire, Champion and Wright assembled the great Red Stocking team of 1869. Only one player, first baseman Charlie Gould, lived in Cincinnati. (Pete Rose's recent Cincinnati teams have fielded as many as five native sons at the same time.) The total season salary of the 1869 Red Stockings was $9,300. Although it is not always a good idea to open budget discussions with Marge Schott, the assertive and tempestuous principal owner of the Reds, one feels compelled to mention that all by himself Pete Rose had earned somewhat more than $9,300 by the time Cincinnati's 1989 season was three games old.

The 1869 Red Stockings traveled more than 11,000 miles through expanding America, an exciting advance party for all the great professional baseball teams—the Yankees, Dodgers, Cubs, Cardinals, and all the rest—that would follow. According to historians at the Baseball Hall of Fame, the records of the '69 Red Stockings are neither complete nor entirely reliable, but the best surviving information suggests that the Red Stockings played fifty-seven games that year.

They won fifty-six and tied one. Under present rules, they would have won all fifty-seven.

Traveling east, the Red Stockings swept teams through New England and subsequently took on the New York Mutuals, who live in history as the darlings of William Marcy "Boss" Tweed, who ruled New York political life from 1859 to 1871 and who loved baseball only slightly less passionately than he loved raping the city coffers, an activity for which Tweed was sentenced to twelve years in prison in November 1873.

On June 16 the Red Stockings defeated the Mutuals, 4–2, a remarkably low score in early baseball. Under the existing rules a batter could direct a pitcher to throw high or low and the pitcher was obliged to comply. The curveball still lay in the future. The split-fingered fastball, whatever that *really* may be, was undreamed of. So these two brilliant primitive teams played a brilliant defensive game.

The *Cincinnati Daily Gazette* reported details the following morning in a story charged with naked ebullience and devoid of the pallid impartiality that certain journalists affect today.

> We are tossing our hats tonight and shaking each other by the hand. We are congratulated and rejoiced with. We are cheered and patted. We are told, "bully for you, boys." All this because we have beaten the Mutuals and because the game was the toughest, closest, most brilliant, most exciting in base ball annals.
>
> Perhaps no words in addition are needed. But I can not refrain from telling you that such excitement I have never witnessed.

The team rolled on unbeaten and when the Red Stockings finally returned to Cincinnati on July 1, riding the Little Miami Road Express, four thousand people appeared to

greet them and a Zouave band, resplendent in uniforms of
gold and white and red, struck up "Hail to the Chief."

Preoccupation with the White House persisted into a
grand banquet at the Gibson Hotel, where Aaron B. Champion announced that if he could either be president of the
Red Stockings or president of the United States, he'd choose
the baseball job.

A club official spoke, as club officials do today, of team
pride: "What [the players] prided themselves in was the tem-
perance principles to which they adhered. In the East they
[were] fed on bread and milk, put to bed at nine o'clock, and
sung to sleep with nursery songs."

The *Cincinnati Gazette* reporter concluded, "Westward
the star of base ball empire!"

The one tie game is not a tale of glory. The Haymakers of
Troy, New York, visited Cincinnati on August 27 and took an
early lead. The Red Stockings came back and by the sixth
inning had tied the score at 17. Calvin McVey, the Red Stockings' $800-a-year right fielder, hit what the umpire ruled a
foul tip. Cherokee Fisher, the Troy manager, insisted that
McVey had missed the ball and struck out. The umpire
stayed with his decision. Fisher then pulled the Haymakers
off the field and left town. Currently such sore-headed action
would lead to a forfeit, and as the rules now decree, Cincinnati would have won, 9–0. But the rules in 1869 were not
codified. The Red Stockings claimed victory and the Haymakers insisted that the umpire was a "homer" and that they
had earned a tie fairly, considering the circumstances.

Betting on baseball developed just about as quickly as the
sport in the wild and heady postbellum North and there is
reason to suspect that Cherokee Fisher was not simply a
sorehead. According to the late baseball historian Lee Allen,
"A group of New York gamblers had placed a large bet on the

Haymakers, and fearing defeat [when the Red Stockings were coming back], entered into collusion with the team from Troy to stop the contest, using any pretext."

The *Gazette* itself published a strong editorial on August 29:

> It was reported before the game was played that large sums had been wagered at the East upon the success of the Haymakers. It was said that John Morrissey alone had staked $17,000 upon the issue. It was said that an [unsuccessful] effort had been made to bribe one of the Red Stockings to lose the game.
>
> [The Haymakers'] conduct was a disgrace . . . but the circumstance is chiefly to be regretted because its tendency will be to lead the public to suppose that base ball, like some other sports, is under the control of the gambling fraternity.
>
> We hope that this single instance, the first that has ever occurred in this city, will not lead to such a result.

Later in 1869, the Red Stockings carried their splendid baseball to California, creating one of those rare and remarkable occasions when a history of sport instructs us on the history of a nation. Their trip in 1869 came during "the year of the golden spike," that year when ties and tracks from east and west were joined, creating the first transcontinental railroad. This moment of true union soon diffused into complaints about the promptness of the trains and the quality of passenger cars and food. Whatever, the Red Stockings rode clear from Ohio to California, through lands still dominated by Sioux and Cheyenne, ten or twelve fellows, with ball and bat and glove, among all those arrows and Winchester rifles. The Red Stockings won all their games near the Pacific and headed back, finally concluding a pioneering season at home in Cincinnati in November with a 17–8 victory over Boss Tweed's mighty Mutuals.

Winter came and passed. The Red Stockings won games in 1870 by 94–7 and 100–2. The Cincinnati team was a wonder of the land and played through 130 ball games without once, ever, having to drink the sour wine of defeat.

That happened, when it finally did, on a forgotten ballyard called the Capitoline Grounds in Brooklyn, New York, against a lineal ancestor of the Dodgers, the Brooklyn Atlantics. The teams were tied at 5, going into the eleventh inning, when the Red Stockings scored twice. But in the bottom of the eleventh, as Calvin McVey was moving toward a ball in right field, an early Brooklyn fan sprang from the crowd and jumped on McVey's back. The ball fell safely. The Brooklyn fan was collared by the police. Brooklyn scored three runs and the Red Stockings were beaten, 8–7. Aaron B. Champion wired home:

> The finest game ever played. Our boys did nobly. But fortune was against them. Eleven innings played. Though beaten, not disgraced.

Brooklyn's comic reputation, or rather the reputation old Brooklyn fans acquired for unpredictable behavior, traces to that day. Ahead lay almost a century of extraordinary activity, from the Dodger fan who physically attacked umpire George Magekurth at home plate in Ebbets Field to another one who wearied of hearing his team belittled in a small saloon on Flatbush Avenue. This fan left but later returned to the bar. Then he silenced the Giants supporter with several shots from a pistol.

Cincinnati and Brooklyn spun out wondrous rivalries, but that 1870 Red Stockings loss robbed the first great Cincinnati team of magic. Baseball people sometimes say that the game is mostly mental, an argument that presumes certain physical standards. A 110-pound man could never catch in the major leagues, regardless of temperament or discipline. You want to catch? Weigh 200 muscled pounds. But given good athletic skills, which all fine ballplayers possess, the psyche assuredly works mightily and even decisively on a ballfield.

The unbeatable Red Stockings had been beaten. Now they could no longer *believe* that they were unbeatable. They scheduled two more games with the Brooklyn Atlantics and split them. On the basis of that three-game series, the Atlantics were accepted as baseball champions of the country for 1870.

The following season the National Association of Professional Baseball Players was organized in New York, and Cincinnati was not awarded a franchise. The Red Stockings broke up, scattering through the new league, from Washington to Chicago. I think it is fair to say that Cincinnati would not again dominate baseball so convincingly until 106 years later, when the Big Red Machine overwhelmed the New York Yankees in that lopsided World Series, ruled by players named Morgan, Perez, Bench, and Peter Edward Rose.

4

Boyhoods

ANDERSON FERRY, OHIO

Pete Rose was trying to tell me about his father, to illumine the shade of Harry Francis Rose. We sat on blue couches in the huge living room of the Indian Hill house. Rose was struggling.

It is not true that Rose is never mute. During the 1987 season, Kalvoski Daniels of Warner Robins, Georgia, a strong young batting star who plays outfield, appeared to have been put out at second base on a routine play against the Mets at Shea Stadium. But Wally Backman, the New York second baseman, missed the bag and umpire Lee Weyer threw out his palms, signaling safe. Daniels climbed out of his slide and reasoning that he had been forced at second walked slowly off the field. Still walking in the base path with great dignity, he was tagged out. The play was a caricature of major league baseball.

The Mets won the game and afterwards Rose contended with the New York press in a set of unexciting interviews. That night, as many nights, the questions were bland. When the last newspaperman had left, I said, "Are you going to talk to Kal Daniels about that play at second?"

"Don't blame the kid," Rose said.

"The umpire was part of it, too," said Tommy Helms.

"You got to call that play two ways," Rose said. "With your hands which Weyer did, but with your voice, too. You got to yell 'safe' or 'out.' Weyer didn't do that."

"The kid's sliding into second base, trying to beat a throw, maybe he doesn't see the umpire's hands," Helms said.

"That's why," Rose said, "the umpire has to use his voice, too. Weyer didn't do it."

"Why didn't you go out there and raise hell?" I said.

"Start yelling at an umpire for a mistake in front of a big New York crowd, he'll think you're showing him up. Maybe *all* the umpires will think you're showing them up. After that, every close call goes against you."

"So you shut up."

"Yeah," Rose said, "but you ought to see my big toe. It's swollen like hell from where I kicked the dugout."

Applied Silence. Silence 101. Not a subject generally associated with Rose, but one that he has been mastering as he applies himself to managing.

Now on the long blue couches in the huge living room, under the drive-in-sized television screen, Rose's struggles with silence were of a different sort. He was trying to describe the most profound emotional relationship of his life, himself and his father, the sunlit days, brimful of admiration and joy, pride and love and even tears.

"My dad," Rose said. "My dad . . . just a terrific guy. Always went to work on time. Ask anybody who knew him. Never late to work. Just a terrific guy."

I waited. Rose threw a sofa pillow at stocky little Tyler, who yelped happily as the pillow struck him, then threw it back at his father.

"It's fun having pillow fights with Tyler," Rose said. Pete was wearing silver warm-up clothes and sneakers. "And it's good for him. Toughens him up. He's not afraid of a pillow today, he won't be afraid of a baseball tomorrow." Rose shot the pillow back at Tyler's shoulder. Tyler giggled and returned the blow.

"They always do that," blond Carol Rose said. "They just love to do that, the two of them."

On the huge screen the Boston Red Sox were playing the Minnesota Twins. The players looked life-size.

"My dad took me with him to games all the time," Pete said. "Football. Softball. He told me I was his lucky charm. Wherever he played, when I was a little kid, I was the waterboy. I mean not every dad does that for his kid. Anywhere he went for sports he took me along.

"And we would talk and I would listen. I know, you're gonna want an example. Well, take a three-base hit, a triple . . ."

There has been no more exciting play in the last quarter century of baseball than one of Rose's 135 major league three-base hits. The ball leapt on a rising line off the bat, tan or black, finding a slot between the outfielders. After you perceived the ball in whistling flight, and two outfielders rushing after it, you picked up a stocky, bow-legged figure running like hell near second base. Number 14. Mr. Rose. He turned second tight and fled for third. The throw appeared in the corner of your eye. Ball and base runner raced down a collision course. Rose jumped out of his full sprint, split the air and came down chest first, raising the infield dirt in a swarming cloud. He skidded, skidded, skidded. Safe at third.

"Some people," Rose said, "who don't know baseball real well would say I made the triple digging so hard from second to third. But my dad taught me long ago, you make a triple between home and first. As soon as you break out of the batter's box, you've got to be thinking third. You've got to come out of the box driving for third. It's not that the last ninety feet aren't important. 'Course, they are. But if you don't break out hard, you don't even *get* to run the last ninety feet, if I'm being clear. You got to stop at second. So that's what my dad meant when he told me how you make your triples. I remembered.

"Something else. When do you go for the triple if you aren't sure you can make it safe at third base? When do you gamble? The best time is with one out. If you do make third with one out, a fly ball will score you. With none out, trying for third on a doubtful play is a bad idea. Stop at second. There's at least three more batters who'll have a chance to drive you home. With two out, don't try for third. Stay at second. You need a base hit almost always to score a run with two outs and the same hit that scores you from third will usually score you from second. Stay in the game. Know the outs. Play like hell." He paused, then said, "I tell people baseball is not all that complex."

"Do you mean what you tell the people?"

"It isn't complex if you learn it right, from the time you're a kid. It isn't complex if you had a father like mine to teach you."

Pete wandered off toward the television and attendant black panels bulging with electronic controls, buttons and levers, radiating digital readouts. These all applied to the projection screen and to the satellite dish, in a far corner of Rose's property, indirectly peeking from Cincinnati across the American continent and clear to Asia.

"Can you get Moscow on that thing?" I said. "Let's watch some hockey."

"I probably could," Rose said, "but I never tried. I ought to pick up the Dodger game. Hershiser's pitching and he's been real tough on my club. I want to see how he's throwing tonight."

Rose tapped three buttons. The Red Sox vanished and Dodger Stadium moved into his Cincinnati living room. Vin Scully was telling a producer that he would get to a public service announcement next inning. (For reasons I had better leave to engineers, commercials aren't always broadcast through the satellites. So while local viewers are being regaled with the wonders of nonfattening, cold-pasteurized Burpo Beer, satellite owners get to hear sportscasters talking among themselves between innings. There have been a few incidents of X-rated language bouncing out to space and back into G-rated households.)

Hershiser was throwing hard. His fastball sank and his curve snapped and blond Tyler Rose, wearing down, faded toward sleep, a tow-headed miniature linebacker now weary of the pillow fights and the tumultuousness of a day.

"Can we get back to your father, Pete?" I said.

"Sure."

"And away from baseball?"

Rose's face set into an unhappy look. Sports defines his memories of Harry Rose, except for death, the time of emergency, and when you go more deeply into Pete than he has previously gone himself, he suffers.

"Baseball was what Dad and I talked about."

"Only baseball? How about girls?"

"I didn't run around much. I was a straight kid."

"Anything else? Homework? Nuclear disarmament? The weather?"

Rose smiled. "Hey, yeah. You know it doesn't snow a whole lot in Cincinnati. Not like back East. No way like Montreal where I played. There was this day, I don't remember which year, a little snowstorm hit town and my dad didn't get back from the job at the bank till nine o'clock.

"I asked him what happened and I can still hear what Dad said. 'They can get a man to the moon in the space program, but they can't get a bus through two inches of snow in Cincinnati.' "

This is as close as Harry Francis Rose will come to entering *Bartlett's Familiar Quotations*. His chances are not outstanding. He was simply, and more than simply, a hard-working man, who struggled with his job and loved his family and touched fame only on a few local ballyards for almost-forgotten teams, then approached fame one generation removed as his son was becoming the most controversial of major league players.

"Can you give me a few more things your father said?"

"Not right offhand." Pete looked uncomfortable. "Hey," he said brightly, "I'll bet you can tell me a lot of things about *your* father."

Harry Francis Rose was born in Cincinnati on January 20, 1912, into a family that would be shaken, not broken, by a divorce, when Harry was one or two years old. After the divorce, his mother, out of Ripley, Ohio, married a railroad man named Harry Sams. Harry never again had much contact with his father, who moved to Indiana. The new Sams family lived in downtown Cincinnati and Harry liked his stepfather so much that he considered going to court to change his name from Rose to Sams. "If he'd done that," Rose says, "then Cobb's record wouldn't have been broken by Pete Rose. Pete Sams, I woulda been." Or even Harry Rose, except for a horse.

When Harry was two years old, he liked to sit on a stoop and stare after the horse carts of peddlers selling vegetables. One particular nag caught the little boy's attention and the peddler sometimes lifted Harry onto the beast. The little boy grinned his delight.

The old horse was called Pete and one day the peddler said to the child: "Come on, kid. Climb up here on Pete. The horse is Pete and you like him so much I'm gonna call you Pete, too." With no more fuss than that, no flourish of hautboys, Harry Francis Rose became Pete Rose; a famous name was thus so simply conceived.

"By the time I met my first husband," says LaVerne Rose Noeth, "everybody was calling him Pete. Even in the family, they called him Pete. I never heard anybody call him Harry. And when we had to put his name in the paper for the obituary, we set it down, 'Harry Pete Rose.'"

The hard records on Harry's early life are brief. He attended Woodward High in Cincinnati, where an I.Q. test placed him in a group of "mentally superior" children. He graduated in June 1930 and eloped with LaVerne Bloebaum to Lawrenceburg, Indiana, on February 22, 1934. The Fifth Third Bank of Cincinnati, which today advertises itself as "The only bank you'll ever need!" hired Harry as a machine accountant; in essence a bookkeeper. He punched and cranked one of those old-fashioned adding machines, poring over his totals hour after hour, day after day. The monotonous task strained his eyes—he suffered from migraine headaches—but Harry Rose worked as hard as he could to improve himself. Sometimes he grew discouraged and talked of quitting. But there were no other jobs, or at least nothing else that paid as well. Harry attended the American Banking Institute for a year and at length became assistant manager of the bookkeeping department. In the late 1950s, he enrolled at an IBM school to learn new technologies. The Fifth Third appointed him assistant cashier in 1963. This Harry "Pete" Rose became an officer of the bank in the same year that his son Pete "Hollywood" Rose became the aggressive young second baseman for the Reds. (The "Hollywood" nickname, Rose says, never bothered him. "Just made me run harder, play harder." Nor, to be sure, did it last.)

LaVerne Noeth winters near Tampa, Florida, today where in her mid-seventies she is still peppy enough to navigate about her retirement village on a two-wheel bicycle. She occupies herself with arts and crafts, swimming, bingo, four children, seventeen grandchildren, and her thirteen great-grandchildren. (Robert Noeth, her second husband, died in 1984.) "You don't have to call me Mrs. Noeth," she said, when we met. "Call me Rosie. Everybody does."

LaVerne met Harry Rose after a softball game in 1932 at Saylor Park, on the western side of Cincinnati. She was, she says, a pretty good softball player herself.

Harry was playing on a team with Buddy Bloebaum and after one game Harry said, "See that girl standing over there? I'd like to meet her."

"I think I can introduce you, Pete," Bloebaum said. "She's my *sister.*"

LaVerne says that she'd had her eye on Old Pete. "I pretended I was going to the softball games to watch my brother play, but I really was hoping to meet Pete. He was the athletic type. I liked that and maybe some people didn't think he was handsome, but I did. When we were introduced I got cold feet. I acted shy."

They courted for two years, riding in Pete's Model A or Model T Ford—nobody seems to remember which it was. They went to movies, dinners, and in the summers swam in the Ohio River. Pete liked hiking. Sometimes they took a ferry boat and walked the Kentucky hills.

In February 1934, Pete said, "Verne, I'm off on Washington's Birthday. The bank is closed. Want to run down to Lawrenceburg to get married?" LaVerne was eighteen. She would have to tell the justice of the peace that she was twenty-one. She went out and bought herself a green dress. ("I don't know why I picked green. I hate green.") She weighed ninety-eight pounds and had long dark hair. The best man, Harry Rose's closest friend, was Norman Dewan.

LaVerne had been keeping house for her widowed father in the Braddock Avenue home for two years and she wondered how her father would react to her elopement. ("It turned out he was so crazy about Pete, he didn't mind.")

Bride and groom moved into the house on Braddock Avenue and stayed there. To this day, the house still belongs to the family.

LaVerne always refers to her late husband as Pete and calls her most famous offspring Peter. Old Pete spent forty years working for the same employer, the Fifth Third Bank, which traces to the ancient Bank of the Ohio Valley. In the nineteenth century, as today, banks merged with banks and acquired others. The Third National Bank acquired the Bank of the Ohio Valley in 1871 and in 1908 the Third National Bank merged with the Fifth National Bank, which, of course, is the origin of that curious name, Fifth Third.

It must have been a dreary job for a man who loved physical activity, sitting deskbound, totaling columns of numbers, staring at the dollars and the pennies, his own and other people's. He was a kind and sporting man, who worked his life away wearing eyeglasses, suffering headaches, in a bank. Harry Rose's leisure-time career suggests that he wanted burningly to become a professional athlete. He wasn't big enough or fast enough for the National Football League and in truth, although the family doesn't dwell on it, his baseball skills were sharply limited. He couldn't hit.

"It was a vision thing with Pete," LaVerne Noeth says. "He didn't have the vision Peter does. He played softball because the ball was bigger. He knew a lot about how to hit a baseball, but he just didn't have the eyes."

Pete says proudly: "My dad grew late, like me. But when he was twenty-one years old, he won an Ohio state boxing championship."

"What division?"

"Special weight. One hundred six pounds."

In those days boxers often used ring names, something they thought would have a catchy sound, and Harry Rose fought under the name of Pee Wee Sams. Club boxing being what it was, Pee Wee Sams's detailed record has not survived. But take it from Pete. His father was the toughest 106-pound fighter in the state.

LaVerne gave birth to two daughters, Caryl and Jackie, and then to the endless delight of the family, the first-born son, Peter Edward, arrived in 1941. "I love sports," Harry Rose told his wife, who already knew what Harry loved. "I'm going to keep playing them for a good time yet. Then Little Pete can take over. Someone from our family should always be playing sports."

Big Pete played football, weekend after weekend, for barely remembered semipro teams. Captain Al's Trolley Tavern in the Feldhaus Sunday League. Christ Church. The Riverside Athletic Club. Saylor Park. The Bengals (an amateur team with the same name, of course, as Cincinnati's National Football League team today).

"The big thing about the football Dad played," Pete said, "was that it was rugged. Just these rugged games and a waterboy, which was me."

In the suburb of Cheviot, Ohio, you can still find the Gumz brothers, Danny and Joe, formerly proprietors of Gumz Cafe and currently operating the Gay Nineties, a dark though spacious blue-collar bar and restaurant on Harrison Avenue. The Gumz brothers were happy to talk about their late friend Pete, sometime athlete for pickup teams they organized decades ago. They loved Old Pete, they said, and they would talk about the man, for as long as anyone would listen, provided they didn't have to break up a game of hearts to do so.

They sat at a large table, under a television set and a few color photographs young Pete Rose had signed. "Old Pete," Joe Gumz began, "was the sports hero of Riverside, Sedamsville, Saylor Park, all those places on the west side of town along the river. He played all sports and he was a helluva boxer, but football was his best. They got to calling him 'Old

Swivelhips' because this son of a bitch, nobody could tackle. He'd make his moves, his fakes, and he could just about run around anybody.

"Then on defense, he played linebacker. And one time when Old Pete wasn't so young, one of the guys on the other team said, 'Gimme the ball. I'm gonna run it right through where that little old bastard is.' They gave the guy the ball and he ran it where he wanted and all of a sudden he gets hit by a Mack truck. That was old Pete, how he played.

"I mean he was about the best competitor we ever saw in Sunday football around here. But if you met him on the street or anywhere else, he was just the nicest guy in the world. There was nothing mean about him. A lovely person.

"After the games, we had pretty good crowds, couple of thousand folks, we'd pass the hat. I guess the money went to pay the officials. Where the hell the money went I never knew. But who in hell had any money then? Coming out of the Depression, nobody had any money.

"Big Pete worked for the bank but for a long time he wasn't much more than a teller, and you know what tellers make.

"So he's struggling, but real happy to be playing sports, and then after a while he starts bringing this little kid around with him. Little kid always did what he was told. Always trying to please. Hell of a waterboy. That was Pete Rose.

"He was like his dad in a lot of ways. I mean, we got an idea here in Cincinnati how famous he is but Pete and his dad, they're the same competitor.

"Like one night in this joint where we are right now, young Pete comes in and we had this pinball machine. He says, 'Joe. Gimme ten dollars' worth of dimes. I'll go in with you and we're gonna beat this pinball machine.'

"I said, 'Get the hell out of here, Pete. Nobody can beat the machine.'

"He said, 'I'm gonna.'

"I didn't go in with him and Pete just beat the living hell out of the pinball machine. Never seen that before or since. Young Pete, everything he's done, he's been one hell of a positive thinker and if you think positive, positive things happen. Am I right?"

The Gumz brothers turned back to their cards.

David Rose, seven years younger than Pete, sat in a hamburger and malt shop on Colerain Avenue, reaching deeply into his memory. He is bearded, intense, and he has not had the easiest of lives.

He wanted to be a ballplayer; you get the feeling that everyone in the Braddock Avenue house wanted to be a ballplayer, even the women.

David played constantly as a child, with his older brother, with his dad, who, David said, treated each boy the same. ("There was no favoritism because Pete was older. If Pete and I both had a game the same day, Dad would make sure he caught a couple innings of each.")

David grew up to star at Western Hills High and went on to play second base for Wytheville in the Appalachian League. Then he was drafted and shipped to Vietnam for fourteen months. He was a machine gunner, first in tanks, then in helicopters. He remembers how the tanks had to be arrayed in a perimeter protecting a base, and the sound mortar shells made as they came in over the Asian jungle. He remembers his seven months as a "chopper gunner," firing out of a glass bubble and hearing, above the helicopter's clamorous engine, the sound of mortal fire coming back at him. He was an airborne combat soldier far from customary skies and he doesn't say much about what that was like, the nights of terror and the fiery days, except he says this: "I still have dreams."

When David Rose was discharged, he bought a motorcycle and "two weeks later a guy come across the yellow line and hit me and that ruined my baseball career right then. Tore up my knees. The surgery was a little primitive, back in 1970." With his baseball dream shattered, David found the strength to gather himself and move on to Tampa, where he became a paramedic. "From a paramedic's point of view," he says, "when you're disciplined and working, every heart attack is pretty much the same, every stroke is pretty much the same, but every automobile wreck is different. With auto wrecks, you never know what you're gonna find. You see death a lot. You get to a bad accident and you just do what you're supposed to do. After you come back from the hospital and you're cruising in your zone, you look over to your partner and say, 'That guy was pretty torn up, wasn't he?' But at the scene you just click and do what you're supposed to do.

"There was satisfaction in that work. A lot of it. I lost a few, but I brought a few back, too."

Early in 1975 Pete put his name to what was projected as a pleasant, low-priced family restaurant in Cincinnati, no more fancy or pretentious than Rose himself. Pete called David and convinced him to leave the Tampa paramedic corps for the family hometown, where there would be a job managing the Pete Rose Restaurant. For a few years the restaurant succeeded, but the Reds forced Pete off their roster in 1979, the year Rose became a Philadelphia Phil. With the native son and celebrity almost permanently away during the baseball season, the Pete Rose Restaurant went the route of Delmonico's, the Stork Club, and the Brown Derby. It closed.

Out of work, David took a municipal examination to become a paramedic, and found himself confronting a strong Cincinnati affirmative action program. "The passing score," he said, "was 75 for blacks and 92 for whites. I

landed in the middle. I got a 90." Though there was an
affirmative program for blacks, there was none for Vietnam veterans, and David's 90 percent score left him unemployed. He signed on with the Cincinnati Water Department as a maintenance man. "It's not bad work," he
said. "I mean I'm tail deep in water and it's real hot in
summertime, but it keeps you physically fit. The one thing
you learn is that the biggest main that bursts is going to go
at 4 A.M. in the middle of the coldest night of the year. That's
guaranteed."

Although the Rose family is no longer so tightly knit as it
was before its central figure, Old Pete, died, David has nothing but praise for his older brother. "Since my dad passed
away, I look to Pete for advice. I mean I look up to him, not
only as a brother, but as a friend, someone who helps me
more than anyone else would. I go to maybe sixty-five Reds
games a year, but you won't see me on the field, or going near
the clubhouse. I don't bug Pete much at all between March
and October. I know he's got a lot of pressure on him and he
wants to be thinking about baseball all the time, but off-
season we see each other quite a lot.

"We grew up together and we played ball together in that
old Braddock Avenue house. We had some great times and
Dad was terrific. Pete wasn't a big kid. I think he was 145
pounds when he graduated from high school, but he was
tough as nails and some competitor. Even at Ping-Pong. Pete
doesn't like to lose at anything. You hear some parents and
even kids say today, 'Well, it's just a game.' I think that's
garbage and Pete thinks that's garbage and my dad thought
that was garbage, too.

"When I was growing up, we learned to play to win. We
didn't care what the sport was, who was playing. Whatever.
The idea was to win. People say, 'What about having fun?'
We like having fun in the Rose family. We're pretty damn

good at having fun. But let me ask you this. Is losing fun? I don't think it is. That's why we play to win.

"Pete, big as he got to be, could have made one helluva halfback, but, course, he didn't know he was going to get that big. That's what got him to focus so hard on baseball. There's probably nobody alive in the world except me who knows how hard he worked to get where he is.

"I don't know how many hours of batting practice I threw to him. At night he'd come home from a date and swing a heavy, leaded bat Uncle Buddy gave him, swing 150 times right-handed and 150 times left-handed in front of a mirror, and not for ego. He was perfecting his swing. He'd say 'low outside' . . . swing . . . 'high inside' . . . swing . . . and move the bat, like he was hitting the ball where it was pitched. My brother's worked at everything he's done. He didn't become a great ballplayer because of size, or because it was born into him. He worked. I've seen that closer than anybody else.

"And then, I want to get this just right, he also keeps a mental edge. See, when a pitcher was getting used to the way Pete was hitting—going up the middle, say—then Pete would change. Pull the ball. Go to the opposite field. Some hitters don't change their style in a career. I've seen Pete change his style three times in a single game."

David had been sipping Coca-Cola and coffee alternately in the little restaurant, as troops of teenagers moved in and out, happy and noisy. "People ask me if I have any resentment against Pete for all the money he's made, all the success. I'm just a regular working guy, getting up toward forty, who likes to play a little softball. And I do that for charity. The answer is I've got no resentment at all. Take Vietnam. I say to myself whatever happened was for the best. I try to keep that positive attitude. I'd love to have been in the major leagues. Dad would like to have seen that too, if he'd lived.

But not making any political judgments here, somebody had to get sent to Vietnam and fire those .50- and .60-caliber machine guns. One of those somebodies happened to be me. Am I gonna kick myself in the tail for the rest of my life? Hell, no. Happened. Make the best of it.

"And Pete, like I say, is a friend as much as he is a brother. I'm proud of my brother. I admire my brother. And I hope maybe that Pete is proud of me, too."

As far as anyone knows, no reliquaries survive in the old Braddock Avenue house, where all the Roses grew from infancy, but there does remain one relic, which the family believes has value, as well it may, provided a buyer can be found. On a summer Saturday in 1944, three years before David Rose was born, Old Pete stationed his son on a home plate he had chalked onto the stone of the back patio. Old Pete had bought his boy a small bat and a sort of semibaseball, a rubber ball covered with hard coating and raised seams. The father tossed the ball softly and Pete, batting right-handed, swung hard and met the ball with a fusion of arm, wrist, body, and effort. He lined the ball sharply into a rear window, which cracked.

"I actually don't remember it real well," Rose says. "Who remembers real well something from when they're three years old?"

LaVerne Noeth remembers. "It's all right if you want to play ball with him all the time," she said to her husband, "but why do you have to do it so close to the house? Now we'll have to have that window fixed."

"What are you talking about?" Old Pete Rose said.

"Fix the window," LaVerne said.

"That's the boy's first hit," Old Pete said. "The cracked window is proof he got it. We're never going to get that window fixed. Never."

To this day, the crack in the patio window remains testi-

mony to Pete Rose's first solid line drive. LaVerne has offered
the cracked window to the Baseball Hall of Fame in Cooperstown and to the Smithsonian Institution in Washington but,
as yet, no taker has come forward. Peter Clark, the registrar
at the hall, says in a noncommittal way, "The window is one
of the more unusual things suggested." He lets the bid-and-
asked negotiation die right there. (In truth, the hall greatly
prefers gifts to items that must be purchased.) Carl H.
Scheele, curator of sports and entertainment for the Smithsonian, says that the institution already has a Pete Rose cap.
"We don't need the window," he adds. "The cap is sufficient."

Pete Rose: "Dad was sincere, dedicated, tough, aggressive.
He had to work his way up. I've had to work my way up. I
know about the headaches he got from his job, but you know
me good. You don't think, do you, when the team plays bad,
and the relief pitcher I pick turns out to be out to lunch and
the game I run turns lousy, just lousy, and now I've got to talk
to twenty reporters about everything that went wrong, you
don't think that keeps my stomach peaceful, do you? Because
it doesn't. So my dad's job gave him headaches. My job is a
great job but it can make me burp. 'Course they're different
jobs, manager and banker, but the thing is we *approached*
the jobs the same. I don't know who it was called me an
egomaniac one time. I don't bear grudges. I forget. But who-
ever it was, he didn't understand. Understood nothing. My
job is a key to my life. Ballplayer. Manager. I *work* my job.
I'm paid damn well to do it. Proud to do it, and do it right.
I look at myself, getting up near fifty years old, got the most
major league hits of anybody ever—that's not egomania,
that's in the record books. The number is 4,256 hits. That's
not egomania. I'm good at arithmetic and the number is in
the record books, too.
    "Best way to describe my father is this. I never heard him

complain. Never saw him drink or smoke. Never heard him argue with my mother.

" 'Cept once he almost did. It was the summer when I was four and one of my sisters needed a pair of shoes. Dad went out shopping and when he came back my mother opened the bag to see what kind of shoes he'd bought her.

"No kind of shoes. None. Instead he bought me a pair of boxing gloves. He said, 'The weather's warm. She can run around barefoot for a while. The kid needs gloves so he can learn how to protect himself.' My mother got a little mad that day."

Although a few incidents on major league fields have given Rose a reputation as a rousing battler, his boxing efforts led him to no glory.

LaVerne Noeth: "Pete was always training little Peter to box. I'd see them outside horsing around, jab, hook, move, that kind of thing. One day when Peter was fifteen, Pete said to me, 'The boy's going to box.'

"I said, 'Oh, God, no!' But Pete had set up a match at the Finley Street Neighborhood House and there was no stopping the two of them."

The bout was arranged for April 11, 1957, as the opener for an evening's amateur card. Pete represented the Jolly Athletic Club of Delhi Hills, Ohio. His opponent, Virgil Cole, represented Finley House. Each weighed 112 pounds.

Virgil Cole was more experienced and unawed by his peppery opponent. He pounded Pete hard in the body and face. Pete's own punches, when he got any off, were wild. Mostly his role in the fight turned out to be target.

During the second round Pete's sister Caryl cried out: "Dad, can't you stop it? They're beating his brains out. They're killing him."

Harry Rose said, "He's all right. He's not getting hurt. He knows how to defend himself." But as the beating continued, Harry's eyes grew wet.

Pete stayed dry-eyed and on his feet, but lost the decision by a wide margin. When the family returned to the Braddock Avenue house, Pete wore his bruises like medals. "Look at me," he told his mother. "But he couldn't knock me out."

After a family conference, Pete's boxing career was closed for good, with a record of 0–1.

At Saylor Park Elementary School, Pete was small, crew-cut, and as he puts it, "always in trouble. Nothing mean. But I was always talking in class or teasing a girl and then I'd get sent to the principal, Mr. Leyland T. Jones. In those days they used to paddle you and Mr. Leyland T. Jones could give you a mean whack on the ass. He used a leather strap. First time I was ever first in anything was at Saylor Park. I led the school in taking swats.

"My grades usually weren't much, so-so, but they really weren't a reflection of my intelligence. There was just other stuff that was more fun than studying. Take a girl's ponytail and put it in the inkwell. Play the air saxophone."

"Air saxophone?"

Pete had been sitting behind his desk in the windowless green office at Riverfront.

"Like this," he said. He stood up and reached for a towel, which he gracefully bent into a shape approximating that of a sax. Then boyishly, dancing a few steps, the great ballplayer pretended to play the towel.

"I was coming through the age of Fats Domino, Chuck Berry, and Little Richard. We'd have school dances at the elementary school and me and a couple of other guys had a band. Only damn band ever that couldn't play a note. We had a guy who couldn't play piano. We had a guy who couldn't play guitar. I was the guy who couldn't play sax.

"Somebody would set up a record and we'd come out on stage with cool hats, you know, fedoras with the brims folded down, and we'd pantomime. I'd blow into the towel like I was playing sax and I'd puff around the instrument, like I was really playing. I'd blow so hard I thought my head was going to explode. 'Course I wasn't really playing a note.

"We weren't that poor, but there just wasn't money enough for music lessons for me or dancing lessons for my sisters. I'd just go to school and come home, work a little at my school stuff, so that when my dad came home we could play ball, or go to a neighborhood ball game, if there was one.

"I don't remember ever wanting to be anything but a professional athlete and it's a good thing I became one because I never prepared for anything else. I know the odds are strong against any single kid making it in professional sports, but when I concentrated I excelled. Like in ninth grade, freshman in high school, I couldn't have been more than five foot nine, but I could dunk a basketball through the hoop. Not fancy the way the pro basketball players do it. My hands were small so I had to get a very firm grip. But when I got the grip I could do it. That's how high I could jump."

Harry Rose never pressed Pete to get a job. He wanted the boy to concentrate on sports. Pete ran with a tousled crowd of neighborhood children who dropped their books after school, played ball until six, when it was time to come in for supper, and after dinner ran out to play some more. "They were always trampling my flowers," LaVerne Rose Noeth says. "I'd shout at them that I'd be glad when they grew up so my flowers would have a chance. But I didn't mind. The children enjoyed themselves so much."

Beyond that, LaVerne was a most passionate fan. When Pete played Knothole Ball, the Cincinnati equivalent of Little League, she paid him a bonus of fifty cents for each hit. Young, crew-cut Pete would reach first and throw fingers into the air, indicating how many hits he had made, how many fifty-cent pieces were coming. (Harry never gave Pete cash for hits. He told LaVerne, "You don't have to be paid for doing what you're supposed to be doing.")

Some Saturdays in his early teens Pete worked as a ticket taker on the ferry that chugged from Anderson Ferry to the Kentucky bank of the Ohio River, where a road led up the hills and toward the major Cincinnati area airport in Covington. Northern Kentucky was wide open when Pete was a boy and stayed that way until the famous Senate hearings that Estes Kefauver of Tennessee conducted in 1950 forced certain crackdowns.

William "Big Bill" Staubitz, a genial and knowledgeable journalist who spent time wrestling professionally and as a deputy to the sheriff of Hamilton County, recalls the flavor of the Kentucky towns so vividly one would think he had tasted them. Which probably he did.

"Cincinnati, as many people know," Staubitz says, "was very conservative, with a large conservative German population and a large conservative Catholic population. That's not to say nobody knew about sin. They just moved it over the river into the towns of Newport and Covington. You could find nightclubs over there, not too much different from the Las Vegas lounges today. Open gambling. Sports bookmaking. Prostitutes. The syndicates ran the action—this was when Pete was a little kid—it wasn't the healthiest situation. I mean there was all this crapshooting and blackjack and the rest and ballplayers from one of the National League teams used to go to one of the joints and bet baseball. Not their own games, but their own league and we don't want that. [Staubitz was saying this in 1986.] I even thought of calling *Life* magazine and having a photographer come in with me and take pictures of these ballplayers betting baseball. Thought about it. Couldn't do it. These syndicate people wouldn't have let anybody with a camera near them.

"Now Cincinnati itself never got near as wide open as that, but on the street beside the Ohio, River Road, there were places with wide-open bookmaking. Mostly it was horse racing, but they did take baseball bets. What the kids would do would be this: hang around these cafes, which served good draft beer, and ferry gigantic schooners of the beer to the houses of the people who wanted it. You'd get copper or tin buckets and you'd run and get your gallon, seventy-five cents, and they'd give you a candy bar while they were drawing it, and that was your fee and you'd run the stuff home, or wherever.

"Pete's father was so into sports and physical conditioning that he wasn't a beer drinker. But all the time Pete was growing up and playing sports Pete ran with a crowd called the River Rats and all those kids knew about beer schooners and sports books before they were fifteen years old.

"People know I covered Pete when he was playing for Western Hills High and they asked me where he got his street smarts. A lot of what he's done, ball playing, public relations, is street smarts carried to a very high level. Pete got his street smarts from the street kids that he knew who came from maybe slightly looser homes. He was around kids like that as surely as he was around his dad, as surely as he was around home plate. Pete's street smarts come from the street."

In many ways Pete lived an American folk-opera boyhood with Cincinnati as his River City. An adoring father. An admiring mother and sisters. Doing enough, but no more than enough, to survive in the prison of the classroom. Watching Dad, the neighborhood hero, playing football, running over tacklers. Sitting with Dad—and feeling almost a grown man—sitting with Dad and Dad's teammates on the sidelines.

Autumns Pete played pickup football himself, a fast and fearless ball carrier, crashing into guards and linebackers at a mighty 115 pounds. When snow came, Pete rode his Flexible Flyer sled down the daunting hill that swept from Hillside Avenue to the river. The river itself. Yet another place to play. With Walt Harmon, a friend who lived five doors away on Braddock Avenue, Pete fished the river, swam the river, and sometimes paddled clear across to Kentucky. If there was nothing else to do, the boys dodged the trains that ran on the tracks close to the Ohio and, in the endlessly inventive manner of city children, they created games.

Behind a restaurant called Schulte's Fish Garden someone had painted a huge mural of a walleyed pike. The boys pitched to each other in front of the mural. The fading fish's eye served as their strike zone.

"You have to picture Pete as this bumpy little guy," says Big Bill Staubitz. "His family cut his hair—they didn't have fashion styling then—and Pete's hair stuck up straight. He looked a little bit like a porcupine. He had a gap between his teeth and he'd spit through it. The way small kids do, he acted tough. But with Pete it wasn't just acting. He *was* one tough little athlete. Always has been, even though he's not exactly little any more."

Trouble came in Pete's sophomore year at Western Hills High. Western Hills mixed River Rats with children from wealthier homes in the hills presiding over the Ohio River Valley. Sports was a unifying motif. The biggest games of the year matched the Western Hills Mustangs against the Elder High Panthers and Pete, despite his small build, became starting quarterback for the Mustang freshman football team. He scrambled and ran and popped short passes, but he was not one of those cannonading quarterbacks who can throw a football from a middle American valley to the Tropic of Capricorn.

When Western Hills organized early varsity football practice for August 1957, most invitees were juniors and seniors. Four ninth graders also were asked. Pete Rose was not among them.

Rose: "I felt just terrible. I try to look at everything positively, but what the hell positive is there about not making a team? And the way it was at Western Hills, if you weren't asked to tryouts, you weren't going to make the team.

"Here I'd been playing sports since I could walk. Dad was a star. Now I was cut. Me. Pete Rose. Mr. Pete Rose's kid, and the coach thought I wasn't good enough to look at. Even these days when I've got to cut somebody from the Reds I end up with a real bad hurt. Usually I have someone else stay in the room with me, a coach, a front-office man, just to make sure we handle everything right. I have to look out for the Reds. That's my job. But I always seem to care strong about the feelings of the feller that I got to tell: 'You aren't good enough right now. Maybe you'll be back.' I don't know how bad that is for other managers. It's very bad for me."

That sophomore year at Western Hills High, his *first* soph-omore year, returns to Rose in blurred, unhappy images. "I didn't do my schoolwork. I missed classes. I remember hanging out. Doing nothing. What was the sense of going to school if they weren't even going to give me a *chance* to play football?

"I'll tell this to every person who listens. There is nothing more important for a young person than getting educated. One thing in my life, if I could do differently, I would have concentrated more on getting educated. I haven't read a whole lot and seriously now I wish I had.

"My career has worked out, which makes me fortunate, but baseball is a tough world. The world is a tough world. And you want to have everything going for you. Not just sports, but sports *and* education."

Bill Staubitz, the journalist-wrestler, had covered Rose's father and now continued to oversee Old Pete's boy.

"Not making that team killed Pete," Staubitz says. "Absolutely devastated him. In the tenth grade he hardly went to school. He became a delinquent, a truant. He struck out. He failed. He flopped.

"I don't mean he mugged people on the streets. I mean he just drifted and flunked everything there was to flunk. When I saw what was going on, to tell you the truth, I lost interest in Pete. He was a punk kid, who wasn't going to make it. Fifteen years old and he was done."

Rose: "My family wasn't happy with me. I wasn't happy with me. It was a bad time."

Staubitz: "We had good quarterbacks in our town. Roger Staubach from Purcell High. Most have heard of him. Steve Tenzy, who went from Elder High to star at Florida State. Ralph Griesser at Western Hills. Those boys could play. Paying attention to them, the ones that were making it, you stopped wondering about that little kid with porcupine hair who spat between his teeth, the kid Pete Rose.

"But there's a rule the whole country has learned by now. Underestimate Peter Edward Rose and you make a major mistake."

Griesser, a tall, deep-voiced man who has been Midwestern sales manager for the Nautilus Company (which builds the famous weight-lifting machines), recalls that Rose lost a year of eligibility because of academic difficulties.

Ralph Griesser: "In my senior year Pete was five foot eight. A developing kid. He tried out for quarterback, halfback, and everywhere on defense. In the end we moved Charlie Scott, a good halfback who went on to West Point, to fullback and we played Pete at half. Pete was one fine receiver coming out of the backfield. He must have gained 400 yards receiving and another 600 running with the ball. He also kicked our extra points and some field goals. We went 7-2-1 and we became the cochamps of the Public High School League in Cincinnati.

"Pete had a lot of the same characteristics in football that he later showed in baseball. Competitive. Tough. No super speed, but excellent quickness. But as a young man Pete was no phenom. College recruiters came to see us and they rated

six or seven others ahead of Pete. His biggest qualities were
not overpowering skills. But he didn't back away from any
man or anything."

Paul "Pappy" Nohr, the retired baseball coach at Western
Hills, lives in a two-story brick home in Westwood, Ohio. A
framed photograph of Ronald Reagan hangs in the den,
along with pictures of many good old boys who played for
Pappy Nohr. He sent no fewer than ten high-school players
into the major leagues, surely something unique in the annals. Among the ten are Clyde "Dutch" Vollmer, the late
Herman Wehmeier, Don Zimmer, Eddie Brinkman, Chuck
Brinkman, Russ Nixon, Art Mahaffey, and the jewel in this old
man's crown, Pete Rose.

"I get more credit than I deserve," said Nohr, who in his
ninth decade was sitting at leisure in his den. "Kids start to
play young out here in Cincinnati and I was just lucky
enough to get the ones I did. When Pete came to school he
was a little fellow and he wanted to play catcher. Now, we
had a good catcher, big guy, name escapes me, so we put
Pete at second base. Pete wasn't the greatest infielder, but he
was learning a new position. He began as a backup. Just a
little kid with stiff hair. We all knew his dad played pretty
rough football.

"Young Pete was a hard worker, but he never did win
honors for high-school baseball. Good bunter. Ran hard. Ran
out everything. But he wasn't the fastest guy on the team.
Attitude, that's what they talk about now, isn't it? The kid
had a great attitude.

"I got this nickname 'Pappy' from a swimming team. I also
coached swimmers in my time. After my daughter was born,
the swimmers started calling me 'Pappy.' Now Pete, he'd
sometimes come back to Western Hills to help with the kids
when he was with the minors or even with the majors. Pete
never called me 'Pappy.' It was always 'Mr. Nohr' or 'Coach.'

Even when he was a real major leaguer, which he is, always will be. He's going to the Hall of Fame."

"Did you ever think Pete was going to the major leagues, Mr. Nohr?"

"Can't say that I did. Too small. Now the guy I thought would make it, could hit the ball a mile, was a contemporary of Pete's, Eddie Brinkman." (Edwin Albert Brinkman, a rangy, bespectacled shortstop, did indeed make the majors. He played fifteen seasons in the big leagues with a lifetime batting average of .224.)

Old Pappy Nohr brightened his den with an old man's snorting laugh. "That shows you," he said, "how much a high-school coach really knows."

After Rose graduated from Western Hills, he briefly considered an athletic scholarship at Miami of Ohio. He could certainly play running back at that level.

Pete: "I wanted to be a pro in sports. Not a semipro like Dad. A real pro. And I just didn't figure I'd get big enough. So I hung with a Cincinnati scout named Buzz Boyle—his real name was Ralph—and I damn near begged. Just give me a chance in the Reds' organization, Mr. Boyle. I'll carry out the bats. I'll water the outfield. A chance, Mr. Boyle. Just let me have a damn chance."

One of Boyle's aides said to Phil Seghi, the Reds' late minor-league director, "I think this stiff-haired kid named Rose deserves a chance."

Seghi, a gentle but pragmatic man, was looking for size and home run power. He said: "We got enough little shits in our organization as it is. We need someone who can really play ball."

Gabe Paul, who ran the Reds for much of the 1950s, said from his Tampa retirement home that in preference to Rose he wanted "a kid from Elder High named Jerry Marx." Marx

signed with the St. Louis Cardinals for $65,000 and now
works in the oil business in Houston. "Shows what a good
baseball man I am," says Paul.

Peter Edward Rose, not the most exciting prospect since
Theodore Samuel Williams, finally was signed after volumes
of supplications from his uncle Buddy Bloebaum. Buddy
Bloebaum was a so-called bird dog. He drew no salary. As all
bird dogs, he was paid only when someone he recommended
actually was signed. He was one of those marginal baseball
men who lived on knowledge, a smile, and well-shined shoes.

"Take the kid," Bloebaum said, pleading both for his
nephew and his bank account. "I know he's small, but people
in our family grow late."

As much for peace as anything else, Seghi and Paul capitulated. Pete would not have to study New Trends in French
Existentialism at Miami.

Rose signed for a bonus of $7,000, which now would not
insure all of his five cars. He was promised an additional
bonus of $5,000 if he made a major league roster and stayed
on a major league roster for thirty days. Gabe Paul and Phil
Seghi were thinking about days. Pete, whom nobody yet
knew, was thinking decades.

"I can't say I knew more than anybody else," says Eddie
Biles, head football coach at Xavier of Cincinnati and later
head coach of the Houston Oilers of the National Football
League. "But I did study Cincinnati athletes hard. That was
my job.

"So I knew Pete from when he was little and I knew Pete's
dad from when he played semipro football.

"Did I know this kid was going to be a Hall-of-Fame hero?
I did not. But I do know this. Pete was given a lot of advantages from his father and his mother both. And he loved to
work. He passionately wanted to learn.

"Now you take a kid like that with the heart of a split pea
and it means nothing. Nothing at all.

"But you look at Pete today and you know he doesn't have the heart of a split pea. He's a guy with a heart as big as a watermelon."

"But watermelons are mushy and pop under pressure."

"Let me correct that," said Coach Eddie Biles. "Pete had a heart just as big as a watermelon that was armored with cobalt steel."

5

Up from the Minors

GENEVA, NEW YORK, 1960

The minor leagues are a country of the young. The players come from towns in rainy Oregon, hill-citadeled Kentucky, sandy Florida. They come with a suitcase and sneakers, riding a dream.

The owners mix misty, adolescent idealism with ethics that would make a junk-bond salesman flinch. No minor-league owner says—perhaps the word should be admits—that he has money. It is a constant corroding struggle to get people into your little country ballpark and to hold off the bus company, which moves your team, the electric company, which powers your lights, and last week's cheap motel, which wants $475 *now* for quartering your players during a three-game series that drew 871 spectators, including ushers, on three May nights of wind and drizzle. It is only slightly less corroding to constantly think of promotions that may increase your home attendance so you can pay half, not a third, of the $475 before a process server, who happens never to have played ball himself, comes rapping in an unsettling way on the club-house door.

The managers are busy, often thwarted men, whose ambitions are fired by a belief that if justice *really* triumphed they would be working many crossbars higher in a baseball organizational ladder that runs today from rookie leagues (Appalachian) to short-season Single A (New York–Penn) to long-season Single A (South Atlantic) to fast Single A (Carolina) to slow Double A (Eastern) to fast Double A (Southern) to Triple A (American Association) before that rare and final step through the golden door opening onto the major leagues. Seven classifications, no fewer than seven, define this country of the young, each closer but every one so distant from the El Dorado of the major leagues.

Somewhere next summer a good minor-league player, tough enough to stand up against ninety-mile-an-hour fast-balls under bad lights, will weep in a glaring laundromat at 1:00 A.M. He is hitting well, but never had to contend with a clothes-dryer cycle before. Aside from that, he misses his mother. Somewhere a minor-league owner will call a major league farm director, whose young talent the owner supposedly is shepherding. He will say, "I'm stuck. Unless you Express Mail $15,000, I'm bankrupting the creditors and folding the team." Somewhere a manager who has been drinking too much will call a team meeting and tell the players he's been fired. He may add, as the great outfielder Pete Reiser once did, after drinking too much and being fired as manager in St. Petersburg, Florida, "Before I go, I want you young guys to know this: None of you sons of bitches will ever make the major leagues."

Those are shades from the dark side of a world, centered on competition and parsimony, illuminated by a glow of hope. Gather ten minor-league players and ask how many expect to make the majors. You could light a country ballpark with the radiance flowing from their faces.

"The minors were good days," Pete Rose says. "Maybe a little nervous. Maybe a little lonely. But real good days. I remember my second year, I was playing for Tampa and we won the championship in the Florida State League. I was making $400 a month. I owned two pairs of pants and three pairs of socks. That's what I had in this world. But we won. The owner decided to give us something to remember our championship. Every player got a Zippo cigarette lighter. That was the most wonderful moment in the world. Wonderful! And I didn't smoke!"

The minor-league players come from cities and towns far from where they are playing. They chatter and prank and play macho games and look for girls, which is not a fierce mission if you are a professional ballplayer, even in the minor leagues. If you're a ballplayer, certain girls—from pom-poms with jiggling bodies and straw-blond hair to the serious, dark-haired ones who signal the onset of seduction with a slow and sometimes exquisite removal of eyeglasses—certain girls seek out the ballplayers. "I guess, I don't want to get in trouble here," Pete Rose says, "you could call that a fringe benefit of being a ballplayer. Whatever you heard, and I heard the same stories, I never was one to play around with a whole bunch of women, be involved with a whole lot at the same time. We'll get to that. In the minors I was a straight young guy. I liked the ladies."

Around minor-league batting practice in twilight at the country ballparks, energy comes bounding from the hitting cage. Young ballplayers love to hit—if you don't love to hit, why begin to play the game?—and they jabber, tease a bit, and work seriously on their swings. You want to hit big in the minors. Only the big hitters advance.

The games are intense, almost always at night, and the young players discover hard realities. Unlike high school or college teams, minor-league clubs play a game every night, night after night, all season long. You have to drive yourself to play baseball seven days a week, down the long reach of a season, play through pain, always play hard, block out the world, block out the pain, play hard to win.

A lonely camaraderie presides. The players share socks, underwear, living quarters, and telephones (if they can pool enough money to cover the phone company's unsporting demand for a deposit), eat together and, of course, work together. They begin the season as strangers. They finish as a team. Everybody is learning all at once how to adjust to one another and, sometimes more difficult, how to adjust to living on your own, in a world where suddenly there are no home-cooked meals.

The low minors are a flare of hope, no more than that, for most. A year or two to play out dreams, poke a few hits, perhaps not enough to advance in baseball. The season ends as summer ends. Blue melancholy invades the clubhouse. The players look at each other, shake hands, and say goodbye, promising to stay in touch at Christmas, "See ya next spring."

But by next spring many are out of baseball, released, in essence fired, at the age of twenty-two.

For most people the minor leagues, that country of the young, are where dreams go to die. But Peter Edward Rose is not most people.

"If I tell you I excelled in sports," Pete Rose asked me, in his lime-green, windowless Cincinnati office, "you wouldn't call that bragging, would you?"

"Dizzy Dean said if you can do something and you say you can do it, that's not bragging. No."

"Except, if I told you that I was a high-school All-American that wouldn't be bragging. That would be something else. Lying.

"See, as hard as this may be for some people to believe, I was a real small kid. I was maybe the second-lightest player on the Western Hills football team. I was fast enough and shifty and you know me, Rog. I'm not the kind of guy who'd back away from a tackler. But in football and in baseball, too, for that matter, scouts look for size. I would say I was a very

good high-school athlete, without being a superstar, which
Eddie Brinkman was at Western Hills. Eddie got a bonus of
$75,000 to sign with Washington and they say they took his
bonus check to the bank in an armored car. I tell 'em I took
my bonus check and cashed it at the corner store.

"Then there was this eligibility thing. After I got discouraged and into all the trouble for ducking classes in my
sophomore year, one of the school advisors said I could make
up the work if I went to summer school. I took that one home
to my dad.

" 'No way,' he told me. 'You can't go to *school* in the summer. It would get in the way of your baseball.'

"I had a pretty great fan right at home, so I left summer
school to the students. I could catch, still can, and play infield,
bat right or left, run. You know whenever I got a base on balls
[1,566 in the major leagues] I always ran to first. Never walk
when you can run.

"I don't know exactly when I first started that, but I know
where I got the idea. Old Enos Slaughter of the St. Louis
Cardinals used to run out his walks. I liked the way he played.
Not the biggest man on the field, but hustling, driving himself every play. Which is how I wanted to play, how I played.
The idea of running out the walks came from Slaughter.
That's probably why some people who didn't understand my
approach tried to give me names like Hollywood and Hot
Dog. But if you're small and hoping you'll grow some more,
hoping but of course you can't be absolutely certain, you
want to keep yourself in high gear every second. If that
makes me a hot dog, pass the mustard."

On Saturday, June 18, 1960, Uncle Buddy Bloebaum called
the Braddock Avenue house with news that transported Pete
to all he has known of paradise. The Reds would take a
chance on the nineteen-year-old kid from Western Hills.
They'd pay him a $7,000 bonus when he signed a contract.
He would be assigned to the Geneva Red Legs of the New

York–Penn League, where he would draw $400 a month. If, down the road, he made a major league roster and *stayed* on a major league roster for thirty days, he would earn an additional $5,000 in bonus money. At its best the contract was worth slightly more than $13,000. In 1986 Rose earned $13,000 every two games.

"Peter ran all over our neighborhood, saying, 'I'm leaving. I'm leaving. I'm going to play ball,' " LaVerne Rose Noeth remembers. "I still have a picture in my billfold of Peter right after he was signed. He was so skinny. I just had two days to get him ready, wash all his dirty clothes, see that he packed right. He was so excited. He'd never been away from home before. Now he was going to leave. Why, he'd never even been inside an airplane."

Rose borrowed one hundred dollars from his mother and bought what he recalls as a sleek 1957 Plymouth. LaVerne remembers the car differently. "When he pulled it up to the house, I almost fainted. I laughed so hard I had to hang on to a telephone pole to keep from falling. He said, 'Come take a ride, Mom,' but I told him no way.

"That car. It had running boards and shades you pull down on the windows. It looked too old to me. I was used to a *decent* car."

Pete: "Eventually, I'd get a Rolls and what I'm driving now: the red Porsche that Mario Andretti customized for me. I like cars. I maintain my cars. If Mom says the first one had window shades, then maybe it did. This was a long time ago. But I had to start somewhere and there were not too many 155-pound second basemen in those days who started out with any car at all."

An American dream was turning toward reality. "I flew to Rochester. After we took off, my first flight, I looked out of the window and wondered what was holding the plane up. A lot of other people have wondered the same thing. But after a while, I just felt so excited about becoming a ballplayer, I could relax a little. I figured I had a great career ahead of me, if I lived."

Geneva, New York, is a quiet college town situated on the northern shore of Lake Seneca, the deepest of New York State's five Finger Lakes. This is two-lane blacktop country and outside the village in late summer hills brim with a bounty of apples and grapes. Carrying an old suitcase, with three bats strapped on, a fielder's glove, and a pair of spikes, Rose walked into the clubhouse at McDonough Park and introduced himself to Reno DeBenedetti, the manager. Then Rose said, with more assurance than he felt, "I'm your new second baseman."

He was indeed. The incumbent second baseman, a Cuban native, possessed a strong bat, but had significant fielding deficiencies. His name was Atanacio Rigal Perez. As Tony Perez, he would play major league baseball beside Rose across most of the following three decades.

DeBenedetti moved Perez to third base; eventually, when Perez found his proper position, he became a first baseman good enough to play in eight All-Star Games. In 1960 Rose was a better second baseman than Perez, which is not limitless praise. Playing in eighty-five games, Rose made thirty-six errors, easily triple an acceptable ratio.

"The truth," says Rose, "is that I wasn't a good fielder. I may have been pressing. I knew I wasn't what you call a natural. But I'd spent so much time as a catcher as a kid, I hadn't played a lot of second base.

"It's important that coaches and young players know how important fielding practice is. Look at a major league team in a good workout. The infielders pick up a hundred grounders each and not just on one day. They do it every day, from spring training to the World Series, if they get that far. Kids love to hit. A lot of kids will hit all day and even miss supper to hit till dark. But there's more than one part to baseball. When one guy is hitting, nine others are out there for field-

ing. And there's only one way to become a good fielder.
Practice. For an infielder, get your body behind the ball.
Figure the hops. Charge every ground ball you can. That's
called playing the ball. Stand there and the ball plays you.
You get tough hops. I don't think this is all that complicated
but not everybody is aware of it. Get up to the plate and take
your swings and then go to your position and work like hell
on your defense.

"Every hitter has slumps and they're discouraging. But
after a while I worked out a mind-set that helped. When I
was in a slump, I was going to work particularly hard at my
defense, my fielding. That way, even if I went 0-for-4, I'd still
be contributing as much as I could to the team.

"That came later. We were in Geneva, weren't we? And
I was gonna need a lot more practice before I had a good
glove at second base."

The Geneva Red Legs of 1960 were a last-place team, and
DeBenedetti was fired in mid-August. Today in Geneva, at
Baroody's Cigar Store and at Ed Smaldone's malt shop on
Exchange Street, you can still find Genevans who remember
nineteen-year-old Pete Rose.

White-haired Bill McDonald, a former member of the Community Baseball Board, which runs the minor-league team,
says Rose was brash and always in a hurry, even when there
wasn't anything he had to do. "He really worked on the ballfield," McDonald says. "He wasn't the classiest-looking young
ballplayer I ever saw, but on the field he worked his butt off."

Charles Hickey, whose family rented Rose a room, says,
"Rose was a great holler guy. Not that everybody liked what
he hollered. He came out with some pretty good terms. You
know it's a small ballpark. The fans sitting close could hear
the terms he used. Some of them would get upset."

Under the brashness and the barracks-room banter, Rose
suffered from homesickness. He called his mother, who traveled to Geneva by bus and stayed in a tourist home for two

weeks. His Aunt Margarette and Uncle Buddy Bloebaum drove out from Cincinnati.

"Something's bothering me," Rose told his uncle.

"What's that?"

"You know I room with four other guys. Well, after we got paid last time, I put my money in the night table. Some of it's missing."

That day the Bloebaums walked Pete, the banker's son, to a local bank, and showed him how to open a checking account.

Rose broke in with two hits in five times at bat, and a sportswriter named Norm Jallow wrote in the *Geneva Times:* "Rose is an aggressive and eager ballplayer at second and gives promise that he could be a good hitter."

Good, but not outstanding that first year. He batted .277. Rose: "I don't believe the reports back to Cincinnati were any too good. I slid headfirst. I played hard. But I didn't lead the team in hitting. And there were those errors. Once I got settled, with the checking account and getting used to Geneva, I watched my language a little more. You know a ballfield in those days. It was like the Army. Men only. The language got rough. But I watched it or tried to and I played so hard that at the end of that year, in a town I'd never seen before, the fans voted me most popular player. I got a matching set of Samsonite suitcases.

"Geneva was a really small town, very beautiful to look at, not much to do except play ball. I left it with memories of some nice fans, a slightly more mature attitude, an idea of how a checking account works, and much better luggage than I came with."

Art Shamsky, who made the Reds in 1965 and starred for the famous New York Mets team that won the 1969 World Series, played with Rose and Tony Perez in Geneva. "We were skinny kids," Shamsky says. "We didn't weigh two hundred pounds among the three of us.

"Pete had incredible energy. He was switch-hitting, of course, but he had trouble getting hits left-handed. There was no way watching Pete in Geneva you could say that he had Hall-of-Fame potential.

"Somebody asked me once if Pete was the most valuable player at Geneva.

"Where the hell did we finish? Nineteen games out of first place?

"There was *no* most valuable player on that team."

Rose: "I knew I had to get bigger and stronger. I took a job in the winter of 1960–61 unloading boxcars. It was hard work, but it built me up. That and nature, the fact that the men in my family grow late. I put on two inches in height that winter and unloading those cars every day and eating good meals, I put on twenty pounds."

LaVerne: "I made sure he ate good meals. I'd drive down to the railway yards and bring him a lunch and cocoa. I was worried all the time he'd hurt himself, unloading those big crates. I was afraid he'd pull one of the heavy boxes on top of himself, or that he'd fall off one of the boxcars."

Rose: "I wasn't gonna get hurt, but I'm glad she worried."

As he moved about from the old Braddock Avenue house to work downtown at the Fifth Third Bank, Harry Rose felt pangs of concern. Now that the caravan to the major leagues had passed him by, Harry had deposited his own boyhood dreams onto the strong shoulders of his older son. With a pure, unwavering desire, he wanted young Pete to make the Cincinnati Reds. Never mind that the dream was implausible. Never mind that the kid was skinny, that he hadn't batted .300 in a low minor league. Implausible dreams are often the most passionate of all.

As a Cincinnati sports star, Old Pete had made acquaintances in the Reds' front office. He asked them what the scouts had to say about his boy. The responses were uniformly guarded. Young Pete displayed oceans of desire. He was a prototypical hungry ballplayer, a significant plus. But turning from attitude to skills, the scouts had fewer positive things to say. Pete's throwing arm was adequate, no more than that. His running speed was good, but not outstanding. His batting style was raw. He swung at too many bad pitches. Aside from all the errors, he had difficulty with two plays a second baseman must make. He did not move well on ground balls hit to his right. He had trouble making a fast pivot at second on double plays.

Harry clung to his dream that winter of 1960–61. Reality was something else. Coming off an ordinary minor-league season, nineteen-year-old Pete Rose seemed on his way to joining that sorrowful army of minor leaguers who play a season or so in obscurity, then are released and have to stop playing professional baseball and go to work.

The first time John Samuel Vander Meer saw Pete Rose, Pete was running like hell to first base. Every time he came to bat that day, whether he singled or grounded out, he ran the same way. Vander Meer noticed, and afterwards approached Rose in the locker room.

"You run to first base like that all the time?"

Rose gazed up from the three-legged stool on which he sat. "I'm looking for a job," he said.

"Keep running like that and you might get one."

Johnny Vander Meer, once a hard-throwing left-hander who led the National League in both strikeouts and walks, is retired to a quiet Florida life in Tampa. Half a century ago sports sections across the country bannered his name in headlines. On June 11, 1938, Vander Meer pitched a no-hitter against the Boston Braves. After three days' rest, pitching the first night game ever played in New York City, Vander Meer shut out the Dodgers at Ebbets Field with another no-hitter. No one in the major leagues before or since has pitched no-hit ball games in succession. After defeating Brooklyn on the night of June 15—the game ended when Leo Durocher flied out with bases loaded—Vander Meer earned a unique nickname. He was Johnny "Double No-Hit" Vander Meer for the rest of his thirteen-year major league career.

In the spring of 1961, Vander Meer was assigned to manage Tampa of the Class A Florida State League. He is a genial, rather low-key man whose career never fulfilled its starry promise. (Vander Meer became a very good pitcher but not a great one. Control would always be a problem.)

"We had a lot of young players we were looking at for the Tampa club," Vander Meer says. "We had a pretty good idea of who our starting players would be, or we thought we had a pretty good idea. Pete was on the scrubinis, the second team, scrubinis. Never was too sure about how you spell that word. The scrubinis were all the kids who didn't know nothing. We played them against the regulars to evaluate whether we were gonna keep them or release them. Pete would run and dive and slide headfirst. I'm not patting myself on the back but I made a pretty darn good evaluation. I told the Reds I wanted to keep this kid. He was going to be something."

Vander Meer spotted the spirit, the drive, and the shortcomings. "The way he pivoted on a double play back then, he wouldn't *ever* get a good major league runner. And then his range was limited, particularly to his right."

Vander Meer told his boss, Phil Seghi, that he wanted to keep Rose, but not as a second baseman. "Let me put him at third or in the outfield." No, Seghi said. He insisted that Rose remain at second. At this point Vander Meer interrupts his story to sound a familiar cry of minor-league managers. "I'd been in the game going on twenty-five years and I'd had that good major league career, but what did I know, right? That farm director, maybe he played some C or D ball, but he was

the farm director, so he knew and I didn't. So at Tampa I had
to play Pete at second against my better judgment."

With his additional height and heft—Rose had reached 175
pounds—the winter boxcar loader blossomed in Florida's
simmering summer. Rose was never a slugger, but it is not
accurate to put him down, the way some have, as a singles
hitter; a "Punch-and-Judy hitter" in baseball argot. (Rose led
the National League in doubles five times.) A Pete Rose spe-
cialty for a quarter century was a 330-foot line drive wal-
loped between scurrying outfielders.

"He got off to a real good start," Vander Meer says. "Every
time I looked up he was driving one into the alleys and
running like a scalded dog and sliding headfirst into third. He
hit thirty triples for me that year. Led the league. Set a
league record for triples that still stands.

"He just hit the ball real well from both sides of the plate.
He was hitting .350 up until midseason, when the average
started to drop but not very much." (Rose batted .331 in
1961.)

"When you got a young player hitting .350 for you, you let
him alone," Vander Meer says. "I'm a firm believer in not
overcoaching. The only thing I ever told Pete was, 'Make
sure you get a good ball to hit. Don't swing at the bad ones.'
I don't know what went on at Geneva, but by the time I got
him in Tampa, and he was twenty years old, Pete Rose looked
to me like one wonderful hitter."

Macon, Georgia, summer of 1962, and the names were Pete
Rose and Dave Bristol and Tommy Helms and Art Shamsky
and everyone was very young and sometimes crazed. That
isn't "May-konn," Georgia. "May-konn" is Northern style.
Pretentious. Too much like Harvard and Yale. George Plimp-
ton and William F. Buckley may be the only people who
would pronounce the word as "May-konn."

This was redneck country. Think redneck, people. And

then you pronounce Macon in the current local manner, a style previously approved by the Confederate States of America. "Makin'," Georgia. "Makin'."

"Actually," says Art Shamsky in his solemn way, "Pete and I just called it 'Makin' Out.'"

That summer the Pete Rose happening was underway. He and Shamsky, Geneva buddies, celebrated their reunion by moving into the Macon YMCA. They were just about twenty-one. They could hit and they could play and all of a sudden reaching the major leagues was something real. Hey, they could do it. The idea then was to play ball like hell, but no one, not even Pete Rose, plays baseball every hour, so the idea was also to have a little fun.

Pete, a take-charge kid, assigned Shamsky to date the telephone operator at the Y. Shamsky is tall, dark-haired, and handsome. The telephone operator was missing two front teeth.

"I'm still trying to figure how Pete finagled me into that," Shamsky says. "I had a fine girl back home, whom I would marry, but nothing for the season and the drawls down there were so thick I had a little trouble making my way. So Pete keeps pushing me at this phone operator missing her front teeth and I'm saying, Pete, I don't think I'm that bad looking. Why should I spend the season dating an ugly girl?"

Rose: "What's more important, Art? The way the girl you're dating looks, or you and me getting free long-distance phone calls?"

Shamsky: "He actually got me to go for it. I don't remember who Pete was running with, two or three different girls over the season, I guess, and all of them were pretty. Sure we got free long-distance calls, but I was the only one who had to spend the summer dating a toothless girl."

Tommy Helms, who himself batted .340 that summer, says that in Macon you could tell Rose was going to be something special. "Running all the time. The headfirst slides. Energy

busting out of every pore." By this time Rose was earning a
better salary. He'd saved some money. He made a long-
distance call to Cincinnati (free, of course) and arranged for
his parents to pick up a new Corvette he'd ordered, and
drive it to Nashville, where he and Helms would meet them.
"If you saw that car," Helms says, "you would remember the
color. Pete picked it out himself. Mint green."

Harry and LaVerne met the boys in Nashville and wished
them a good trip back to Macon. Rose drove, a twenty-one-
year-old in a new green Corvette with out-of-state license
plates. Presently Rose and Helms were standing before a
justice of the peace in a small, forgotten Southern town.

No one remembers exactly the speed at which Rose was
clocked. A corollary question might be, how fast could a new
mint-green 1962 Corvette go?

"We're professional ballplayers," Rose told the judge. "We
have to get to Macon for a game."

This failed to awe. "Now I want you boys to empty your
pockets and your wallets," the judge said, "and just put all
your money right on that table there in front of me."

With two troopers in the wings, the judge counted the
collective funds of Rose and Helms, a sum of about $200.

"Now I figure," the judge said, "that you boys need about
$8 worth of gas to get yourselves back to Macon. The court
will keep the rest. That's your fine for speeding.

"Take $8, just $8, no more and then you're free to go.

"Have a safe trip to Macon and good luck in the ball game
tonight."

Dave Bristol, who was managing his sixth minor-league
season at the age of twenty-nine, just a few years senior to
some of the players, established a curfew. For Rose at
twenty-one, a curfew was something like a speed limit—one
more barrier to break.

One night he and Shamsky were behaving as immoder-
ately as they possibly could and returned to the YMCA after

even the room clerk had fallen asleep. "But there was somebody down from the Reds' minor-league organization," Shamsky says, "and he could stay up very late. So there was some possibility we might get caught. Then they could fine us, yell at us, and all that."

Aside from the front entrance to the Y, the building could be breached by proceeding up a fire escape. The bottom flight, so to speak, of the fire escape remained parallel to the ground about eight feet in the air, to discourage such breaches. Going down, in a real emergency, that bottom flight would swing into a vertical position when someone moved onto it, and provide decent access to the ground. But at rest the flight stood sideways, eight feet high.

Shamsky stands six feet two. He jumped, snagged a rung, and began climbing. Rose followed. "We were up maybe two levels," Shamsky said, "and suddenly a big light hits me. I look down and I see a fat cop, he looks like one of those Japanese sumo wrestlers, and in one hand he's got a flashlight. In the other hand he's got his gun."

"Come down or I'll shoot," the sumo wrestler–Georgia cop called.

"Pete," Shamsky said, in an urgent tone. "What do I do?"

"I'd say, Art," Rose said, quite calmly, "you'd better go down, or else the cop will shoot you."

After some talking, Rose and Shamsky avoided arrest. As they remember it, in the excitement they also avoided being fined.

Often the players made road trips not by bus but in station wagons, eight players riding in each. "If you were gonna sleep at all some nights," Rose said, "you'd have to learn to sleep sitting up. Sometimes I could. Sometimes I couldn't."

"I was driving a wagon one night," Shamsky says, "and I could hear Pete talking away in the back."

Rose wasn't sleepy. "How long is the trip gonna be, Art? There's nothing to do. I'm going nuts."

Shamsky made a perfunctory answer and continued driving a two-lane highway at sixty miles an hour. Suddenly, at the top of the windshield, two human palms appeared. Rose had opened a window, climbed to the roof of the wagon and crawled forward in the wind.

"I was just having fun," Rose says.

"I saw those hands," Shamsky says. "I couldn't believe it. I stayed on the road but don't ask me how."

Dave Bristol—the full name is James David Bristol—is a Macon native with a flat-featured face, a little country shrewdness to the eyes, and a wide mouth that seems about to curl into a smile. You could have a little fun with Dave Bristol. You might want to think twice, however, before sitting in with him for an evening of stud poker.

Bristol played infield in the Reds farm system for a decade from 1951 to 1961, scrapping, struggling, and never advancing within radar range of the major leagues. He played in places like Geneva; Palatka, Florida; and Visalia, California. A career baseball man and, it seemed, a career minor leaguer. But the Reds were alert to Bristol's quick intelligence— he put himself through Western Carolina College—and in 1957, when Bristol was twenty-three, he was appointed playing manager at Hornell, a small town along the southern tier of New York State with a franchise in the New York–Penn League. After that, he has managed or coached, nonstop, including jobs running the Reds, the Milwaukee Brewers, the Atlanta Braves, and the San Francisco Giants. In 1989, Bristol's thirty-eighth season in baseball, Rose hired him as the Reds' third-base coach.

"Have I known Pete?" Bristol says. "You'd be right if you guessed we go back a ways together and from the first time I had him down in Macon, Pete was the greediest player I ever saw.

"Greedy is the word, and that's no knock. A lot of ballplayers, when they get a couple of hits up front, they cruise. They've done their night's work. Particularly if the game is one-sided, they don't bear down on their last at-bats.

"Not Pete. If he got two hits, he wanted three. Get three hits, he wanted four. He kept coming at them, coming at them, never stopped.

"One game in Greenville, North Carolina, we had a big first inning, Pete was 0-for-2. As I say, Pete Rose keeps coming. When that game was over, Rose was 6-for-8."

When that season was over, Rose had batted .330, led the South Atlantic League in runs scored with 136 and led the league in triples as well, with seventeen, that headfirst slide into third becoming famous through Georgia and the Carolinas.

A spring later, Fred Hutchinson, who managed Cincinnati, spoke up so persuasively for this intense young player that Rose was promoted to the Reds, just before his twenty-second birthday.

He telephoned his father. "Dad. I made it. I'm with the Reds."

Tough Harry Rose, the unstoppable semipro running back, said, "Congratulations. We always knew you would."

Harry repeated the news to LaVerne in the living room of the Braddock Avenue house where she sat crocheting an afghan.

LaVerne put down her needles and began to weep. Soon tough Harry Rose was weeping, too.

"We were so happy," LaVerne says. "Why, my husband was just the proudest man, the proudest father in the world.

"If only he could have lived to see all that his kid has done . . ."

6

A Rose Grows in Cincinnati

CINCINNATI, 1963

It was not exactly the coming of Peter the Great, Piotr Alexseyevich, the Bronze Horseman of Pushkin's poem, who swept in as Czar of Russia in 1689 and, historians tell us, single-handedly created Russian civilization. It was, instead, the coming of Peter the Rose, a skinny, crew-cut kid whose constant chatter irritated veterans and whose intensity and drive seemed altogether too strong to be believable. "I was just so damn happy to be with the team," Rose says. "I figured then, I figure now, anybody who doesn't like life in the major leagues has got to be crazy."

Although no one knew it at the time, the brash, skinny rookie was point man for an era of glory and other blessings that would last sixteen seasons in Cincinnati until a general manager named Dick Wagner let Rose go to Philadelphia, because of a disagreement about money (Wagner's version) or because of the publicity surrounding alleged marital discord (Pete's belief). "Hey, who you gonna believe," Rose asks intensely, "Dick Wagner or me?"

"It's your book, Pete."

"Then take it from me. I know what's going on. If there hadn't been a divorce, Wagner wouldn't have let me go. The year before I put people in the ballparks like nobody else. You remember my forty-four-game hitting streak? In 1978 that was the biggest story in baseball. You don't let a hitter like I was then get away from you just for a few thousand bucks."

It is trying sometimes to keep Rose in strict chronology. His mind and his tongue are so quick that unless you're careful he can be playing the ninth inning while you're still leading off in the first. "Back then," Rose says, focusing into the deep past with a certain effort, "I had nothing. I mean when I was a rookie, I had my Corvette, but I didn't exactly own major league clothing. Jeans and T-shirts and sneakers. That's what you wear in the minors. And you do your own laundry. But the first month with the Reds it hit me that I really was a big leaguer. It was time to start dressing like a big leaguer. I went for a wad. Five hundred dollars. Ties. White shirts. Sports jackets. Good slacks, and I kept 'em pressed. When I went back to the old neighborhood, after the games at Crosley Field, the people couldn't believe this well-dressed guy was me."

The 1963 Reds were a good but not outstanding team, with a substantial veteran penciled in at second base, Don (the Blazer) Blasingame, coming off a season in which he had batted .281. "Second base wasn't up for grabs with Blazer there," Rose says. "But, hell, I still wanted to grab for it. Look at it this way. Down in Macon they gave me $3.50 a day for meals. Good nutrition is important so breakfast would set me back $2.00. That meant for the whole rest of the day I'd have a big buck and a half to eat on. What happened? I'd eat all right, but I had to dip into my own money, if I wanted more than a candy bar, which I did. With the Reds in 1963, the meal money was $10.00 a day. Not a fortune, but that would cover what it cost, even with steak. With all respect to Blasingame, I wanted that $10.00 a day meal money for myself. Let somebody else try to feed his face three meals for $3.50."

Rose was a rookie on the run. Some days he jogged the five miles from the spring-training field at Redsland to the Tampa Causeway Inn. "I couldn't arrange to bring my car down—nowadays I have a Porsche or two shipped—and I couldn't afford to rent a car, and the veterans who could weren't talking to me much. They were for Blasingame. They probably guessed I was a threat to his job, which is what I was trying to be. So how was I gonna get from the field back to the motel? Hitchhike? I was in a major league camp. A major league camp for the first time in my life. Major league ballplayers don't hitchhike. That's bush. So I'd get out of my uniform and into jeans and sneakers and I'd jog the whole five miles. No big deal. Besides, it strengthened my legs."

Fred Hutchinson, who managed the Reds from 1959 into 1964, was a tall, black-haired two hundred pounder, a former pitcher whose gait suggested a black bear approaching supper after having missed lunch and possibly breakfast. Hutchinson's bearing and his strong-jawed look concealed a nature of remarkable sensitivity. Once when he was managing the St. Louis Cardinals, a newsmagazine asked me to write a cover story about Stan Musial (whose National League record total of 3,630 hits Rose broke in August 1981). Hutchinson spoke so well during one late supper that I kept my notebook empty, for fear the act of taking notes might stifle the marvelous flow. At length Musial appeared and pointed to the notebook. "Got that thing filled yet?" Musial said in his forever genial way.

"I'm afraid I haven't helped him, Stash," Hutchinson said to Musial. "I've been doing my best, talking for forty minutes, and he hasn't taken a single note."

A regret that lingers is that I didn't burst out with the truth: "Hutch, you've been wonderful." But we were all macho long ago and couldn't say such things.

Rose, the extrovert's extrovert, intrigued Hutchinson, an essentially contained man except when one of his teams played listless ball. (Then Hutchinson could close the clubhouse door, rant, and even throw chairs.) He invited Rose to the Reds' camp in 1963, but did not press to have him added to the roster. Blasingame was solid and the jump from the Sally League to the majors could well be longer than Rose could manage, even adding in the headfirst slide.

On March 10, 1963, the Reds began their exhibition season in Tampa with a game against the Chicago White Sox. Rose had worked out all morning and, curiously for him, late in the game he gathered his gear and started toward the locker room. He hadn't played. He didn't think he was going to play. Why hang around?

"Where are you going, kid?" said Mike Ryba, an old coaching hand with the Reds who had pitched major league ball for the Cardinals and Red Sox.

"They don't need me," Rose said.

"Stick around, kid. You never know."

With the game scoreless in the ninth, Hutchinson looked about. No sense in wearing down his regulars in March. "Rose," the manager said. "You're in at second."

In his first time at bat against major league pitching, Rose doubled. That came in the eleventh inning. In the fourteenth, he doubled again and scored the winning run. "I've never left early, never even *thought* of leaving early, ever since."

The two happiest Reds were Rose and Hutchinson. Hutch told one friend, "You know Blasingame is popular with his teammates, but from what I've seen of the kid, if I had any guts, I'd stick Rose on second and forget about him."

For the rest of that spring, Rose batted .290 and the night

before the regular season opened, Hutchinson said, "Pete, I've had them book you into a hotel room. I don't want you going home."

"Why not?"

"I'm promoting you to the Reds. You're our starting second baseman. The word is going out and I don't want the neighbors bothering you all night."

Earl Lawson, a Cincinnati baseball writer for decades, remembers that Rose's promotion was "roundly unpopular" with the veterans. "You heard talk," Lawson says, "that they were using Pete only because he was a local boy and that would put more customers in the stands. A lot of the regulars said Rose couldn't get around on a good fastball. In fact, during spring training I asked eight players to give me the final squad that the Reds would start with. They all worked at it for a while. Rose only made one player's team. That player was Don Blasingame." (By July Blasingame would be gone from Cincinnati, shipped off to that classic third-world baseball team, the Washington Senators.)

Rose started slowly, three hits in twenty-five at-bats, and Hutchinson benched him. "Not because I had lost any faith in Pete," Hutchinson said, "but because I was trying to take some pressure off the kid. I knew he was a local boy and that his father was coming to every game." By mid-May Rose was back in the lineup, ripping line drives that ballplayers call frozen ropes.

The veteran Reds maintained walls of silence. Rose could chatter all he wanted in his new-won kingdom. They didn't have to chatter back, or even listen. Only two established Reds gave Rose attention. One was Vada Pinson, a sleek and swift center fielder, who had batted .343 in 1961. The other was Frank Robinson, who became the only man to win the Most Valuable Player award in both the National and American leagues.

Rose: "The other guys just wouldn't hang with me. Even

my roommate. One night on the road, I get back to the hotel room and I can't get in. My roomie has the chain across the door. You can figure out why, what he was doing. He wasn't alone. But what about me? It's midnight and I'm out in the hall. I don't have to give you the guy's name. I said right up front, I'm not Jim Bouton.

"So I got nowhere to sleep but the lobby and I go down the hall to where Vada Pinson is bunking and he says, sure, kid, there's an extra bed in here. You're welcome.

"Next morning Vada says we'll eat breakfast in. Room service. I wasn't sure what room service was. I never heard of room service in the minors. Eat hearty, Vada told me, and I ordered good and Vada picked up the check. To this day I remember what it was: $12.75."

"Here was this kid," Pinson says, "who wanted to be a major leaguer more than anything in the world. But he was so raw, he just didn't know how. Frank Robinson and I took a little time to show him. Dressing. Tipping. Basics like that. No big deal. Just a little kindness to a youngster."

"I hung around with Vada and Frank all the time," Pete says. "They're black guys. That meant nothing. They were *nice* guys."

A few months into the season a Reds official—Rose won't name him, either—called in the rookie. "I got a friendly tip for you," the man said. "What you're doing is bad for your image."

"What's that?"

"Hanging around with niggers."

Rose fled. "They could tell me a lot of things in that front office. They were my employers and I'd do what they said. But to call terrific ballplayers like Frank Robinson and Vada Pinson niggers . . . I've gotten excited on the ballfield and used some language, but to this day that's one word nobody in the world will hear me use."

"And?"

"And what? I kept hanging out with Frank and Vada."

Rose had a rousing rookie season on a team that finished a strong fifth in what was, in 1963, a single-division ten-team National League. Great stars kept the league ablaze: Willie Mays and Willie McCovey in San Francisco; Hank Aaron with the Milwaukee Braves; and Roberto Clemente, entering his prime at Pittsburgh determined to show, as Clemente told anyone who listened, "Latin ballplayers are *good* ballplayers, not hot dogs."

For his starting Cincinnati salary of $7,500, twenty-two-year-old Pete Rose got to see magnificent pitching very close. Sandy Koufax was too good for the league. He pitched eleven shutouts and won twenty-five games. Sadly for the batters, there was no higher league on earth; they had to face the heavy heat of Koufax, every four days all summer long. When the Dodgers won the pennant, the New York Yankees of Mickey Mantle and Roger Maris, a team not distinguished by humility, went forth to battle Koufax in the World Series on a cold, sun-bright October afternoon in the Bronx.

Bobby Richardson, a high fastball hitter, led off for the Yankees. Koufax threw Richardson three high fastballs and struck him out. Then he gazed into the Yankee dugout, the left-hander from Olympus considering mortals, and the look said to many: "I'll pitch into your power and I'll *still* strike you out." Koufax struck out fourteen more and the Dodgers swept the Yankees, who seemed relieved to pick up loser's checks and beat it hence.

A shade beneath Koufax, batters could swing against his formidable teammate, Don Drysdale. Bob Gibson alarmed batters for the St. Louis Cardinals. Juan Marichal, master of five pitches, high-kicked his way to twenty-five victories for the Giants. A left-handed gentleman from the Pleistocene

Age, Warren Edward Spahn—actually Spahn was only forty-two—won twenty-three games for the Braves.

"When I was a kid," Rose said, "and my dad couldn't get to Crosley Field, I'd hang around outside. Skinny little crew-cut kid and I'd go up to strangers and say, 'Got an extra ticket, mister?' Sometimes it worked. Sometimes I got into the ball-park that way. And now the guys I'd begged my way in to see, Spahn, Stan Musial, like that, I was playing major league ball on the same field with them. And in the town where I grew up. I was still skinny and crew-cut when I was twenty-two. Can you imagine what that meant to me, Rog?"

"Your dad, Pete, was he out watching you every night?"

"Every night he could. I was running out walks and sliding headfirst, but one night I must have loafed a little, going from first to third. After the game my dad was waiting outside the clubhouse. He wanted to know if I had flu. I told him I was fine. He said he thought that I must be sick, not hustling all out on one play.

"Some dad, he was. He cheered me and he gave me tips but he always put in the same phrase. 'Keep hustling.' How could you not hustle if you had a dad like that, a great dad like mine? How could you not hustle to show him he had the son he had always wanted to have?"

Rose hustled in 1963 as though possessed. He batted .273 in 157 games, cracked 25 doubles, and scored 101 runs. You couldn't miss him with the drive, the energy, the chatter sometimes coming out among little whistles through gaps in his teeth which, in later years, cosmetic dentistry dammed. "He's just a little slappy with the bat," Hutchinson said, meaning Rose slapped at some pitches rather than swinging straight through. "That'll pass. He's going to be some hitter." Rose already was some hitter. He was selected as the National League Rookie of the Year.

Even then, he had begun to like racehorses. The action of the track excited him. "Racehorses are athletes, like ballplayers," he says to this day. One day at the races he was studying ponies through binoculars and then not studying ponies any more. His eyes had picked up one Karolyn Ann Engelhardt, comely, miniskirted, auburn-haired, full-busted. "I like to look at horses," he says, "but there are other things, too."

Pete moved in slowly, politely. Karolyn was an ebullient Cincinnati girl, a sports fan. She knew who Pete Rose was. They dated. He bought her jewelry. Very quickly, they found themselves in love. Karolyn had been raised a Roman Catholic and they set their wedding date for January 25, 1964, at St. William's Church in Cincinnati. Karolyn Engelhardt was suddenly Pete Rose's rookie of the year.

Life with Rose proceeds along several tracks, all rapid. After the wedding Rose had to scurry to a banquet room where he sat on the dais for the Cincinnati baseball writers' dinner. He had agreed to speak. On this occasion, he kept it short. "I'm going for more doubles next year," said Rose the bridegroom. "I'm no longer a single man."

Genial laughter. Rose jumped off the dais, ran down a hallway, and vaulted into his Corvette. He ran some Cincinnati red lights, but even so arrived at his own wedding reception hours late. "It was okay," he explained later. "There were maybe a thousand people, but nobody got upset."

What about Karolyn? Wasn't she annoyed that her husband was late to his own wedding reception?

"Karolyn always understood a ballplayer's life," Rose said. "She did what she had to do. She recepted all the people very nicely."

With years, the love grew hard for both of them, but at first they were a pair of free spirits, matched in heaven, mated in Ohio. Their spirits were about as wild and free as any can be in Cincinnati, fountainhead of Taft conservatives, world headquarters of Procter & Gamble, the company which for years advertised its Ivory soap as 99 and 44/100 percent pure. (The town is somewhat looser today. It now houses Cincinnati Microwave, a company that purveys radar detectors to drivers who want to break speed limits without getting ticketed and are not excessively concerned with purity.)

Pete and Karolyn flourished and in time she was hosting a radio talk show out of nearby Covington, Kentucky. Karolyn won new fame for herself when she was announcing an evening's menu of sporting events. "In hockey," she said, "the Stingers will be playing at home tonight. Puck-off time is 7:35." For a time after that she was Karolyn "Puck-off" Rose.

The country was entering an age of casual murder. When Rose unseated Blasingame at Crosley Field, John Kennedy was president, more confident after the Cuban Missile Crisis passed and with it the shattering imminence of a nuclear shoot-out against the Soviet Union of Nikita Khrushchev. Kennedy had not, in fact, accomplished much as president but his patrician style excited the country. Most believed that given time he could accomplish a great deal. Time stopped for John Kennedy on November 22, 1963.

Lyndon Johnson was inaugurated and, with the support and encouragement of a Kennedy cabinet, he led the country into war in Vietnam. Martin Luther King arose, first as a leader of a boycott against Southern bus companies, later as the most eloquent speaker of the time. With King preaching, orating for peace and civil rights, blacks rioted in inner cities and set fires across Harlem, Detroit, and the Watts district of Los Angeles. In the sixties many wondered how the country could remain one country, among the ragged, smoldering canyons that split black and white society.

Draftees, both black and white, fled to Canada to escape military service. At length a Democratic senator from Minnesota, Eugene McCarthy, ran against the war in Democratic primaries. He did so well that Robert Kennedy improvised his own instant antiwar platform and ran himself.

Johnson, foreseeing his political death, announced he would not run again. But havoc was abroad. Martin Luther King was murdered in April 1968 and the spirited debate between Gene McCarthy and Bobby Kennedy ceased a few months later when Kennedy was assassinated in California. The Democratic party could not recover and, in 1968, the American presidency passed into the hands of Richard M. Nixon. It was a decade remembered in a large sense as one remembers nightmares. One would like to forget but one cannot.

The Vietnam War touched the Rose family when Pete's younger brother, David, was drafted. "We worried when Dave was over there," Rose says. "We're no different from other families. What family wouldn't worry with a kid in Vietnam?

"I got over myself with Joe DiMaggio. The Army asked us to go out to base hospitals and visit the wounded. We saw some guys shot pretty bad. That's all I know of war firsthand, kids busted up and blinded by shrapnel. They gave me a temporary rank of colonel, but I don't think I'd make much of a military man. Salute and tell the troops, 'Go kill. Go kill. Go kill.'

"I like things a helluva lot better without the salute and telling the troops something else. 'Go to right when they throw you that outside slider. Come on. Hit the hell out of the ball.' "

As a wedding gift in 1964, the Netherland Plaza Hotel gave Pete and Karolyn Rose free use of an expensive bridal suite. Art Shamsky and his wife, Randee, helped the Roses check in.

"Hey, Art," Pete said. "That's one tremendous suite they got for us. Why not save yourself a hotel bill tonight and bunk in with Karolyn and me?"

"This is your wedding night, Pete, not ours."

"No problem. We're all friends, aren't we?"

Karolyn said nothing. She simply stared. When Shamsky begged off, her look showed relief. "You know, Pete," she said, "it's better that we be alone. I really am a rookie. You're going to have to teach me."

The Shamskys said good night and Rose said that he would teach Karolyn everything he knew.

The couple began housekeeping at Fort Knox, Kentucky, where Rose was serving a hitch with the Ohio National Guard. At 7:00 A.M. on March 14, 1964, Rose was separated from the service. He sped 210 miles, working his way around an Ohio River flood, to Greater Cincinnati Airport, where Pete dropped himself off. He had to catch a plane for spring training. Karolyn's eyes were wet. He was flying away from her on her twenty-second birthday. "I knew it was her birthday," Rose said. "But I had to report. You don't get days off for wives' birthdays, or your own birthday, not that I'd want one. That's how it is when you're a ballplayer."

It was eleven at night before Rose arrived at the International Hotel in Tampa, the Reds' spring-training base in 1964. He proceeded directly to Art Shamsky's room. "I'm here," Rose announced. "Get your glove."

"For what, for God's sakes. It's nearly midnight."

"To have a catch. I want to get loose."

"Where are we gonna have a catch?"

"In the hall, Art. The room looks kinda small. The hall would be fine."

"I'm going to sleep, Pete," Shamsky said. "You can play catch all day tomorrow."

Rose reached the ballpark at eight the next morning. Some hours later a right-hander named Bob Purkey was ready to throw batting practice. Rose jumped into the cage, lay down four bunts and then, with his first swing, lined a pitch deep into the left-field corner.

"Hey," he shouted at Pinson. "I'm back, Vada. I'm back."
Pinson grinned. "You didn't have to tell me, Pete. I noticed."

As Rose bounced around spring-training camp, reporters asked him about the sophomore jinx. That question, directed at a rookie of the year, is, in Johnny Bench's phrase, a given. Second base will lie between first and third, and lie there every spring. Umpires will wear blue. And reporters will ask a rookie of the year about the sophomore jinx.

Some great rookies simply picked up the pace in their second year. Ted Williams's batting average moved from .327 to .344. Stan Musial sprang from .315 to a typical Musial .357. But enough rookies stumble in their second season to fuel the question across decades. Besides, it helped fill columns in the spring before sporting pornography exploded upon us and offered up such baseball tales as Margo Adams.

Joe Black won fifteen games for the Dodgers of 1952 and started three more in the World Series. "What about the sophomore jinx, Joe?" someone asked in the spring of 1953.

"That's all psychology," Black said. "Rookies hear about the sophomore jinx and that makes them worry about the sophomore jinx. Then their heads get messed up and they have an off year. I majored in psychology at Morgan State College. I know about these things. The sophomore jinx is not going to psych me."

That sounded like a fine, well-reasoned, if not a classic Freudian, answer. Then as a sophomore Joe Black won not fifteen games but six.

Rose did not study psychology, or much of anything except sports, in his five years at Western Hills High, but he is a sound intuitive psychologist. He didn't want to talk about the sophomore jinx, he told reporters. That was negative thinking. He intended to think positively. There wasn't any such

thing as a sophomore jinx, anyway, he said. It was just something reporters made up.

So saying, sophomore Pete went into the worst slump of his
career. By late June, Hutchinson had to bench him. Rose was
batting .214. "I couldn't understand what was happening. I
was worried as hell. I was telling this to Walt Harmon, who
I played ball with as a kid, and Walt didn't have a clue,
either. But he had one good idea. He told me to talk to
my Uncle Buddy. You know. The guy who got the Reds to
sign me."

Buddy Bloebaum was sympathetic and professional. Rose
was holding his hands too high. He was swinging defensively,
as if afraid to strike out. "Lower your hands, Pete," Bloebaum
said, "and attack the ball."

Rose the attacker smacked eight hits in the next two
games. He was on a tear and with him came the Reds. The
1964 pennant race was wonderfully exciting, sweeping into
the final week of the season. The Phillies, with Richie Allen,
not much more hitting, and a deep pitching staff, had been
leading. Then they lost ten in a row. The Reds came charging, along with a good Cardinal team driven by Bob Gibson,
Curt Simmons, Ken Boyer, and Lou Brock.

On September 27, the Reds swept a doubleheader from
the Mets and moved into first place by one game. They lost
to Pittsburgh on September 29 and fell into a tie with the
Cardinals. Going into the last day of the season, the Reds and
the Cardinals were tied, with records of 92–69. The Phillies
were one game back at 91–70.

With everything to win on the final day, and victory insur-
ing at least a playoff, the Reds rolled over at Crosley Field.
The Phillies beat them, 10–0. The Cardinals won their game
in St. Louis and went on and won a seven-game World Series
from the Yankees. Shocked by Koufax the year before, the
Yankees now ran into Bob Gibson, who struck out thirty-one
in three starts. "Say," Mickey Mantle asked a cocktail wait-

ress. "Doesn't anyone ever throw a change-up in the National League?"

"That was one big baseball year," Pete Rose says, "but the biggest thing for all of us Cincinnati Reds went a long way beyond the ball games. Fred Hutchinson got sick."

Hutchinson was forty-five when lung cancer struck him. "It was something to see the way this big, strong guy hung on," Rose says. "It was sad, but it was inspiring.

"We saw Hutch go from 220 pounds to 140 pounds with the cancer and he never once complained. Tough. Really tough. More than baseball tough. He was a man.

"He had this cough and he was getting skinnier every day, but Hutch was a fighter. He'd come into the clubhouse to conduct the meetings and after a while, looking at Hutch was like looking at a skeleton. But I'll tell you this. That skeleton was in charge.

"I was a kid. I'd never seen cancer before. Never seen courage like Hutch's, either. We all knew he was sick. You couldn't *not* know that he was sick. But he ran the meetings the way he always had. He didn't want sympathy. Strictly baseball. Never mind my cancer. Go out on that field and play like hell.

"Damn, we tried. We would have walked through walls for Hutch."

On August 12, Hutchinson had to step down and Dick Sisler replaced him. But, still fighting, Hutchinson returned in civilian clothes on the last day of the season. After the Reds lost that ball game, someone said, "Too bad, Hutch. The ballplayers should have won this one for you."

Hutchinson coughed and cleared his throat. He was dying. "No," he said. "They should have won it for themselves."

At Hutchinson's urging, Rose flew to Venezuela for a season of winter baseball. The stricken skipper said he thought that might further improve Rose's play at second base.

"They loved Pete down there," says Damaso Blanco, a
Venezuelan who played briefly for the Giants. ("I was Willie
McCovey's designated runner," Blanco says. "If Willie got a
hit in the late innings, I ran for him.")

Many American athletes come to regard winter ball as not
much more than an extra season in the sun. "They come
down and don't put out," Blanco says. "Not Pete. One night
his team was ahead, 20–3, and he hit a line drive between the
outfielders. A sure double. Maybe a triple. Gary Kolb, who
played for the Cardinals, knew the score. He knew his team
was down by 17 runs. So he didn't run after the ball. He just
trotted slowly. Pete doesn't play that way. He went all out
and reached the plate, an inside-the-park home run, with a
headfirst slide. They gave him a standing ovation. An American player hustling like that with the game already won. The
fans couldn't believe it. They cheered and cheered."

Rose: "That's the way you're supposed to play baseball.
There's nothing so special in what I did. The fans paid for
their tickets. How can you *not* go all out?"

On November 13, Rose was riding a bus to a ballpark in
Caracas, seated beside Reggie Otero, who coached at Cincinnati in the summer. Otero listened to a portable radio, a
broadcast in Spanish.

Suddenly he gasped and began to sob. Otero pointed to the
radio. "The news . . ."

"Hutch . . ."

"He die."

Like Otero, Rose broke into tears. "Hutch had faith in me.
He gave me my chance. I just wish he coulda lived to see me
hit .300."

After Hutchinson's death, Rose batted over .300 fourteen
times in fifteen seasons. Back from Venezuela in 1965, he
blossomed into the best all-around second baseman in the
league. He was also ticketed at 4:30 on the morning of July

9 in Newport, Kentucky, for running a red light. The trooper learned that Rose didn't have his driver's license with him, either.

Rose was no stranger to traffic courts. The judge bumped him with a $10.00 fine, plus $3.50 in costs. "But this is also going to cost me 18,000 boos," Rose said, "and $500.00 for breaking curfew."

He was wrong. Dick Sisler fined him $250.00, and, to Rose's delight, nobody booed. Instead the crowd cheered Rose when he was given a color television set in a brief ceremony at home plate for leading all the Reds in balloting for the All-Star team. (Rose made the National League All-Star team thirteen times between 1965 and 1985; an all-star second baseman in 1965 and an all-star first baseman twenty years later. He would also start all-star games at third base, in right field, and in left, a total of five different positions. No one has come close to matching that combination of endurance and versatility nor is it likely that anyone ever will.)

The Reds of the mid and late 1960s were neither very good nor very bad. Dick Sisler couldn't win with them in 1965 and a journeyman named Don Heffner replaced him for 1966. The year endures in certain Cincinnati annals as unique. It was the season Charlie didn't hustle.

"That spring I was twenty-four," Rose says, "and feeling pretty good about myself. I'd cracked .300. I led the league in putouts at my position. And suddenly in training camp the manager told me, he didn't ask me, that he was moving me to third. You know how hard I'd worked to become a good second baseman and now, when I about had it down, as much as you can have anything down in baseball, they move me off to a place I'd never played.

"Aside from me personally, I didn't think the switch would help the team. Help, hell. I thought it would weaken the club at two positions, second and third.

"Some of the reporters wrote that I was sweating in spring

training, trying to learn a new position. The truth is I didn't sweat enough. I just didn't work hard at learning third. I know that doesn't sound like me, but it's true. I wouldn't accept the move. I was just stubborn."

The Reds began abysmally, losing eleven of their first fifteen games. They dropped into last place. Rose made two errors in one inning. His batting wobbled. The new .300 hitter was having trouble batting .200. In the dugout during one early game, Rose turned to a backup infielder called Chico Ruiz. "You're hitting better than me," Rose said.

"I haven't been to bat this season, Pete."

"I know. And you're still hitting better than me."

Before April ended, Rose moved back to second base and Tommy Helms, one of the Macon madcaps, took over third. Rose celebrated by going on a 12-for-26 batting run. He went on to hit .313 for the season.

"Nine years later," Rose says, "I was back at third base, and this time I just about broke my butt, learning the position. When I got the award as Most Valuable Player for the 1975 World Series, I was a third baseman. I think I learned some things along the way. When I was playing, I always tried to think like a manager. Where's the game at? What are the moves? Where's the ball? That's important. Now here you have one manager telling the best second baseman in the league, me, he's got to go play third. It doesn't work and the manager gets fired.

"Now in 1974, I played a good left field. I made only one error the whole year. Then they moved me to third and I do great.

"What's the difference in the two moves?

"The first manager told me to play third. Sparky Anderson *asked*. You don't tell a good ballplayer to move. You ask him.

"I've never forgotten that.

"If Sparky Anderson had asked me to catch, I wouldn't have smiled, but I would have done it.

"It happens he didn't have to ask me to catch. He had another guy who could handle things behind the plate.

"Johnny Bench, just the best catcher I ever saw."

Observers watching the passion of Rose's play across the years have concluded that he would play baseball for nothing. For free. For zero zero zero dollars a year. That is a reckless assumption to make about any professional athlete and particularly inappropriate in Rose's case. "Pete has always been what we call a 'hard sign,' " says Sheldon "Chief" Bender, that soft-voiced, sandy-haired grandfather, who has spent more than two decades as the Reds' director of player personnel. (The Reds have had five different presidents across that period, but only one director of personnel. Bender is a municipal asset in Cincinnati, gifted in his judgments of talent, organized, unobtrusive, and invaluable, as all the presidents from Francis L. Dale [1967] to Marge Schott [1989] have recognized.)

"There's nothing wrong with being a hard sign," Bender says, "except it made my job a little more difficult when I had to be the one to do the signing. Pete always wanted the last dollar that he could get. He'd give you fits."

Rose: "Yeah, but once I signed a contract, I stayed with that contract. When I was closing in on Cobb and half the country was watching, I could have said, 'Hold it. I'm not getting paid much for what I'm doing. I'm gonna sit right now, unless I get a better contract! But I didn't do that, did I? I didn't hold anybody up. A contract is like giving your word. Don't break it."

When Rose came up with the Reds he was earning $7,500, then $1,500 above the minimum salary for a major league player. By 1965, he had moved up to $13,500. Now, with a .312 year under his belt and as the best young second baseman in the league, he wanted to be paid $25,000. The appearance of lawyers and agents who negotiate on behalf of ballplayers is a recent phenomenon, born in the 1970s, along with free agency and the death of the so-called reserve clause, by which a team exercised a sole and noncompetitive option on a ballplayer's services from the time he first signed a minor-league contract until, weathered and worn, he was good enough only for old-timers' games. The one-on-one negotiation was classically loaded in favor of the ball club. The player was unlikely to be schooled in contracts, much less the art of bargaining. Wearing street clothes, stripped of his ball-field glamour, the ballplayer walked in to face a baseball man who had been negotiating fifty contracts a year for decades.

Baseball lore resounds with stories of penurious owners underpaying the help through guile, deceit, or simple cruelty. A workaday Brooklyn outfielder named Gene Hermanski completed a solid .290 season in 1948 and told a newspaperman that he was damned if he was going to play another year for the $7,500 he had been earning. He then walked into the office of Branch Rickey, probably the most guileful and sometimes the cruelest of baseball negotiators. Half an hour later, Hermanski reappeared wearing a grin.

"Get your raise, Gene?" the newspaperman asked.

"No," Hermanski said, still smiling, "but Mr. Rickey didn't cut me."

It was in this persistent, atavistic, some said feudal climate that Pete Rose walked in to see Phil Seghi in early 1966 and make his case for $25,000.

Rose had statistics at the ready, batting average, runs scored, hits—209, most in the league. "Aside from that," he said, "the fans really like me. They're noticing the way I play."

Seghi handed Rose a contract. The salary was filled in, not at $25,000 but at $17,500. If the baseball times were indeed feudal, Rose was about to flunk his serf test.

"You gotta be kidding, seventeen five. I oughta walk out of here with this contract right now and take it right to Earl

Lawson. This would give Earl a story for his newspaper all right."

Seghi grabbed back the contract. "We could go as high as $21,000."

"You could go higher." Rose held his line. The Reds needed him. He was indeed popular, the hard-driving play picking up fans, and some detractors as well, all around the National League. Rose was about as unobtrusive as a Hell's Angel in an art gallery. He had indeed led the league in hits. He got his $25,000.

Later Rose would remark that one of his ambitions was to become the first $100,000-a-year singles hitter. He didn't make proper allowance for inflation and the explosive baseball salaries of the 1980s. Eventually Rose's salary reached $1,000,000. Besides, the ambition as he stated it was touched with curious hype. The phrase was catchy: $100,000-a-year singles hitter. It summoned up contrasts with other $100,000 players: Ted Williams, Stan Musial, Joe DiMaggio. All were masters of the long ball.

But these days, in one of those curious contradictions that appear in dialogues with Rose, he does not like to be remembered as a singles hitter. "You saw me," he said. "I had some power. I led the league in doubles five times. I got 746 doubles in my career, which is 22 more than Ty Cobb. I got the most doubles in the history of the National League. Tris Speaker is the only major leaguer who ever lived who got more doubles than me, if I'm not mistaken. Are my figures right?"

Rose is always right when citing batting statistics and absolutely unimpeachable when the statistics are his own. "I was no Punch-and-Judy hitter, popping humpback liners over the infielders' heads. I hit for good power in the alleys." He was content to call himself a singles hitter when he was trying to earn six figures. Indignation appears when somebody else calls him a singles hitter; indignation and enough numbers to occupy arithmetic classes in a dozen Cincinnati grade schools for a semester.

Talk with Rose sweeps from topic to topic, the tongue hard at work moving double-time, in rhythm with the mind. "I bargained hard, but I had to have the hits to do it. You couldn't go into a front office with a .210 average and say anything more than, 'Please sign me again.'

"In 1966 now, my best big-league year up to that point, I batted .313 and I hit sixteen home runs.

"I'd kid with fans on the banquet circuit. That year, '66, I went 11-for-14 against Warren Spahn and 13-for-15 off Bob Friend. At the end of the season they both announced they were retiring. I'd tell the fans, 'The 1967 season hasn't started yet, and already I'm down to .270.'

"That's having fun. Negotiating a contract isn't having fun. I wouldn't joke. I'd give them the numbers and make my case. For my first couple years with the Reds, I worked winters. I had to be a car salesman in the off-season. A lot of people don't remember those days any more, when major league ballplayers had to take winter jobs to support their families.

"My first year with the Reds, I told you, $7,500, 1963. My last season with the Phillies, 1983, I figured it out, I was getting paid $10,000 a game. *A game.* No wonder people don't remember when ballplayers had to work winters.

"Seems like old times. Seems like *ancient* times. I can understand. Come on. Let's go to the bank and visit my money."

The Reds were building slowly, very slowly, toward the Big Red Machine, quite literally a squad of all-stars that peaked in the mid-1970s. Except at All-Star games, there has not been as good a ball club since. But the 1960s were seasons in which the Reds were more exciting than successful. Tony

Perez was in place. Rose was in several places. Dave Bristol, who replaced Heffner as the Red's manager halfway through 1966, asked him to play outfield in 1967. Asked and not told, Pete cheerfully headed for the fences, making room at second base for his old Macon buddy, Tommy Helms. Johnny Bench appeared. But there were weak spots and the pitching was uncertain. The Reds were contenders, without being winners, a situation Rose had to face again as a manager some twenty years later.

Rose's progress from good hitter to great hitter became so vividly clear in 1968 that he moved beyond *The Sporting News* and onto the hyperbolic pages of *Time* magazine. The unsigned story was headlined, "$100,000 Worth of Singles."

> In an age of the impotent bat and the omnipotent pitch, the National League's Cincinnati Reds are a curious anachronism. Their mound staff is a monument to mediocrity, but Red batsmen are rattling the fences from Crosley Field to Candlestick Park. The team batting average is .270, tops in either league by 18 points.
>
> Best of the bunch is Pete Rose, 26, a brassy, bristle-topped Irishman, whose flip tongue and frenetic brand of baseball have injected fresh breath into an increasingly stale game. . . . Equally notable is his penchant for playing every second as if his spikes were hot out of the forge.

The English language—the late Red Smith called it "the Mother Tongue"—gets surprising massages in newsmagazines. Can you "inject" fresh breath? Of course you can. Just as surely as you can inhale penicillin. Is Rose an Irishman? *Time* mentioned his Uncle Buddy Bloebaum. Why, walking the streets of Castlebar in County Mayo, you just bump into one Bloebaum after another. Rose's ancestry is Scotch, Irish, and German, which would seem to have made him a brassy, bristle-topped American.

Whatever. An athlete from the increasingly stale game of baseball had cracked *Time*'s frenetic sports section. Obscurity and Rose were becoming strangers.

Mateo Rojas Alou, called Matty, a fast, feathery left-handed batter, was having a good run with the Pirates. He won the batting championship in 1966 (.342), finished third in 1967 (.338), and was, if one bets on such things, the favorite to win the championship in 1968.

At the top of the final week of the season, Rose was hitting twelve points higher than Alou. "Pressure," he says, "I'll tell you what pressure is. It's going for your first batting championship the way I did it." Abruptly, Rose lost his touch and went 1-for-12. Over the same period, Matty Alou went 9-for-12. With three days left in the season, Alou, streaking, and Rose, slumping, were tied at .331.

On Friday, September 27, Alou went hitless in four turns at bat in Chicago. That night in Cincinnati the Reds played a fifteen-inning game with the Giants. Rose went 1-for-7.

"You look like an old woman the way you're swinging the bat," Tommy Helms said.

"I know. I know. But I don't know what to do about it."

"Come out early tomorrow," Helms said. "Take extra batting practice." So on September 29, half a year after spring training and with 147 regular-season games behind him, Rose reported early to Crosley Field. He spent twenty-five minutes working on his swing.

Gaylord Perry, a six-foot-four-inch right-hander who would win 314 major league games, was pitching for the Giants. Periodically batters accused Perry of throwing spitballs and an occasional accuser was Pete Rose. "You gotta cheat to get me out," Rose would call and Perry, in the manner of sensible accused spitball pitchers, declined to respond. "I wasn't saying I threw the wet one and I'd have been stupid to say I didn't throw the wet one," Perry said subsequently. "If I had the hitter looking for it, that was one more thing for them to worry about. Their problem. Not mine."

That Saturday after the extra batting practice, Rose cracked out four straight hits, sliding into second with the fourth, his forty-first double and springing up in jubilation. "Man," Rose said to Hal Lanier, the Giants' shortstop, the closest mortal. "Isn't that something?"

"Yeah," Lanier said. "It sure is. The other guy has just gone 4-for-4."

"What other guy?"

"Matty Alou."

Gaylord Perry turned on the mound. "Got enough?" he shouted with a grump.

Dave Bristol's greedy batsman did not hesitate. "I'll take another," Rose said. And he did. Five-for-five going for the batting title. "With the fifth hit, I stopped worrying," Rose says. "A five-hit game. That felt so good, I got nine more five-hit games before I quit. I was two points ahead of Alou. I figured out the numbers. On the last day, I could win the championship if I went 1-for-4 and Alou went 2-for-4. So on the last day, September 30, I really needed that one hit." The pennant race was finished. Bob Gibson had pitched 305 innings for St. Louis with an earned run average of 1.12. The Cardinals won easily behind this most intimidating of modern pitchers. Still, more than 27,000 fans paid their way into Crosley Field where the Reds would play the Giants. The lure was Rose's run at the batting championship.

The fans welcomed him with an ovation. Rose responded by cracking a double off Ray Sadecki. He had his hit. He won the title by three percentage points. "And that," Rose says resoundingly, "is playing under pressure. I got real good at that."

"And damn," says Dave Bristol, "if he didn't go through the same thing the very next year."

This time the opposition was Roberto Clemente. "I had a

little lead going into that last day," Rose says, "but I couldn't
figure Clemente was going to fold. Clemente was not a folding kind of player. And I'm in right field and the fans have
their portable radios and they're shouting, 'Better get on,
Pete. Clemente got a hit. Better get on, Pete. He got another
one.' The fans were right. Clemente went 3-for-3 that day."

Coming up for his final turn at bat, Rose felt he needed a
hit. He couldn't be sure what else Clemente might accomplish. "What do I do?" he said to Tommy Helms.

"Lay one down," Helms said.

"He put down a blueprint," Dave Bristol says. "The kind
of bunt you want to show to all your players."

"I beat it out," Rose says. "I had my hit. I ended up batting
champion for the second year in a row. The number was
.348. The batting championship, on the last day of the season,
two years in a row. Players talking to me, fans talking to me,
and what I got to do is hit. I got to block out all the talk and
hit. When a young ballplayer comes 'round and asks me
about pressure, I have a couple of pretty good stories to tell
him, am I right?"

The oldest established professional baseball franchise was
beginning to stir around the Cincinnati Kid. A solid, reserved
baseball man named Robert L. Howsam signed on as general
manager in 1967. Before he moved out in 1979, quiet Bob
Howsam had won renown as architect of the Big Red Machine.

Crosley Field, the Reds' historic ballpark, possessed buck-
etsful of charm. The outfield in left and center fields sloped
up toward the fence. The slope antedated warning tracks
and was built to let outfielders know when they were racing
into a collision. Across the street, beyond the left-field fence,
rose a laundry building, topped by a sign for a local product,
Burgomeister Beer. From good seats, you could follow the

flights of routine home runs that cleared the fence, longer ones that crashed into the laundry, and very long home runs—I saw Carl Furillo hit one—that carried onto the laundry roof. Then some would exclaim what almost everyone had seen: "He hit the ball on top of the laundry!"

The right-field bleachers early were called the Sun Deck. The first major league night game was played at Crosley on May 24, 1935. With time and the ascendency of night baseball, the Sun Deck became the Moon Deck. Crosley Field was an intimate ballpark, where fans sat close to the field; they could hear the chatter of the infielders and, as in Rose's batting race against Clemente, the ballplayers could hear the customers.

Whether it was the genes, the water, or Burgomeister Beer, the crowds at Crosley Field always seemed to contain a wonderfully disproportionate number of well-proportioned blondes. Even the grouchiest newspapermen—old baseball writers elevate complaining to a saga—liked their three-day stopovers in Cincinnati. If the blond baseball fans failed to command attention, the press-box food—good German cooking, sauerbraten and red cabbage, steaming as it was borne from the kitchen—prompted another sort of salivation.

Like Ebbets Field and certain other storied parks, Crosley Field was compact. With wedges, shoehorns, and perhaps a gift to fire marshals, you could cram in a crowd of almost thirty-seven thousand. In only four years of Crosley Field's fifty-eight-year life did the Reds draw more than one million fans at home. Modern major league economics required greater attendance than that and the solution was Riverfront Stadium, a huge concrete cup erected close to the Ohio River and, since the Reds draw from three states, Ohio, Indiana, and Kentucky, close by Interstate 75, as well.

The Riverfront playing surface is mostly plastic grass. The

concrete cup is mostly anonymous. Indeed, all-but-identical stadia have risen in Pittsburgh, Philadelphia, and St. Louis. In none does one get a sense of place. Each is a representative of that modern development, the homogenized, plastic baseball-football field. Uniquely in Cincinnati the press box is soundproofed (and, to be sure, the steamy sauerbraten and red cabbage are history). Reporters watching home runs see fans open their mouths and raise their arms, but cannot hear the cheers.

But the strong argument for a new ballpark in Cincinnati was simple: money. Since Riverfront was opened in 1970, Cincinnati home attendance has exceeded two million ten times.

Rose's contribution to the transition was characteristic. On June 24, 1970, he hit the last triple in the history of Crosley Field. On July 1, he hit the first triple in the history of Riverfront Stadium. The Kid could triple on plastic as well as on grass. A suspicion grew that the Kid could play the game.

After the 1969 season, when the Reds finished third in the National League West, Howsam replaced Dave Bristol with George Lee Anderson, called Sparky, a salty, peppery baseball man and part-time used-car salesman out of South Dakota, who had never played a major league game. Anderson came up in the Dodger organization when the Brooklyn infield was peopled with athletes named Reese and Robinson. "Compared to those guys," he says, "I just plain couldn't hit." Anderson had a quick mind, a charming way with the press, a gift at handling major league ballplayers of all varieties, and a way with English seldom seen since the debut of Mrs. Malaprop in *The Rivals* and the debut of Casey Stengel, several centuries later in Ebbets Field. "Sparky was master of the double negative," says Jim Ferguson of the Reds, "and if you needed a triple negative really badly, he could give you that, too."

Still, a writer left uncharmed by Anderson was either deaf or an unreformed grammarian. I once needed twenty minutes of his time. "If you ask me for twenty minutes," Anderson said, "you get an hour. 'Cuz when I'm talking to you I'm advertising baseball, the Cincinnati Reds, and George Anderson, who used to have to work winters in a used-car lot."

"Used-car salesmen have a reputation for cheating," I said after a while.

"And that's wrong," Anderson said. "The people are the cheats. They come in trying to get something for half what they oughta pay. They kick the tires and they say they saw the same car other side of town for a thousand dollars less. That's a lie, but you can't say that when you're a salesman. They kick the tires again. They give you fits. All I did selling cars was defend myself. I never cheated." The look in Anderson's eye cried out that he never wanted to sell second-hand cars again.

In addition to a full complement of coaches, Anderson enlisted key players as his lieutenants. This is a sophisticated managing technique. Instead of all demands and commands coming from the manager and coaches, some now came from fellow ballplayers. Joe Morgan, the great second baseman, would become the driving leader of the Reds' black players. Tony Perez took over the Latins. And all this began on Thursday, October 23, 1969, when Anderson appointed Pete Rose as team captain. In the excitement, publicist Tom Seeberg split an infinitive. "The Reds' outfielder," Seeberg wrote in a press release, "becomes the first player to officially be named captain in the Reds' lengthy history."

"Pete's won the batting championship twice," Anderson said. "He deserves to be recognized like a Willie Mays or a Hank Aaron. People would rather see him go up to home

plate with the lineup card than me. I believe in having take-
charge players on a club. It pulls a team together. Pete fits
that description perfectly. We're not giving Pete anything he
hasn't already earned."

Rose was entering his eighth season as a Red. Not yet
twenty-nine, he was the senior member of the team. It was
going to be a very good year.

As captain, with a second consecutive batting championship
behind him, Rose was about to crack the $100,000 barrier.
"Chief Bender called me at 8:30 in the morning. This was
early January 1970. He said to come on in. When I got there,
Chief said that he wanted to sign the team captain first. We
talked back and forth for two hours and this one time it
was enjoyable. I was entertained while we were talking contract. Bender left his radio on all the time." The final figure,
$105,000, made Rose the first Red ever to earn six figures and
made serious winter news in Cincinnati where, Johnny Carson has said, "Big news can be: city of Covington buys new
cement mixer."

The *Cincinnati Post* ran a story saying "only a few people
in the Greater Cincinnati business community will earn
more this year than Pete Rose." The few included Neil McEl-
roy, board chairman at Procter & Gamble ($325,000) and
Federated Stores chairman Ralph Lazarus ($213,000), but
did not include Paul Brown, the head coach and creator of
the Cincinnati Bengals, the National Football League franchise. For inventing the Bengals and running them, Brown
was earning $80,000.

Rose: "That salary felt great. It meant I was appreciated,
not just for the stuff on the field, but for promoting baseball
and the Reds all year round. That felt real great, being appreciated and there was something else that felt real great,
too. I had more money." The day of the entrepreneur had
reached Ohio. Rose, who once sold cars by winter, and

Johnny Bench, who once pulled cotton in Oklahoma, now pooled assets and bought an auto dealership on their own.

By way of celebrating the opening of Riverfront Stadium, the 1970 All-Star Game was scheduled in Cincinnati on July 14, a hot, muggy Bastille Day along the Ohio. Home plate was the fortress Rose would storm after a game that was a splendor on plastic grass.

The American League led, 4–1, in the ninth inning with the formidable Jim (Catfish) Hunter throwing hard sliders. Then Dick Dietz of the Giants homered and successive singles knocked Hunter back into the clubhouse. Willie McCovey singled off Fritz Peterson and Roberto Clemente lined a low slider safely to right field against Mel Stottlemyre, tying the game.

Rose's turn. The winning run was in scoring position with two out. Stottlemyre struck out Rose, with a hard, low breaking ball. Rose's turn, but not his last one. The teams stayed tied until the twelfth inning when Rose singled sharply off Clyde Wright, who would win twenty-two that year for California. Another single advanced Rose to second. Then Jim Hickman lined a sharp single to center field and Rose fled for home plate, the winning run.

Amos Otis, the center fielder, made a strong throw that buzzed in three feet up the line toward third base. Ray Fosse, a fine young catcher, positioned himself up the line, blocking home plate.

Rose whipped through a tight turn at third, came home all out and started diving into his headfirst slide. In a millisecond, he changed his mind. "I saw Fosse's shinguards. If I'd slid headfirst, I woulda broken both collar bones."

Running with all the speed of youth, Rose bent out of the slide, straightening to save his clavicles, and crashed full into Fosse. He made first impact with his left shoulder.

The men collided with a force that shatters bones. Rose knocked Fosse into a backward somersault. Then he spun with great violence to the ground. Rose was safe. The National League had won the All-Star Game, 5–4.

Rose got up slowly, limping. Fosse did not get up. He was able to rise from his sprawl to his knees. Rose fluttered over him asking Fosse if he were all right.

He was not. His left shoulder was so battered in the collision that Fosse could never again hit with his former power. Television caught the play and ran it and reran it into the night.

Suddenly, but not for the last time, a large portion of the country was talking about a character named Rose. Since the Reds hadn't made the World Series since 1961, the year Rose won the Zippo cigarette lighter in Tampa, few American League fans had seen him play. Who was this kid Rose, people wanted to know, and how the hell could he play baseball so viciously? Didn't he know that the All-Star Game was an exhibition, a showcase, an extravaganza like the ice follies? What kind of person would run over a nice young catcher like Fosse? The same kind of person who'd crumple a follies figure skater with a ferocious body check that drove her lissome carcass into the boards.

Right? Not quite right. Fosse talks freely about the play. "A lot of things were going through my mind," he says, "when I was waiting for Otis's throw. This wasn't an ordinary ball game. The president of the United States had thrown out the first ball. I was young, just twenty-three. I was playing with guys like Frank Robinson and Harmon Killebrew, tremendous names to me.

"There's a bad play a catcher can make in that situation. The ¡Olé! shot. Get out of the way. The runner goes by like a charging bull and you wave a tag at him, like a matador.

"That's the wrong play. The right play is block the plate. I knew 65 million people were watching on TV. Aside from that, I wanted the respect of my peers. I wasn't going to look like a fool and get out of the way. I was the Cleveland catcher, not the San Diego chicken.

"I didn't know Pete at all until the night before the game. Then we met at some function and he invited me over to his house and we sat up half the night talking baseball.

"Talking baseball. But I didn't really know what kind of player Pete Rose was until the next night. We both made the plays we thought we had to make. A couple of aggressive ballplayers doing their jobs."

Inane criticism persists, surfacing once a year at All-Star time. "People forget," Rose says, "that Fosse played the next game for his ball club. I couldn't play the next one for mine. I only missed ten games with injuries during all the 1970s and three came out of that play."

Do you think maybe you hit him too hard? Some say you could have scored with a conventional slide.

"Look. I'm the winning run in the All-Star Game in my hometown. I just want to get to that plate as quickly as I can." Rose grins his Huck Finn grin. "Besides," he says, "nobody told me they changed it to girls' softball between third and home."

This single play secured Rose's notoriety and, as John Erardi of Cincinnati points out, secured Fosse's place as the answer to a trivia question. (Obviously, name the feller Pete Rose ran over at the 1970 All-Star Game.) In time, Rose presented Fosse with a baseball. Above his signature he wrote: "To Ray Fosse—Thanks for making me famous."

Famous Peter Edward Rose was, and getting more so. Fine columnists and broadcasters seemed almost to vie with one another to celebrate the Cincinnati Kid, now twenty-nine. Jim Murray of the *Los Angeles Times* described Rose as "The Big Red Machine's cloud of dust, the original He-Was-Here-A-Minute-Ago. In Cincy they tell of the time his uniform was

hung up to dry on a railing and it stole second base." The late
Wells Twombly of the *San Francisco Examiner* wrote that
Rose's style was so out of fashion in the laid-back Age of
Aquarius that Rose could not possibly be real. "His jaw is so
firm," Twombly wrote, "that a blacksmith could forge
horseshoes on its point and never disturb the owner." When
Rose ran to first on a base on balls against the Dodgers, Vin
Scully said, "Pete Rose just beat out a walk." On another day
Rose missed a two-strike pitch and sprinted back to the dug-
out. The late Cincinnati broadcaster (and Hall-of-Fame
pitcher) Waite Hoyt said, "Rose even runs out his strikeouts."

Of course Pete Rose was real. He was real and becoming
a legend all at the same time, a legend with basepath dirt
smudged over his legendary uniform. "Hustler Pete Rose
Baseball's Best Ad," proclaimed *The Sporting News*. In the
article that followed, Earl Lawson told a personal story. Lawson had seen his daughter Nancy, "then a twelve-year-old
tomboy," playing in a pickup baseball game with neighborhood boys. Nancy laid her bat to a pitch, clubbed it, circled
the bases, and slid safely home headfirst.

Concerned lest Nancy injure herself, Lawson called,
"Don't do that!"

Nancy answered, "Pete does."

She then embroidered a pillowcase with the words: "I love
Pete . . . Nancy." She slept on it for several nights and then,
Lawson wrote, "blushingly presented it to Pete."

Rose later called Lawson for lunch and arrived with a
package. "Nancy cherished the knit skirt and sweater set
Pete gave her," Lawson says, "long, long after she had out-
grown it."

Under Sparky Anderson in 1970, the Reds won 102 games.
The race in the National League West was effectively over
by Labor Day. Johnny Bench hit 45 home runs. Tony Perez

hit 40. Rose batted a generic Rose .316. The Fosse collision
kept him in the dugout for three games, but he played right
field in 159 and over the entire season made only one error.
The catcher, turned second baseman, turned third baseman,
now led every right fielder in the major leagues. His fielding
percentage was .997. (The competition included Al Kaline
and Roberto Clemente, both of whom could run and catch
a fly.)

The Reds swept the Pirates in the League Championship
Series, then decided on three-of-five. The first game was
scoreless for nine innings. Rose singled home a run in the
tenth off Dock Ellis and the Reds went on and won, 3–0.

Ellis's recollection of that game is unusual. "I had a drink
or two the night before," he says, "and I didn't feel good in
the morning. We could get a little wild in the old days. Somebody drove me to the ballpark in a Volkswagen Beetle. I'm
hung over and six foot three and I'm trying to fit into a Bug.
I felt worse when I got to the park, so I took about ten
greenies [pep pills] to snap me out of it. Then I went out to
pitch. I remember Rose getting a hit off me in the tenth, but
I have no memory at all of the first nine innings."

"Dock. You've forgotten nine innings of shutout ball you
pitched in a league championship playoff?"

"Absolutely. It must have been that ride in the Volkswagen."

The Reds took the second game, 3–1, and in the third game
snapped a tie in the eighth inning when a pinch hitter named
Ty Cline walked, and Rose and Bobby Tolan singled, secur-
ing a 3–2 victory.

The World Series belonged to Baltimore. Specifically it
belonged to Baltimore's third baseman, Brooks Robinson.
Robinson's fielding captivated a country that didn't know
third base could be played at such an acrobatic level. Robinson batted .429. The Orioles won the Series, four games to

one, and *Sport* magazine named Robinson most valuable player and presented him with a Dodge Charger.

Rose was gracious in defeat and not above plugging his auto dealership. "Hey," he said, "if we knew Brooks wanted a car that bad, Johnny Bench and I woulda given him one, and we'd maybe even thrown in a radio for free."

7

The Thrill
of the (Plastic) Grass

CINCINNATI, 1970

John Patrick Harmon became sports editor of the *Cincinnati Post* in 1951 and kept his job until 1985, writing columns, running a changing sports staff, and twilighting a bit with a television sports program. Earnest, grizzled Pat Harmon worked hard because that is his nature and also because he had no choice. While covering the Ohio River sports beat, Harmon, who was raised as an orphan, fathered no fewer than eleven children. He tells a number of stories about rotating pairs of shoes. How the eleven children kept their socks straight is a book Harmon intends to get to when he finds time. (He is now curator of the National College Football Hall of Fame.)

"One of my greatest thrills," Pat Harmon says, "has been knowing a Pete Rose in three different generations.

"Peter the First was the most famous athlete Cincinnati ever had in the local leagues. He played baseball and basketball and boxed when he was young but he's best remem-

bered as a football star, who played in the Feldhaus Sunday
Football League until he was forty-two years old.

"I interviewed him on television five years later and asked
if he felt he should still be playing football. He said, sure he
should. If he'd known all the teams were switching to the T
formation, he would have kept on playing; he could still
make it fine as a T quarterback.

"I said, the games get pretty rugged and suppose he had
to make a tackle at the age of forty-seven. There was a folding
chair in camera range. Suppose, I said, that chair was a defensive player who'd intercepted one of your passes.

"Big Pete moved fast. He was up and suddenly he made
a diving tackle of the chair. The chair, of course, collapsed.
It was in pieces. Pete was fine. He was a rugged character.
I don't think I'll forget that. Ol' Pete putting a flying tackle
on to a chair—this was live television—when he was forty-
seven years old."

The Fifth Third Bank stands on an edge of Fountain Square
Plaza, which is to Cincinnati what Times Square was to New
York City before havoc seized Manhattan streets. Clement L.
Buenger, the president, recently listed the assets of the Fifth
Third as somewhat more than three billion dollars.

A pleasant, soft-voiced woman named Fran Carter super-
vises the accounts of smaller area banks that maintain balances of their own at the Fifth Third. "I started here in 1951
in the bookkeeping department," she says. "Big Pete was my
boss. He was one of those great people to work for. If I were
out of balance at the end of the day, Big Pete would stay into
the night, helping balance the ledger to the last penny,
which we all had to do in those days. To the penny.

"We have a bank picnic every year and Big Pete played
in the softball game. He always brought his family, including Little Pete, who's Big Pete now. We knew Little Pete

when he was small. We watched him grow. When he got to be a big leaguer, his father was so very proud, bubbling over. Not braggadocio. Big Pete was a humble man. But very proud.

"When Big Pete was playing football, some Mondays he'd have to come to work on crutches. A lot of younger football players used to go at him. 'Let's get the old man.' That sort of thing. But he wouldn't complain and he wouldn't miss work. In those days at the bank, your accounts had to balance to the penny and you *never* missed work if you had the strength to get out of bed."

On December 9, 1970, Harry Francis Rose was reviewing overdrafts in his office on the third floor off Fountain Square. Shortly after eleven o'clock, he said to Fran Carter that he wasn't feeling well. "I think I better go home."

"Let me call a taxi for you," Fran Carter said.

She thought he might be suffering from indigestion or flu. The idea of something worse never entered her mind, nor did it enter the mind of Big Pete Rose. "I don't need a taxi," Mr. Rose said. "I can just take the bus."

He told some others he was leaving and waited for a bus, out of sorts, but apparently not gravely ill. He rode the bus to Anderson Ferry, walked two and a half blocks uphill, and climbed eleven stairs up to the doorway of his home. La-Verne Rose rushed to meet him, surprised that he was home so early.

He put one foot inside the door and said, "I don't feel good." He fell forward, dying of a massive coronary. Harry Francis Rose was fifty-seven.

That was the early afternoon when Pete was having his haircut and the barber answered the phone and blurted out the awful news and Pete could not believe his father was dead and thought surely that the dead one had to be his mother.

"Dad was just so rugged and he never complained and he meant so much to me that I couldn't accept that he was gone, that I wouldn't hear from him any more, ever again, 'Keep hustling, son.'

"I couldn't accept it, I wouldn't accept it until I went to the funeral parlor and saw Dad's body in the coffin.

"That broke me up like nothing else.

"I had to accept it then. I had to go on with my life. I . . ."

Rose stumbles here. He cannot find a phrase for his emotion.

I remember one composed by Robert Frost, when the poet was writing about a shattering death in his own family. "My love for someone else does not extend to going crazy because they go crazy or dying because they die."

Like Frost, Pete Rose was going to have to find the courage to be new.

A squabble can serve as therapy. An argument moves your mind away from the dead and toward the quick—the people who are arguing with you. As Rose recovered from his father's death, he ran into an argument waiting to happen.

Had Pete Rose, captain of the pennant-winning Cincinnati Reds, come through with a good season in 1970?

Not really, decreed Bob Howsam. Rose's batting average dropped from .348 to .316.

"Wait a minute," Pete Rose said. "I led the league in hits with 205. I got thirty-seven doubles and fifteen home runs. I stole twelve bases. For a lot of guys, a year like that would be a career."

"Not the kind of year we expect from you," Howsam said.

The issue was money. Howsam wanted Chief Bender to sign Rose in 1971 for the same salary, $105,000, Rose had earned in 1970.

"I'm not gonna do that," Rose told Cincinnati sportswriters. "I guarantee I won't play for $105,000. I realize $105,000 is a lot of money, but there's a principle here. I did what they wanted. I got the most hits in the majors [along with the Chicago Cubs' Billy Williams]. I deserve more money."

And if the Reds don't come through with more?

"I'll sit out 1971. I got things going for me off the field. I own this bowling alley and it's full every night."

Rose was three months away from his thirtieth birthday. Is it possible to imagine a thirty-year-old Rose spending the soft nights of summer watching strong-armed ladies and beer-bellied gentlemen miss spares? No, it is not possible to imagine that. Rose was mining the media for whatever loose gold could be found among the seven hills of Cincinnati.

In 1970, and in all the decades before, ballplayers could not declare themselves free agents. If they wanted more money than a ball club offered (and if the differences were serious), their best attack was to carry their case to the press and, through the press, to the public. That was a stressful, dangerous approach but it was the only one available. (Joe DiMaggio carried a demand for $40,000 into the press in 1938 and the *New York Herald Tribune* described him as headstrong and greedy. When the Yankees held to their figure, $25,000, DiMaggio capitulated and found himself forced to sign his contract in front of gloating Yankee executives and two dozen reporters. Ed Barrow, the general manager, then told the reporters that DiMaggio was not yet in shape to play and if he wanted to make road trips with the team, he would be required to pay his own expenses. The trouble with trying your case in the press is the same as the trouble with trying your case before a jury. You can lose.)

"In '70 the Reds offered every other starting player a raise," Rose says. "Not me. Someone in the front office actually told me on the phone that the team could get along

without me for the next year. What was I supposed to say to
that? Please take me back, mister. Please take me—and my
205 hits—back. That didn't make sense. So I had to tough it
out. I tell the writers I got my bowling alley. I tell the Reds
be fair and if you won't be fair to me at least be fair to
everybody else. Take the $105,000 you're offering me and
spread it around to the other players. Have a very fine year
without me, guys. I'm tied up, bowling for dollars."

Rose wanted $125,000. He also, burningly, wanted to play.
He telephoned Earl Lawson in Florida on March 5. "I should
be down with the team," he said. "I want to get going."

"Chief Bender tells me you want a $20,000 raise," Lawson
said.

"I'd settle for $5,000."

Lawson sought out Bender. Rose made a plane reservation.
Bender reported back to Lawson that Howsam now would
not agree to any raise at all. Rose canceled his ticket. "Set 'em
up in alley number 2," he said without much cheer.

Backs arched. Bender suggested that if Rose had come in
asking for a $5,000 increase in the first place, he would have
gotten it. But it was too late now. He would have to play for
$105,000 again. Rose said, no increase, no contract. *The Cin-
cinnati Post* ran a headline: Rose Compromise Offer Ignored.

Rose: "This was no fun at all. I started getting mail from
fans telling me that $105,000 was a lot of money, which I
knew. I wanted to get into shape. But I was feeling stuck.
What did the Reds expect? That I'd win the batting championship *every* year? I mean, were they telling me that was
the standard I had to meet to get a raise?

"So I finally called Bender and said, look, the cost of living
is going up. You got to at least keep me even. If I play for the
same this year, I'm actually making less, when you consider
buying power, am I right? I got 205 hits and led the majors
and you want me to play for less?"

"Let me work on that," Bender said.

Bender and Howsam consulted economic indices. The cost of living had risen a bit more than five per cent. They offered Rose a bit less than one half of a 5 percent adjustment: $2,500, lifting the offer to $107,500.

Rose accepted and flew off to Tampa wearing a green suit. "I'm unhappy," he told Pat Harmon. "I'm no phony. I'm not gonna tell you I'm happy when I'm not happy. This is the smallest raise I ever got."

"He would have been a lot more unhappy," Harmon wrote, "if he couldn't have switched from his green suit into a Reds uniform."

Building his exceptional team, Bob Howsam intended to avoid paying exceptional salaries. The hard line with Rose got that message across. Thrift, boys, thrift. That's the order of the day. The love of money is the root of all evil.

Rose: "I guess that was not exactly an upper for the team."

Howsam sat back among his certificates of deposit in 1971 and watched the developing Big Red Machine finish fourth, four games under .500. None of the stars, Tony Perez, Johnny Bench, batted within 20 points of .300. None, except Rose. Having what the Reds would insist was another off year, the man in the green suit batted .304.

On November 29, 1971, Bob Howsam concluded an eight-player trade with Houston that approached larceny. He shipped three Reds, including Tommy Helms, to Texas. In return he landed five players including Joe Leonard Morgan, a five-foot seven-inch second baseman out of Bonham, Texas, who, Rose says, "was the smartest ballplayer I've seen." From that day forward, the Reds dominated the decade.

Indeed, across the 1970s, Cincinnati won more games and more championships than any other team: six Western Division championships, four National League Championships, two World Championships. Across the span from 1972 through 1977, six seasons, the National League most valuable player was a Red on five occasions: Bench, Rose, Morgan twice, and George Foster. All this world-class excellence worked in one of the smallest cities in the major leagues.

Rose: "I don't think that with the present structure, free agency and all, any team can ever dominate that way, that long again. I mean we had fellers who could *play*. We averaged more than ninety-three wins a year. Remember I said winning is the most fun. Nobody else in baseball had anywhere near as much fun in the 1970s as the Cincinnati Reds."

The pitchers never measured up to the position players but Sparky Anderson pulled starters and long relievers with such decisive dexterity that he won the nickname of "Cap'n Hook." (In the argot, a manager removing a pitcher "hooks" him, which in turn comes from vaudeville, circa 1910, when an entertainer performing poorly was literally hauled from the stage by a giant hook.)

Rose had twice won Gold Gloves as a right fielder. Now Anderson asked if he would switch to left field. (Cesar Geronimo, who came from Houston with Morgan, could catch fly balls about as well as Rose and had a stronger throwing arm. Geronimo, a limited offensive player, won four Gold Gloves in Cincinnati.)

"I think the switch will help the team," Anderson said. "And it can add years to your career."

"My arm isn't bad," Rose said. "I threw out thirteen runners last season."

"Add years to your career, Pete," Anderson repeated. "I'm asking you for the good of the team."

Rose nodded. "Okay. Whatever I did in right, Roberto Clemente and Hank Aaron stole my thunder anyway."

Rose: "I like Sparky. Always have. But I know he used to sell used cars and now he musta been using one of his sales pitches. Add years to my career, going from right to left? The only way I could see that happening was if the walk from the dugout to left field was shorter than the walk to right field. And that wouldn't add years. The most it could add would be a couple of innings.

"But he asked me and mentioned the good of the team so I went along. What bothered me was Sparky being a little phony, pumping me up. I always played pumped up. He didn't have to bother.

"I knew myself as an outfielder. I'd never say I had the arm of a Clemente or a Carl Furillo because I never did. But my years in the infield made me a better outfielder. It's all one game. At second I had to learn to charge the ball hard. I took that with me into the outfield. I got to the ball quick and I got rid of it quick. Take a slower man than me, or someone who can't charge balls like I could, it pretty much balances out arm strength.

"I know a great throw is spectacular, but I think that's one part of baseball that gets overrated, just because it is so spectacular. You know how many major league games I played. Three thousand five hundred and sixty two. The most ever. The most anybody ever played. How many of those ended with a guy being thrown out at the plate?

"I don't have a stat for that, but very, very few."

Some would argue. An arm like Clemente's, just the existence of that arm and awareness of it in a runner and a coach, make a man pull up at third and not even try to score the winning run. The game ends with a pop up, but one play earlier the winning run was frozen ninety feet distant from home plate. A great throwing arm is not only spectacular, it's also a factor in how the base runners advance, how they dare to advance.

Rose: "I'm not saying it's not important. I'm saying some people rate it too high. The first thing an outfielder has to do

is get to the ball and do that quick. You can't throw the ball
before you have it. You can't throw air. The scouting reports
stress throwing arm a lot. They don't all stress how the outfielder charges the ball. I'll give you two guys who played a
little infield, then switched to the outfield. Man, could they
charge the ball. One was Mickey Mantle. The other was
Willie Mays."

Rose had spent the winter of 1971–72 growing and trim-
ming a beard. The Reds then, and the Reds today, enforce a
rule which forbids Cincinnati players from growing facial
hair.

Rose: "I don't happen to think that's the greatest rule ever
invented. The Reds are my employers and I do what I'm told,
even when I don't agree, which I don't particularly on
beards. I mean if Jesus Christ came back to earth and wanted
to play third base for Cincinnati, am I supposed to tell Him,
'All right, sir. But first you got to shave'?" Rose's eyes twinkle
a bit. He has criticized management, oh so mildly, and perhaps won the support of fifty thousand ministers.

His own beard did not survive that February. The Gillette
Company hired him to do a commercial, a morning's work
for $10,000. In the contract Rose agreed not only to shave on
camera, but to remain clean-shaven for two years after the
commercial was taped. Gillette did not want bearded ballplayers hawking its blades. "That makes commercial sense,"
Rose says, "but if I'm not mistaken, the Cincinnati Reds are
not in the razor-blade business."

The 1972 Reds were a strong team, and getting stronger.
Dave Concepcion, the rangy young Venezuelan shortstop,
couldn't hit much yet. Third base was a problem and would
remain one until Rose moved there in 1975. But Johnny
Bench led the league in home runs and runs batted in. Tony
Perez had a solid year. Morgan batted .292 and stole fifty-

eight bases. Rose, the slightly reluctant left fielder, led the National League in hits for the fourth time.

In April Rose turned thirty-one. "A certain dream," wrote the late Si Burick in the *Dayton Daily News,* "is developing in Rose's mind. He goes into this [1972] season with 1,724 major league hits. He honestly believes he has time to reach 3,000. He estimates that might take him eight years." (It took him six.)

It was during the 1972 season that someone first joined the names of Rose and Cobb significantly. Reviewing old numbers—so much baseball history survives in its statistics—Bob Hertzel of the *Cincinnati Enquirer* prepared a chart covering the first ten seasons of a number of great batsmen. Two had hit safely more than two thousand times. These were Paul Waner and Stan Musial. Rose placed seventh on the all-time list. "Behind him," Hertzel wrote, "are the likes of Rogers Hornsby, Ted Williams, Willie Mays, Honus Wagner, and the immortal Ty Cobb."

Rose: "I was surprised. The day before Hertzel's story ran—it was August—I hit a single to center off Jon Matlack of the Mets and that was hit number 1,881. That made me the all-time leader of the Reds. They stopped the game and gave me the ball. I was thinking I could maybe make 3,000, but I wasn't thinking Cobb. I wasn't *up* to thinking Cobb.

"I thought I could go strong until maybe thirty-seven and that would be it. Three thousand. A good number. Turned out when I was thirty-seven I felt about the same way I did at twenty-seven, and that year I got 208 hits for the Phillies."

Far to the south an echo sounded. "It is hard to realize that it has been ten years since Pete Rose was sending Middle Georgia baseball fans into shock with his amazing antics at Luther Williams Field," Tommy Desselle wrote in the *Macon Telegraph.* "It was 1962 when Rose burst on the local scene as a member of the Macon Peaches. He didn't just capture a city. He captured an entire area, an entire league. He was voted all-everything. He hit, he fielded, he ran, he hustled . . ."

No one, not even Rose, recognized it yet, but the countdown to Cobb had begun. Tyrus Raymond. Kid Charm. The most spiky peach that ever grew in Georgia sunshine.

And here was praise for Cobb's rival, Peter Edward Rose, gushing from a Georgia type font.

Lordy be.

The Reds won their division and then won a close and exciting championship series from the Pittsburgh team of Willie Stargell and Clemente. Rose batted .450 in the playoff. Joe Morgan hit two home runs. But the series ended with a mistake.

The teams were tied with two victories each in a best-of-five series and the Pirates carried a one-run lead into the ninth inning of the final game. Bench slammed a home run off Dave Giusti and the score was tied at 3. Two singles followed. Bill Virdon, the Pirates manager, brought in a big right-handed relief pitcher named Bob Moose, who got two outs. Then Moose threw a wild pitch and George Foster ran across home plate at Riverfront with the winning run.

Rose: "So here's this real competitive series, with a lot of great baseball, and it ends with a pitcher throwing the ball away.

"What was I saying before?

"It didn't end with somebody getting thrown out at home."

The Oakland Athletics of 1972 were one of baseball's more curious teams. The owner, a slick and swaggering Chicago insurance man named Charles Finley, liked nicknames. He believed ballplayers with nicknames sold tickets. Arguing his point, Finley said, "Who the hell ever paid to see George Ruth?"

By Finley's edict, James August Hunter became Catfish Hunter; Johnny Lee Odom became Blue Moon Odom; and Vida Rochelle Blue remained Vida Blue. Not even Finley would tinker with the sound of Vida Blue.

Toupeed Charlie Finley hired a caustic, driving character named Dick Williams as manager. The A's brawled with others and among themselves, and grew mustaches. Finley ordered them to grow mustaches. Such passion for facial hair from a man who wore a wig might be material for a Freudian monograph.

Beyond all that, Oakland offered wonderful, winning baseball. A non-Philistine Goliath named Mike Epstein played first base. The young Reggie Jackson worked right field. The team had Sal Bando at third and quiet, gifted Joe Rudi in left. Hunter, Ken Holtzman, Odom, Blue, and Rollie Fingers, the king of the mustaches, were key pitchers. None had an earned run average higher than 2.80.

A backup catcher, part-time infielder, occasional outfielder, was born Fiore Gino Tennaci in Russellton, Pennsylvania. Finley did not impose a nickname on Tennaci. The catcher spun his own: Fury Gene Tenace. Few noticed. Few notice backup catchers.

Then came the Series. Fury Gene swatted two home runs in his first two times at bat. He hit homers in games 4 and 5 as well. Oakland moved ahead, three games to one. Rose rallied the Reds in game 5 when he drove Catfish Hunter's first pitch into the stands. Tenace responded with a three-run homer. Rose had the last say, singling home the winning run in the ninth. The Reds tied the Series in game 6, but in 1972, Fury Gene Tenace owned October. He got two more hits in the seventh game and batted in two runs. Oakland won the game, 3–2, and with it the World Series.

Who on earth is this fellow Tenace, who hits for average

and power, plays infield, outfield, and catches, sportswriters
and fans wanted to know? Was Fiore Gino Tennaci the second coming of Peter Edward Rose?

Not exactly. After his four-homer set against the Reds,
Tenace played in three other World Series. His batting average ranged from .000 to .222. He never hit another Series
home run. His regular-season average never reached .265.
Gene Tenace was just a workaday ballplayer, a world away
from Pete Rose.

Rose: "But for a week against us, he was Ruth and Cobb.
What I liked about him was that he played so hard, but I'm
reaching there.

"How much can you like somebody who beats your brains
out?"

Howsam continued to sit on salaries. Rose: "I organized a
Reds basketball team and we played around the Cincinnati
area in the winter. I was a guard. Good defense. Wherever
we played, we made friends for the Reds. But management
started worrying one of us might get hurt. I'd tell 'em we
were athletes. Basketball kept us in shape. You can get hurt
slipping off a curb. Were they gonna tell us not to cross the
street? I guess they figured I was defying them. What's the
word? Oh, yeah. Headstrong. I was headstrong.

"In 1972, I led the league in hits with 198. Our attendance
kept going up. We played a seven-game World Series. Who-
ever it was held stock in the Reds, they didn't have to sell
matches Christmas Eve. They were making money.

"But Howsam didn't seem to be my biggest fan. I'm an
All-Star, got the most hits of any Cincinnati player ever. I'm
going on thirty-two and I'm playing great.

"I go in to see Howsam and here's how he starts me off:

" 'How old are you really, Pete?'

"They know my age. My birth certificate is on file right
here in town. It's not like I'm Zsa Zsa Gabor.

"As soon as Howsam starts on the age thing, I know we're going to a contract war again. I figure I'll have to call Henry Kissinger to negotiate for me before I get to spring training."

Rose wanted $120,000. The Reds offered $115,000. Someone planted a story that the Reds were paying Johnny Bench $150,000 and that this had reduced Rose to a green, seething blob of avarice. He was jealous; his ego demanded that he be the highest-paid player on the club.

Rose countered, sharing his thinking with a sportswriter. He didn't care what Bench earned. Bench was a great player. Well, maybe he cared a little, but that wasn't the main point. The main point was "the numbers I was posting."

For the last three years, the Reds had been giving him contract fits. "During that stretch, I averaged .307. I scored 313 runs. I got 595 hits. We won two pennants. The Reds home attendance was 4,916,049. But getting even tiny raises was like squeezing lemon juice out of a turnip. You can't do that, can you, squeeze lemon juice out of a turnip? Well, that's the idea."

Some ballplayers would have buckled, taken the club's first offers, bought themselves peace. Rose bargained as hard as he played. If the Reds tried to use the press against him, he would use the press against management. Tell him he can't have a beard in the summer and he grows one in the winter. Tell him basketball is dangerous and he says, "Well, maybe I ought to stop sliding headfirst. Just come in to the bases, pitty pat. Sliding hard is dangerous, too."

No one in the front office then admitted it, but a suspicion lingers that the Cincinnati Kid was not the Cincinnati management's favorite character.

Why didn't he just come in and beg, like some of the others? What was he trying to do with all those salary demands, bring free enterprise into baseball? Didn't he appreciate that the Reds gave him free uniforms, including free baseball caps, every season?

The guy was not only a hard sign, he was too damn independent.

Better check the records. Was Rose really born in Cincinnati or is that just a story he made up?

Look up the registry in Moscow. See if Rose wasn't born there.

To the front office Rose looked like more than a Red. He was a bit of a Bolshevik.

As an actor, Rose is self-taught. "Pete," says Nancy Sarnoff, who arranged a score of commercials for him, "isn't at his best when he has to stick rigidly to a script and do retake after retake. But let him be spontaneous and he's just wonderful."

The Vitalis Company hired Rose to push Vitalis Dry Control, a men's hairspray, and loosed him with a saucy blond model. Women journalists were barred from baseball clubhouses until 1977—an issue of not-so-quiet fury to feminists—but here, in the Vitalis commercial, came an actress named Victoria Medlin with a jiggle-hipped stroll, strutting and bouncing into the Reds locker room. She caught a baseball soft-tossed by relief pitcher Clay Carroll toward relief pitcher Tom Hall, casually hooked the ball over her shoulder, and closed on Rose, who stood in front of his locker, combing his hair. All parties, the ballplayers and the actress, were clothed.

"This is the year for sharing," Medlin announced to the camera, "so Pete Rose and I use the same thing on our hair." She reached into Rose's locker and held up a can of Vitalis Dry Control. She continued to push the product and Rose continued to brush his hair, deadpan, as though blond actresses in locker rooms were common as spikes.

Finally Victoria Medlin considered the well-combed hair. "Hey, looks nice, Pete," she said. Rose allowed himself a suggestion of a smile.

Abruptly Medlin slapped his stomach. "Now work on the gut," she commanded. Rose's double take was splendidly droll.

Not every hair stayed in place for Rose during 1973 and no one cared. He won the batting championship for the third time in six seasons (.338). He hammered 230 hits, which led the league by thirty. Rose was hitting about three weeks ahead of everybody else. "I know this sounds corny," Joe Morgan said, "but anyway it's true. Playing on the same team with Pete is inspirational."

The Reds won the West and moved into a playoff with the New York Mets. Rose had no idea what trouble he was sliding into *this* October.

Tom Seaver started the first game for the Mets and held a 1–0 lead into the eighth inning. Rose homered, tying the score. Johnny Bench homered in the last of the ninth and the Reds won, 2–1. The Mets won the second game, 5–0, and the scene was set for a rousing main event.

The Mets hit the ball hard in game 3 and going into the top of the fifth inning held a 9–2 lead. Rose bounced a single through the middle off Jerry Koosman. ("That kind of hit isn't luck. You get it by *trying* to go up the middle and driving down on the ball.")

Joe Morgan grounded toward first and John Milner snapped a throw to Bud Harrelson, forcing Rose. Harrelson's strong throw to first caught Morgan. As it did, the focus was moving back to second.

Rose slid hard, feet first, trying to block Harrelson from throwing. The shortstop jumped and the men collided, no harder than runner and fielder bump around second base across a hundred summer nights. Then Harrelson jumped on Rose.

"Cocksucker," he said.

"You don't know me that well," Rose said.

The word infuriated him. He pummeled and shoved Harrelson to the ground, "triggering," the late Arthur Daley wrote in *The New York Times*, "a free-for-all of sprawling immensity."

Harrelson is listed in *The Baseball Encyclopedia* as weighing 160 pounds. He has since claimed his real weight was 146. Rose at 190 put Harrelson down easily. "That's as much as I wanted to do. I didn't want to really hurt the guy. I just didn't want him to get away with calling me that name."

Wayne "Red" Garrett of the Mets sprinted over from third and jumped on top of Rose, who was on top of Harrelson. "That's what did it," Sparky Anderson said later. "Without Garrett, you got a little one-on-one scrimmage that peters out."

The benches emptied. Benches always empty in ballfield brawls, but here intensity surged so mightily that the bullpens three hundred feet away emptied also. Pedro Borbon rushed in from the left-field bullpen to help out his Cincinnati teammate. As he closed in on the scene, Borbon landed a right on Buzz Capra's face. Don "Duffy" Dyer, a six-foot Mets catcher, threw a right at Borbon. Fifty players milled and punched and shoved.

The late Ted Kluszewski, a Cincinnati coach, was a 230-pounder with arms so huge that he used to cut off his uniform sleeves so that his biceps could have room to flex. Rose's part in the brawl ended when Kluszewski threw those mighty Polish arms around him and dragged him away. Others continued to punch and shove and mill for fifteen minutes.

At length two Reds hauled Borbon from the scene. Borbon picked up a baseball cap and snapped it onto his head. "Hey, man," someone said. "That's a Mets cap you have on."

Borbon whipped off the cap. It was dyed New York blue. Borbon sank his teeth into the baseball cap and bit a chunk out of the bill.

Since this was the fifth inning, many of the 53,967 fans at Shea had been drinking beer for two hours. They roared and growled as drinking crowds at ballparks will when players tussle on the field. (The violence was more perceived than real. Harrelson suffered a scrape over his left eye. His sunglasses broke apart and bloodied his forehead when he was wrestling on the ground with Rose. No one else was more than bruised.)

The double play ended the Reds turn at bat and now Rose jogged to his defensive position in left field. Fans pelted him with beer cans, the new missiles of October. Rose ignored them briefly, then began to throw cans back into the stands. The drinking crowd was being challenged. Garbage poured down from the upper deck. A whiskey bottle landed heavily near Rose.

He had no helmet. He trotted in and Sparky Anderson jogged out to meet him. "Spark, that was a Jack Daniels bottle that somebody just tried to bounce off my head."

"That's enough for today," Anderson said. He motioned his players in from the field. Fans continued throwing cans and bottles.

"We better get this straightened out," an umpire said to Anderson.

"Let me know when you do," Anderson said. "Until then my players stay in the dugout. Pete Rose has contributed too much to baseball to die in left field at Shea Stadium."

The situation moved into the lap of Charles "Chub" Feeney, a law school graduate and professional baseball man who was president of the National League before the bearded, polysyllabic appearance of A. Bartlett Giamatti. "What we had here," Feeney says, "was a possible forfeit. The home team is responsible for crowd control. I wasn't going to order the Reds to take the field. The crowd was frightening, particularly the people upstairs in left field. I thought that maybe I should go out there and reason with them. And then I thought, they might throw things at *me*. I didn't want to get killed any more than Rose did."

Feeney walked into the Mets dugout and approached two secure heroes of New York. Yogi Berra was managing the Mets. At forty-two, Willie Mays was playing a final season. (He could hit no more than .211.) Feeney explained the forfeit rule. Berra and Mays walked out to left field and pleaded with the fans. The missiles stopped. With a hundred New York City police officers keeping order in the left-field stands, the game resumed.

Rose came to bat in the ninth inning and Jerry Grote, the Mets catcher, said, "If you're on base when this thing ends, you better get the hell off the field in a hurry."

Rose singled up the middle. Ed Sudol, the first-base umpire, said, "You be careful, Pete, when this is over."

Rose: "I'm thinking we can come from behind. We still got a chance to win and Sudol and Grote are scaring me to death. All our guys were at the top of the dugout, holding our bats. It was the ninth inning. I guarantee they weren't getting ready for batting practice."

The Mets won, 9–2, and Rose sprinted from the field. Time and the hour had run through October 8, but on October 9 the teams would play in Shea again.

Someone decided in the interests of crowd control that Rose and Harrelson should shake hands at home plate before the next game began. M. Donald Grant, an investment banker who ran the Mets, put the issue to Harrelson.

"I don't really want to," Harrelson said, "but okay. If Rose will, I will."

Bob Howsam put the same request to Rose. "No," Rose said. "It won't be honest. It wouldn't be right."

"It'd do more than cool the bottle-throwers," Howsam said. "It'll make you look good."

"I won't shake hands with him," Rose said. "Not in the

middle of this series. I don't care how it would make me look. I'm not gonna do something I don't feel."

Rose: "Man, do I remember the next ball game. I wasn't playing the Mets. I was playing *New York City.*"
The fans at Shea greeted him with signs.

ROSE IS A PANSY!

The fans didn't know Rose that well, either.

ROSES DIE. BUDS BLOOM.

The pun is the lowest form of humor.

After some ritual jeering when Rose's name was announced in the lineup, the fans quieted somewhat and the teams went about playing a tight ball game. They were tied at 1 in the twelfth inning. Then Rose, the much despised, lined one of Harry Parker's fastballs over the right-field fence for the home run that won the game. He did not simply touch home plate. He jumped on it with both feet.

Something like 70 percent of the Shea Stadium crowd recognized what they were seeing. The competitor of the age. Something like 70 percent of the Shea Stadium crowd cheered gritty Pete Rose, running his home run home.

"The pregame handshake," Dick Young wrote in the *Daily News,* "would have been contrived. Pete Rose doesn't do it that way. He went out and beat the Mets with a home run. He didn't beg the fans to like him. He *made* them like him. That's his way. The way of a professional."

In the Mets clubhouse, Bud Harrelson said, "I'm going to call Pete or send him a telegram after this series is over. When all that junk was coming down on him, I hoped a couple of those animals throwing it would come on the field, so Pete could deck them."

The Mets won the final game, then lost the World Series to Oakland in seven games. Feeney wrote Harrelson and Rose in November, informing them that each was being fined $250 and would have to submit personal checks to the league office before he could play in exhibition games the following spring. Feeney added: "You have my personal regards and hope you have a good winter."

"I can't believe it," Rose said in Cincinnati. "Mostly I was holding Harrelson. He was the one who called me the name. He was the one who really wanted to go. I was just grabbing, trying to keep the fight from getting worse.

"Why didn't Feeney fine Wayne Garrett and Jon Matlack? The films show they threw punches at me when I was down.

"Why didn't he fine the Mets management for not being able to control the crowd?"

"He did say he wanted you to have a good winter," a reporter said.

"But he forgot to wish me Merry Christmas and Happy New Year," Rose said. The reporter described Rose's manner as sardonic.

Sardonic Pete Rose was selected Most Valuable Player in the National League for 1973, narrowly edging Willie Stargell, who had hit 44 home runs for the Pirates. Howsam summoned him for contract talks in February.

"I hit .338 with 230 hits," Rose began.

"Let's not talk statistics," Howsam said.

Rose settled lower into a chair, thinking, Here we go again. Howsam surprised him. He talked leadership and hustle. Within one hour he agreed to pay Rose $160,000 for 1974.

Rose: "That was the easiest negotiation ever and I got the biggest raise of my career. The summer before, when the team was on the road, Howsam and I made it a point to have breakfast once a week. We'd talk about little things, who was dogging it, who needed a boost. He'd point out some things he thought that I could do as captain that Sparky maybe couldn't do as manager. Talk to someone one-on-one as player to player. It could have made him understand that I was more important to the team than he had known.

"He said he looked at me as the team leader now, so I guess it was all those breakfast talks.

"Or it could have been the whiskey bottle that did it."

It was a merry winter. Rose was hired as baseball's entry in a network TV competition called "Superstars" where he got to bowl, golf, lift weights, and play tennis with athletes renowned in other sports. He was new to tennis but beat the great skier Karl Schranz, 7–6. The match turned when Rose made a diving forehand return. "I ripped my pants and skinned my knee and I broke the crystal in my Mickey Mouse watch. But the shot was a winner and that's what counts."

Bowling went badly. Baseball had been cutting into Rose's bowling practice time. He finished seventh in a field of ten with a score of 141. But he surprised everyone in weight lifting. The big fullback, Franco Harris, won that event, pumping 265 pounds of iron over his head. But Rose, who many still viewed as a powder-puff singles hitter, jerked 210 pounds, a formidable lift even for a slugger.

He would not win the overall competition. (A soccer player, Kyle Rote, Jr., finished first.) But going into nine holes of golf Rose was struggling against John Havlicek of the Boston Celtics for fourth place. On the second hole, Rose hit a low line drive into a lake but the golf ball did not sink. It skipped and landed in the fairway on the other side.

"If I hit toward that water," said Stan Smith, the tennis player, "talk to my ball, will you, Pete?"

Smith hooked his drive off the course in Rotondo, Florida.

"Is that out?" Smith asked.

"It's out of the state," Rose said.

By the end of eight holes, Rose was twenty-three strokes over par, which is about the way he plays golf. Havlicek, an

experienced golfer, was having a wretched morning. He was
twenty-two over. "I'll get him," Rose told a reporter as he
walked from the eighth green to the ninth tee.

Havlicek drove out of bounds. He drove again and split the
fairway. Then Rose hit and drove his ball long and straight.
He outdrove Havlicek. He hit the green with his second shot
and holed his ball with two putts. After eight holes, in which
he had not shot lower than six, Rose parred a hole when he
had to and beat out Havlicek for fourth place. "Put me head
to head with anyone in a pressure situation," Rose said, "and
I'll win."

He had long since mastered the give-and-take of father-son
banquets. Now, moving upscale, he advanced through formal dinners at which guests arrived in private planes. The
Industrial Fuels Corporation, a company that brokered coal,
invited him to address its annual dinner-dance in Pikesville,
Kentucky.

Among the 190 guests—including twenty McCoys and one
Hatfield—there was not a single coal-miner's daughter.
These weren't coal-mining people. These were the people
who owned the mines. "Their women," reports the Cincinnati writer Willard Bailey, "were haute couture. They flew in
a band from the Greenbrier Resort. They gave their mines
down-home names like Quicksand, Mousie, and Defeated
Creek, but you wouldn't say these were down-home people.
They were fancy."

Rose dressed in a dinner jacket of brown, with patterns of
green and rust and eggshell. His bow tie was chocolate-col-
ored velvet. Everyone sang "My Old Kentucky Home," then
Rose began:

"Who would have thought an innocent Cincinnati boy
could go to New York, slide into second base trying to break
up a double play, and wind up nearly starting World War III?

"I'm standing out there in left field when, zing, a bottle of whiskey goes right by my head. That made me mad. But I *really* got mad when I saw that it was empty. . . .

"Seriously, folks, I loved every minute in Shea Stadium. Where else do you get to go to the zoo three days in a row for free?"

Rose took some questions. "We hear," someone said, "that you have to play for New York or Los Angeles to get big-time publicity. Do you have trouble getting publicity playing for the Reds?"

"Look at it this way," Rose said. "I been featured on the cover of *Sports Illustrated* magazine three times. That ain't bad for a white guy."

He was working the room. (When questioned seriously about the relative strengths of black and white athletes, Rose answers that no one knows. "You got great athletes in black and white and brown. I don't go with the idea blacks are dominating. Look at the medals the Russians win in the Olympics. All the Russian athletes I've seen are white.")

He was working the room with enormous energy. One guest suggested Rose could be the next Johnny Carson. That seemed excessive. But clearly Rose led the major leagues in one-line jokes.

Talking to mobile-home dealers a week later, he put on an earnest face after being told most had suffered through a slow year. "When you come eye to eye with a potential customer," said Pete Rose, motivational lecturer, "if he don't buy, you lose. The object in baseball and selling is to win. You hear the cliché, it's not whether you win or lose, it's how you play the game. To me, that's a bunch of *toro poo-poo*. If you don't win, you haven't accomplished nothin'."

Pete's speaking fee reached $1,500, outstanding for the time. One evening Karolyn Rose, herself a competitor, told a visitor she was speaking to the wives' club of a machine tool company. "They're paying me $100."

"See here," Rose said in a burst of spousal pride. "How

many women in Cincinnati get paid to speak at banquets? I'll bet there ain't another one."

Pride preceded teasing. "A hundred isn't bad, Karolyn, but I know how you could get it up to $1,600."

Karolyn looked wary, then said, "How?"

"Take *me* along."

Rose had dropped the other shoe but on this one occasion, the last line belonged to somebody else. "To tell you the truth, Pete," Karolyn said, "your name didn't even come up."

Superteam had a remarkable off year in 1974. The Reds won 98 games, but finished second. A young Dodger team won 102. Nobody batted .300, not even Captain Rose. He hit .284, the first time in a decade he slipped below .300. Still he led the leagues in games played (163), runs scored (110), doubles (45), and he led the major leagues in fielding percentage for an outfielder. Across those 163 games, Rose made only a single error.

Esquire magazine, rather carefully laid-back with sports stories through various regimes, celebrated with a valentine of a profile. The magazine assigned a *New York Times* reporter named Judy Klemesrud to write the story; few women had composed profiles of ballplayers even as late as the mid-1970s, and Klemesrud jumped into her idea of the sports world as hard as Rose jumped onto home plate at Shea.

"Pete Rose," Klemesrud wrote, and who could argue, "never does anything half-ass."

The story rings with a kind of tomboy charm but halfway through a stab of sex appears. "We get into a Stingray," Klemesrud writes, "and as we head toward the city, I notice Rose has the habit of driving with his right hand on the wheel and the left hand on his crotch. I ask him about baseball groupies, and whether it is true that Rose likes to ogle girls while he's on the road."

The transition in that paragraph is compelling. At one moment Judy Klemesrud is looking at Rose's crotch; from there she immediately asks about his sex life.

Rose's answer was a model of press relations. "You don't have to worry about groupies on my club because we got a bachelor, Johnny Bench, and they all swarm around him. I liked to go see the Statue of Liberty and Fisherman's Wharf, but once you've seen 'em, you've seen 'em. So I just watch TV."

Once I asked a beautiful woman whether she'd had a love affair with an orchestra conductor who'd been hovering over her cleavage for an evening, after conducting a vigorous performance of the *New World* Symphony. The woman's response was the most sensible thing I would ever hear her say: "I don't have to tell you everything."

If you assume Rose followed the same thinking with Judy Klemesrud, you will get no argument in this volume or probably anywhere else.

"There is a definite star quality," Klemesrud wrote. "He has a thick head of dark auburn hair, sparkling brown eyes . . . His beefy five-foot-eleven-inch body is reminiscent of a fireplug, but he looks awfully good in his clothes, which tend to be very form fitting. So is his white knit uniform—so tight, in fact, that you can easily see the outline of his boxer shorts. . . ."

Two years later, in a landmark case, women journalists won the right to interview naked athletes in the locker room.

Watergate was unsettling the country and informed people wondered why a character as calculating as Richard Nixon tape-recorded himself into disgrace. The most reasonable explanation seems to be the arrogance of power.

In the demimonde of baseball, a parallel arrogance was about to bring down the feudal system that club owners had

created in the nineteenth century and had preserved
through at least three challenges that carried to the Supreme
Court. The era of the free-agent ballplayer was about to burst
upon us, with remarkable suddenness, although it would be
fifteen years before $2 million annual salaries became rou-
tine for preeminent ballplayers.

Rose: "I never made $2 million from a baseball contract,
or even close. If this was the 1970s, I mean if I could still play
like that, I'd probably ask Reuven Katz to get me $3 million.
And I'll bet you he could do it, too. Come in, in his quiet way,
Reuv would, and pull some numbers, and never show a bead
of sweat, and demonstrate why at $3 million, I'd be a bargain.

"People say, they said it long ago, do ballplayers make too
much money? Most of the time when they're asking that,
they're telling you they think they do.

"You hear about someone working in a ghetto, maybe not
all that safe, trying to educate kids for $25,000. How do you
balance that with a ballplayer at $3 million?

"Don't pay the ballplayer less. Pay the ghetto teacher
more.

"Everybody—ballplayers, lawyers, doctors, teachers—has
a right to bargain for as much as they can make.

"The ballplayers were fortunate to have Marvin Miller run
the players' association [the major league union] and I've
personally been fortunate to have Reuven Katz bargaining
for me.

"You got no major leagues without the players. That's obvious, am I right? The players take what they can, free enterprise, and, if I'm not mistaken, no ball club has gone bankrupt in the history of the two major leagues.

"Besides, major league baseball signed a contract with CBS
in 1989 that's worth $1.1 billion. Billion.

"When did you last see a billion, outside of a report from
the U.S. Treasury?

"CBS couldn't pay baseball the money if it wasn't there. The owners don't pay players money they don't have."

Manumission, free bargaining, for ballplayers came in two giant steps. Catfish Hunter had signed to pitch in 1974 for $100,000, part of which would be deferred to lower Hunter's immediate liability to the Internal Revenue Service. But as tax experts, including Reuven J. Katz, point out, there is no such thing as a free lunch. The liability that Hunter delayed would pass on, in somewhat different form, to Charlie Finley.

Finley demanded that Hunter take all his $100,000 in one year. Hunter refused and demanded arbitration. John Gaharin, the arbitrator chosen by major league baseball, and Marvin Miller, chosen by Hunter's side, split their vote. The third panelist, the late Peter Seitz, was a professional arbitrator and, coincidentally, an unregenerate fan of the old Brooklyn Dodgers. He sided with Hunter. The contract was voided. Hunter could now sell his services to the highest bidder, which turned out to be the New York Yankees, who agreed to pay him $3.75 million for five years, in salary, deferred payments, and other benefits. ("My dad was a farmer in Carolina," Hunter said, "and some years he made about $200. We ate what we grew. That's how we lived.")

Marvin Miller next asked two players to test the validity of the standard major league contract, specifically the clauses that required a player to give an exclusive option on his services to the team for which he was playing. The so-called reserve clause, actually several clauses, had denied ballplayers the right to seek bidders. Instead, all anyone could do— Ted Williams in Boston, Joe DiMaggio in New York, Pete Rose in Cincinnati—was to bargain with the club that already employed them. As owners frequently pointed out, any player who didn't like their final offer was perfectly free to spend his summer pumping diesel fuel in a truck stop.

Two pitchers, Andy Messersmith of the Dodgers and Dave

McNally of the Montreal Expos, played through the 1975 season without signing contracts. They received the same salaries they had earned in 1974. By not signing, Miller argued, they were now free of the reserve clauses, now free agents.

Why would the Dodgers and the Expos pay Messersmith and McNally without contracts? Both were fine pitchers. (Messersmith won nineteen games for Los Angeles. McNally developed arm trouble and won only three.) But more critical to the owners' decision was an unshakeable belief that baseball's reserve clauses were above the law. Walter Francis O'Malley, who moved the Dodgers from Brooklyn to Los Angeles with aureate success, had been a practicing attorney before elbowing his way into control of the Dodgers. He was now the most powerful individual in the baseball establishment. ("When O'Malley wants a cup of coffee," Red Smith wrote, "it is [Commissioner] Bowie Kuhn who asks, 'One lump or two?' ")

As the establishment was about to learn, O'Malley, a ruthless, brilliant businessman, was—in O'Malley's English—a lousy lawyer. Messersmith and McNally maintained that they were now free agents and, when organized baseball dismissed their argument, went before the same arbitration panel that had heard the Hunter case.

The vote was again two to one, with Peter Seitz, the swing man, siding with the ballplayers in a sixty-seven-page decision. Kuhn at once dismissed Seitz from the panel of arbitrators who could decide baseball questions because he "did not understand the structure" of the game.

Seitz replied mildly that he was not Lincoln freeing slaves. "I am just interpreting the renewal clause as a lawyer and arbitrator." Lawyers for organized baseball attempted to overturn the Seitz decision in federal circuit and district courts. Each time judges cited a Supreme Court ruling, on the books for fifteen years, that denied *any* court the power to overrule an arbitrator's decision in a labor case.

Rose, like other ballplayers behind him, would reap a bountiful harvest.

Coincidentally with the decision, baseball—*Time* magazine's "increasingly stale game" of the 1960s—began reasserting a love-lock on the American heart. Professional football had moved toward dominance, some said, because its quick-paced violence matched America's random violence during Vietnam. If any single event can be said to have turned American consciousness back to its ancestral team sport, it was the 1975 World Series, which ran across eleven days of October in the purist confines of Boston's Fenway Park and on the plastic grass in Cincinnati.

In the spring of '75 at Tampa, Rose took a few minutes off from shagging flies, borrowed a glove, and started taking throws at first base.

"Why you playing there?" Sparky Anderson asked.

"Just havin' fun."

"If you really want to help us," Anderson said, "put away the first baseman's mitt and go play third."

"For practice, Spark?"

"For the season, Pete. If you move to third, we'll have an outfield of [George] Foster, Cesar Geronimo, and Ken Griffey. We need pop [run scoring]. We'd get the most that way."

"I haven't played thirty games at third in my life."

"I'm not telling you, Pete. I'm asking."

Rose nodded and started toward the clubhouse. A few reporters speculated that Rose was headed there to call Reuven Katz. Pete loved to be paid, they knew. He'd probably demand a $50,000 bonus for switching positions.

Rose: "I was not going to the telephone. I was going to the equipment man to get a [protective aluminum] cup. Sure I'd play third. Sparky's reasoning was right. But I didn't intend for third base to turn me into a soprano."

The Reds ran away with the National League West, winning it by twenty games. They swept the championship series from the Pirates and moved on to Boston to match themselves against a good Red Sox team that included five .300 hitters in the batting order and a deep pitching staff that wheeled around the left-hander Bill Lee, of baseball's Woodstock generation, and Luis Tiant, a bald and guileful Cuban émigré, called affectionately, by Harvard Spanish majors, El Tiante.

The Boston Red Sox had not won a World Series since 1918, when Babe Ruth was still a pitcher. The Reds had lost the last three Series they'd been in and Rose's Reds had lost two in the 1970s. Each ball club had something to prove: October staying power. The teams and their ballparks stood in distinct contrast, which fed the sense of competition. "Riverfront is synthetic baseball," wrote Peter Gammons in the *Boston Globe*. "Steely and sparkly and aseptic." He likened Riverfront's hops and caroms to "playing marbles in a bathtub." The Reds had finished 64–17 at home. But could they play on grass? That seemed to be Gammons's question.

On Saturday, October 11, the Red Sox won going away and the *Globe* headline employed internal rhyme and announced: "El Tiante Elegante; Red Machine Pffft . . . 6–0."

Rose hit the ball hard—"on the squash," wrote Bob Ryan in the *Globe*, but got no hits. "I saw Tiant perfect," he said. "I wish I could say he was great because he shut us out. But he wasn't. We were hitting our line drives at their fielders, which was not what we were trying to do."

Sunday brought a tense and exciting game. Coincidentally, the Boston regional football team, the Patriots, was playing the Cincinnati Bengals, back in Ohio. Paul Brown, the great football coach, decreed that no World Series reports could be flashed on the Riverfront scoreboard. Brown had taught

high-school English; he could spell civic pride. He spelled it
f-o-o-t-b-a-l-l.

The Bengals defeated the Patriots, 27–10. Bengal fans
brought portable radios and as the football turned dull, they
began to cheer the happenings in Boston. Bill Lee pitched a
strong game for the Red Sox, but the Reds scored two in the
ninth and won, 3–2. The football game was done by then. Still
fans remained in Riverfront, the scoreboards dark, for group
radio listening. Rose got two hits. Bench and Ken Griffey
powered the ninth-inning rally. Game 2 was not only exciting, but something of a rarity. It was followed simultaneously
by fans in two ballparks.

"What's your impression of the World Series?" a reporter
asked Bill Lee.

"My impression," Lee said, "is that the World Series is
tied."

"What's your impression of Boston?" another reporter
asked Rose.

"Outstanding lobster. Worthless weather."

New York City, the newspapers said, was going bankrupt.
President Gerald Ford and Vice President Nelson Rockefeller issued contradictory statements and the teachers' union,
of all underpaid cabals, had to lend the city money to meet
a payroll. The National Catholic Opinion Research Center
announced the results of a survey, seeking to learn why
fewer Catholics were attending church. The hierarchy's
stands against divorce and effective birth control were
blamed.

More people were talking about a tenth-inning play in
Cincinnati. The Red Sox tied the score in the ninth inning on
a two-run homer stroked by Dwight Evans, the sixth home
run of the game. Marbles kept flying out of Peter Gammons's
bathtub, scuffing his tiles.

Cesar Geronimo singled, leading off the last of the tenth.
Sparky Anderson sent in a skinny Bahamian outfielder

named Ed Armbrister, who bunted. Catcher Carlton Fisk, a Boston strongboy, moved for the ball and bumped into Armbrister. He flicked Armbrister away with his glove and threw the ball into center field. As the throw sailed high, Fisk turned and shouted at Larry Barnett, the home-plate umpire, "Interference." Geronimo raced to third, oversliding the bag.

"No interference," Barnett said. The Red Sox stormed him and argued for five minutes. Then Roger Moret walked Rose and Joe Morgan singled home the run that won the game for Cincinnati, 6–5.

The Red Sox cursed in their clubhouse. "Armbrister came up under me as I was going for the ball," Fisk said. "I felt like I was hit by a linebacker."

"There were three outs on that play," Bill Lee said, "and none got called.

"Out one. Interference at home. Armbrister should have been called out and Geronimo sent back to first.

"Out two. When Fisk came up with the ball, he actually tagged Armbrister. I saw it.

"Out three. After Geronimo overslid third base, Rico Petrocelli tagged him. But the ump there had come up toward home. Nobody called the play."

The country happily turned away from Ford, Rockefeller, and Catholic crises and concentrated on an umpire named Larry Barnett. "It looked to me," Pete Rose said mildly, "that Fisk just ran into Armbrister and that's not interference."

The Boston writers were finding Cincinnati provincial, even quaint. A detachment from the 101st Airborne Division presented the colors at Riverfront. "In Boston," commented Mike Barnicle (of the *Boston Globe*), "a mother's march for peace would be preferred." But peace was less and less the order of the time. (When the Series returned to Boston for Game 6, Umpire Barnett requested and received twenty-four-hour police protection for himself and his family.)

Pete at age ten.

Pete in junior high school.

Western High School second sacker Pete Rose turning a pivot in the late 1950s.

Pete's dad is number 28 in the front row;
Pete, on the right, served as waterboy.

Pete and his dad.

Pete's dad playing b

Harry Francis Rose,
a.k.a. "Big Pete."

Rookie Pete Rose.

Pete in his first year of pro ball
in Geneva, New York.

Pete at the time of his military induction.
His hairstyle didn't change much.

Pete being congratulated by his
platoon sergeant, Sgt. Lester
Axson, on being named National
League Rookie of the Year. Pete,
in his third week of a six-month
Army basic-training program,
was waxing a kitchen floor
when notified of his selection.

Pete and his first wife, Karolyn, on their wedding day.

Karolyn and their two children, Pete Jr. and Fawn, at the ballpark in 1978.

In 1981, Pete Jr. served as the Phillies' batboy while watching his dad pursue Ty Cobb's record.

Fred Hutchinson with Ralph Houk.

Opening day in Cincinnati in 1965 saw Pete going up in the air to grab a high pickoff throw from pitcher Jim O'Toole in an attempt to get Milwaukee's Mack Jones off second base.

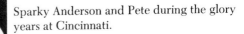

Sparky Anderson and Pete during the glory years at Cincinnati.

In the 1970 All-Star Game at Riverfront Stadium, Pete scored from second on Jim Hickman's two-out single. Both Pete and Indians catcher Ray Fosse were injured in the collision.

The night before the game, Fosse and Pete, who had just met for the first time, spent most of the evening talking baseball together.

Charlie Hustle.

The National League playoffs
in 1973 reached a climax when
a routine double play erupted into
a wild bench-clearing brawl when
Pete took Bud Harrelson out on
a hard slide at second.

According to Pete, the incident was
ignited by just one word Bud said to him.

Loyal Mets fans still haven't
forgotten this wrestling match.

Two of the game's greatest—
Johnny Bench and Pete Rose.

A typical
Pete Rose slide.

The 1975 World
Series between
Boston and
Cincinnati is
considered one of
the greatest ever
played. That's Rico
Petrocelli waiting
for the throw.

The Big Red Machine, with Johnny Bench in the driver's seat. Left to right: Bobby Tolan, Tony Perez, Lee May, and Pete Rose. Ironically, Tolan managed Pete Rose, Jr., in his first year of pro ball in the New York–Penn League.

Pete gets some free advice from long-time friends Dave Concepcion and Tony Perez before taking the field as the Reds' player-manager for the first time in August 1984.

Player-manager Pete Rose in action in 1985.

Pete takes the long walk back to the dugout as the scoreboard lights up saying it all, "The End," after he struck out in the ninth inning to end his forty-four-game hitting streak on August 2, 1978.

In 1978, Pete took part in a barnstorming tour of Japan. The Yomiuri Giants won, 7–6, in this game.

Pete and a Phillie teammate,
future Hall-of-Famer Mike
Schmidt, in 1979.

First baseman Pete Rose being
introduced in his first game as a
Phillie in Veterans Stadium in 1979.

Joe Morgan and Pete Rose, two Reds
stars, talk baseball in the 1983 World
Series as teammates on the Phillies.

Pete signs a one-year deal with the Expos.

Pete as an Expo in 1984.

Expo outfielder Pete Rose flags down a gapper in a spring-training game. Pete was a spry forty-three years old.

Hit number 4,192, on September 11, 1985.

Pete and his son share the emotion of Pete's record-breaking hit.

Reds owner Marge Schott congratulating Pete on his record-breaking hit.

Pete and his son, Pete Jr., now a player in the Orioles chain

Pete, Tyler, wife Carol, and five-day-old Cara Chae. Pete is looking forward to her first birthday.

The late Commissioner of Baseball A. Bartlett Giamatti announces a lifetime ban for Pete Rose in New York, August 24, 1989.

ose accuser Ron Peters outside the federal ourthouse in Cincinnati, June 16, 1989, after eing sentenced to two years in prison on rug and tax charges.

Paul Janszen was one of Pete's main accusers regarding alleged gambling on baseball. Janszen later sold his story to *Penthouse*.

John M. Dowd, the Washington attorney who conducted baseball's investigation of gambling allegations against Pete .

Longtime friend and advisor
Reuven J. Katz.

Reuven Katz
and the
only three
ballplayers he
represents—
Johnny Bench,
Pete, and
Tony Perez.

Pete makes
it clear at the
August 24 press
conference:
"I did not bet
on baseball."

The fourth game belonged at last to the redoubtable Luis Tiant, who threw 163 pitches, easily a game and a half, along the way to a 5–4 victory. "My impression of the Series," Bill Lee said, "is that it's tied again."

Tony Perez hit two home runs and the Reds won the fifth game, 6–2, at Riverfront. No more marbles flying out of a bathtub now. The teams moved back to Boston where a nor'easter lingered and dropped 2.7 inches of rain on Fenway Park. Five days elapsed between Game 5 and Game 6.

Rose: "Everybody was talking baseball. All that time just added to the suspense. Could Boston beat us twice in their home park? Which team was the rain helping most? Then, when we finally did get back, we played the best ball game I played in ever, up till then."

The temperature on October 21 was a tolerable sixty-four. Tiant came back, and the Red Sox jumped ahead when Fred Lynn hit a three-run homer in the first inning. The Reds tied the score in the fifth. Tiant aged in a hurry. The Reds moved ahead by 5–3 in the seventh and added one more in the eighth. Then, in the last of the eighth, Bernie Carbo, who broke in as a Red, tied the score for Boston with a three-run pinch-hit home run: 6–6.

Now everyone knew or sensed a run would come hard. The Red Sox loaded the bases with nobody out in the tenth. The Reds turned them back. Next time Rose came to bat, he turned to Carlton Fisk and said, "Can you believe this game?"

What an extraordinary moment! In the midst of a wonderful World Series game, one of the players had turned to another to comment on the wonder, even as its fabric unfolded, a baseball cloth of gold. It was almost as if, in the midst of a transcendent *Hamlet,* one actor turned to another and remarked, "Can you believe this script?"

Fisk merely nodded. He is a New England Yankee. Then, in the twelfth inning, he drove a high fly down the left-field line. He ran a few steps toward first, twisting his bulky body as if to apply English to the ball. The baseball carried into the foul pole. Boston won, 7–6.

Some have called this the best of all World Series ball games. The idea that there is a single best game, a single most dramatic hit, is popular with certain television interviewers, magazine editors, and amateurs, who like to argue foamy-lipped in loud sports bars. Was Game 6, 1975, better than Game 5, 1956, when Don Larsen threw 97 pitches for the Yankees and let no Dodger reach base? Was it better than Game 7, 1926, when Grover Cleveland Alexander of the St. Louis Cardinals came out of a bullpen in the Bronx—he was thirty-nine years old and had pitched nine strong innings the day before in beating the Yankees of Ruth and Gehrig—and struck out Tony Lazzeri with the bases loaded, preserving victory? Was it better than Game 3, 1911, when Jack Coombs of the Philadelphia Athletics, a twenty-eight-game winner, bested Christy Mathewson of the Giants, who had won twenty-six, 3–2, in twelve innings?

Rose: "I can't say it was. What I can say is that the sixth game in '75 was the most exciting, competitive game I ever saw or played in. That's more than 4,000, counting playoffs and all. The most exciting competitive game and we lost. I might feel differently if things hadn't worked okay in Game 7."

The Red Sox sprang ahead with three runs in the third inning. Tony Perez hit a two-run home run for Cincinnati in the sixth. The Reds tied the score in the seventh and won in the ninth, 4–3. Rose batted in the run that tied the score. Joe Morgan knocked in the run that won the Series.

Rose hit .370 and *Sport* magazine selected him as Most Valuable Player of the Series. The award was a compact car called a Pacer which, someone remarked, Rose could hide in the trunk of the white Rolls Royce he had bought for himself and Karolyn. ("I didn't hide it," he says. "I sold it.")

Five of the seven games in this grinding Series were decided by a single run. When it was over, somebody asked
Rose if he felt worn and weary. "The other way," he said.
"I'm *sorry* it's over. I wish spring training started tomorrow."
Toward Christmas *Sports Illustrated* awarded Rose a Grecian urn and anointed him Sportsman of the Year. In the
issue that celebrated Rose, Ron Fimrite wrote:

> The sheer force of his personality was felt most compellingly
> in the sixth inning of the final game. The Reds had closed an
> early 3–0 Red Sox lead to 3–2 on Perez' home run. . . . There
> was someone on base for Perez to drive home only because
> Rose, sliding with typical fury into second, had intimidated
> Denny Doyle into throwing wildly to first on what would have
> been an inning-ending double play. Now, with the Red Sox
> about to come to bat, Rose gave an astonishing performance.
> He set about rousing his teammates, as if they were troops on
> the front line. He bellowed encouragement, pounded his fist
> into his glove and bounced about the infield with an enthusi-
> asm that was contagious. He seemed to grow physically in
> stature, to tower over the situation. Even in the stands his will
> to win could be felt. Though they still trailed in the game, it
> seemed inevitable the Reds would win. It was a highly
> charged moment of a kind rarely, if ever, seen in a major
> league baseball game. Rose had stirred his teammates, hard-
> ened professionals, to a collegiate pitch.

Rose: "And, of course, I never even been to college. Now
that I think of it, forget Game 6, where we got beat. Game
7 of the 1975 World Series was the best game I ever
played in.

"It's all right, isn't it, for me to change my mind in the
middle of a book?"

"You changed it in the middle of a chapter."

"If we could all get younger, you know what I'd like? We'd
play Game 6 and Game 7 all over again tomorrow. If I'm not

mistaken, far as anybody knows, that would be the best doubleheader of all time."

The Reds won their division by ten games in 1976 as this great team reached full, radiant flower. The Reds led the National League in runs, doubles, triples, home runs, stolen bases. They batted .280 as a team. They could also field ground balls and catch fly balls. They led the major leagues in fielding percentage.

They swept the league playoff from the Phillies and then played a connoisseur's World Series against the Yankees. I remember visiting the home of Reuven J. Katz for a pre-Series party. The conservative house in a conservative neighborhood was decked with a loud red-and-white banner: "WE'RE REDS HOT."

Ballplayers and enthusiasts milled inside. Sparky Anderson sipped coffee and looked unhappy. "Everybody's writing that the team is so great we have to win," Anderson said. "So if we win, it's just expected and if we lose, you know they're going to blame the manager."

Under Billy Martin, the Yankees liked to run and steal. Early in the first game, Lou Piniella, who couldn't run fast, reached third base and took a six-inch lead. After the next pitch, Johnny Bench threw to Rose at third. He fired out of his catcher's squat and I had not known before that anyone could throw out of a squat that hard. Piniella was safe; he had only to move his toe-plate. "But we put on that little pickoff," Rose says, "just to show the Yankees Bench's arm." Billy Martin saw Bench's arm and his passion for a running game subsided. (The Yankees did not steal a base until they were trailing by three games.)

Sparky Anderson stopped worrying about blame. There was no blame in Cincinnati. Rose: "We blew 'em out. We knew we could do it and we did." The Reds swept the Series in four games and gave the country a lesson in the art of playing baseball. Seven Reds regulars hit over .300. Bench, playing the catcher from Olympus, hit .533 and was MVP. Rose hit .188. "But the worse I hit the harder I was working down at third. You know my theory. If you aren't contributing with your bat, work twice as hard with your glove. Contribute any way you can.

"And even though my bat was cold, I did that. I contributed.

"Everybody talks about '75, the year I won the car. Sure I'm proud of that.

"But I'm just as proud of the way I played in 1976.

"I wasn't hitting. I didn't let myself get down. I played in their face. I probably had the best .188 World Series of all time."

8

No Longer a Red

CINCINNATI, 1978—"THE STREAK"

In a long-ago era, when Ruth and Gehrig reigned, persistent barking sounded across the dog days of August: "Break up the Yankees." You heard that in Cleveland and Detroit and even in New York, where municipal dissidents wearied of pennant races dominated by a single team, a single starting lineup. Break up the Yankees. Dismember the patricians. Give the proletarians a chance.

But after Ruth and Gehrig came the teams of Joe DiMaggio and after *that*, a period, 1949 to 1953, when Casey Stengel's Yankees won the World Series five times in a row. "How can you root for the Yankees?" a forgotten actor tartly asked Red Smith at the Players Club in New York. "It's like rooting for U.S. Steel."

Essentially, the Yankees positioned themselves to become the dominant team in baseball in 1920 when the organization bought Babe Ruth's contract from the Boston Red Sox for $125,000 plus a loan of $300,000 to one Harry Frazee, the Boston owner. The Yankees still dominated four decades later when CBS bought the franchise for $10 million in 1964. But within two years of the CBS purchase, the Yankees finished last. The Yankees championship survived boom times, a great depression, World War II, Korea, cholera, dengue fever, the urban crisis, and plague. They could survive anything except CBS.

The Reds of 1975 and 1976 were as dominant as some great Yankee teams, assuredly a tribute to Bob Howsam, Chief Bender, and the Cincinnati scouting staff. But two years is a brevity. Except as press-box humor, you didn't hear cries of "Break up the Reds." Besides, there was no need. In two misbegotten moves across three seasons, the Cincinnati Reds broke up themselves.

On December 16, 1976, the Reds announced that they had traded Tony Perez and a relief pitcher named Will McEnaney to the Montreal Expos for a pair of journeyman pitchers, Woodie Fryman and Dale Murray. McEnaney had saved games 3 and 4 of the World Series. Perez, who was 34, had hit .313 against the Yankees in October.

Rose: "They were thinking in the front office that Tony's batting average for the season had fallen off to .260 and that he was over the hill. They were going to move Danny Driessen, who was about ten years younger, to first base. I *think* that's what they were thinking. It could have been money, too, getting rid of Tony's salary. When you look at the record and what they did with me, you have to figure the people in the front office, at the top, were *not* saying we're gonna have a dynasty in Cincinnati, we're gonna pay for the dynasty and make a fortune. You have to figure this new setup, free agency, scared them more than it should have. I don't for sure know what they were thinking at the top and it turned out their thinking wasn't that great. Tony Perez over the hill in 1976? When we finally got him back to Cincinnati nine years later in 1985, Tony hit .328. He was more king of the hill than over it."

Intense, bespectacled Dick Wagner had moved in as Howsam's assistant and would become team president in 1978.

Wagner was a serious character, even grim, who indulged himself in outbursts of nastiness.

Rose: "Like Wagner always called Reuven Katz my *agent.* Reuv went to Harvard Law School. Reuv is my *lawyer.* He charges by the hour for the work he does. He could have made a lot more charging a percentage. But he wouldn't do that. I know the word here. Ethical. So here's a man who went to Harvard Law. An ethical attorney. And Dick Wagner tells the writers he's an agent."

Tony Perez convened a press conference to announce the trade. Leaving the organization he had started with in 1960, Perez conducted himself with dignity and no bitterness. With the reporters present, Johnny Bench hugged Perez and burst into tears.

Rose: "It was emotional for all of us. My kids, Fawn and Petey, got home from school and *they* started crying. In the summer they used to play with Tony's boys, Victor and Eduardo. Now Victor and Eduardo weren't even gonna be in the same country."

The Reds' Wagner had dealt a remarkable ballplayer, probably a Hall-of-Fame player, whose base hits might possibly be replaced. He had also traded something irreplaceable: an uncomplaining competitor who embodied and provided some of the drive and élan that moved the Big Red Machine. That done, the bad deal concluded, a star discarded like an extra joker, the Reds became embroiled in a contract fight with Rose that has no match in the annals. The Reds against the Rose. Near Fountain Square it began to look as though the Civil War was back.

Rose: "We had the best team in the major leagues in the mid-1970s. There's no question about that. We also drew the most fans in the major leagues. In '76, our home attendance was over 2.6 million. No other club came close. The Dodgers, with that tremendous population area, drew 300,000 less than we did. Plus the Reds had extra income from the play-

offs and the World Series. I wasn't asking anybody for a contract that paid me what they didn't have. I wasn't trying to
take Dick Wagner's food stamps."

Rose had earned $188,000 in 1976. "I first thought I
wanted maybe $225,000 for the next year, for 1977. Then I
thought some more. The number changed. It got bigger.
People wrote that I wanted to be the highest-paid player on
the Reds. I wouldn't have objected, but I wasn't gonna get
into an argument about me and Bench and Morgan. Who was
best? We were all-stars. Who was the best? It varied with the
day. Besides, I wasn't only thinking Cincinnati.

"I read the papers. I watch television. In November, Reggie Jackson left Baltimore for the Yankees. Five years, $2.9
million. That's $580,000 a year. Now I'm not gonna get into
an argument about me and Reggie, either. I'm just saying,
which is true, after 1976 I was a helluva player on a helluva
team that was drawing more than anybody else in baseball.

"What was I worth? I asked for $400,000.

"Dick Wagner flipped out."

The Reds had an option on Rose's services for 1977; he
was under contract to play for Cincinnati until 1978. Indeed, baseball rules provided that the Reds could unilater-
ally renew the contract for 1977 at the same salary figure,
$188,000, that Rose had earned in 1976. But checks and
balances were coming into baseball as the players' union,
under soft-voiced, wily Marvin Miller, consistently out-
thought and outmaneuvered the owners, who were arrayed
behind their tall, rigid, and ultimately shortsighted commissioner, Bowie Kuhn.

Were the Reds to renew Rose at $188,000 for 1977, he
would automatically have become a free agent when that
season ended, at liberty to offer himself to the highest bidder
for 1978. This was one quid pro quo worked out through hard
bargaining by Miller. In later years the owners, trying to
recapture what they had lost, conspired to suspend meaning-

ful bidding. Ramifications of that remain before the arbitrators. But through the late 1970s, baseball owners still bid seriously against one another, in one of the game's infrequent spasms of free enterprise.

So after 1976, the Reds management had clear alternatives. Respond seriously to Rose's $400,000 demand. Or, with moaning noises appropriate to whales in heat, the Reds could resist Rose's salary demand. They could then congratulate themselves on their own fiscal responsibility and, oh yes, lose their homegrown star.

Negotiations between Dick Wagner and the Reds on one side and Reuven Katz and Rose on the other went slowly; poorly would not be too strong a word. The Reds were facing the reality of free agency all at once. They didn't care for that. Their executives had a legitimate long-range concern that the Cincinnati franchise could not match New York or Los Angeles across a decade of bidding wars. Beyond that, there seemed to be strains of personal animus toward Rose. He was combative, independent, loud, loud as his suits, in the button-down river town where Procter met Gamble.

Quite beyond that, Wagner was no admirer of Reuven Katz. Perhaps it is inevitable that hard negotiators come to dislike each other; they spend most of their time together arguing. Perhaps not.

Come February, with spring training days away and no satisfactory contract in sight, Rose took to the media and gave Earl Lawson a story that the *Cincinnati Post* ran on its front page.

Lawson: I know you're having problems with management on salary. Is it conceivable you could play out your option this season?

Rose: I don't know if baseball at Cincinnati is going to be as much fun for me as it was. Tony Perez is gone.

If you'd asked me the same question last year, I'd have told you I wanted to play my whole career in Cincinnati. I owe a lot to Cincinnati and the fans. But the people who run the club now aren't from Cincinnati and I think I've repaid the fans by what I've done on the field. This is the place to play, but if I can get double the money somewhere else and set myself up for life, I don't see any reason why I shouldn't. We make a third of what some of the other players make. You can say a lot of ballplayers are overpaid. This may be true. But they're still getting it.

Lawson: Is there any special team you would want to play with if the Reds decide to trade you?

Rose: An offensive team and a contender. I wouldn't be worth a dime to a team that was gonna lose 100 games. . . . Offensive teams, the Phillies, the Dodgers. Up-and-coming teams. The Yankees. I need 650 at-bats to get 200 hits and get my runs batted in and scored. It's like if I was a passing quarterback I couldn't play for Ohio State. I'm an offensive player. I couldn't go to a team which played 1–0 and 2–0 games every night.

Rose's comments, the *Post* maintained, "were as hard hitting as when he's swinging the bat." That didn't scan but made the point. Rose was telling the Reds through the media that he was ready to move on if pushed, and that his thinking had reached a level at which he had decided specifically where he would be willing to go. After impulsively dealing Perez, the Reds were in no position now to deal Rose. Four hundred thousand dollars, Rose said, was a fair competitive annual price for his services.

Rose: "I didn't mention the million I wanted to Wagner

and neither did Reuven Katz. We didn't want to cause a heart attack."

In taking on Reuven J. Katz, Dick Wagner found himself facing a contained and skilled negotiator, whose courteous manner and soft voice tended to conceal the passionate determination with which he represented a client.

"I've only represented three ballplayers," Katz says. "Pete, Johnny Bench, and Tony Perez. It's obvious, from the record books, how each contributed on the field." Katz is a Cincinnati native, Harvard Law School, a good athlete, a fan of Cincinnati baseball and Reds ballplayers for most of his sixty-five years. He rejoiced at Cooperstown, in the summer of '89, when Bench was inducted into the Hall of Fame. He would like to see Rose and Perez follow. He is fond of all three, sometimes referring to them as his adopted sons. Beyond that, it would please Reuven Katz to become the only lawyer in the annals all of whose baseball clients made the Hall of Fame. "I have nothing," Katz says, "against batting 1.000."

His position on *Rose v. Wagner* was well considered. He asked Wagner to take into account Rose's willingness repeatedly to change positions for the good of the team. Had any ballplayer of Rose's caliber in Rose's time moved about so much? The answer, of course, was no. From Katz's point of view, the answer was what made the question worthwhile.

Next, as a Cincinnati native and resident, Rose contributed to the team on a year-round basis. He attended banquets when the team asked him to. He made appearances during wintertime season-ticket drives. Rose was both an ultimate team player and a twelve-month-a-year Red.

These things were so. There was no arguing with them. And now perhaps, Mr. Wagner, we can turn to hits and runs and doubles. If my numbers are correct, Mr. Wagner, and you'd know more about this than I, my client, Pete Rose, just led the National League in all three.

Do ball clubs pay extra for team spirit? Not significantly. Do they offer a bonus for the athlete who makes jokes with the Reds Rooters of Crestline, Ohio? Not as such. What Katz was doing at this stage was setting a climate. My boy Pete's a hard-working, loyal employee. Our boy Pete's a jolly good fellow. Then, amidst the jollity, by the way, Dick, how much are 215 hits, 42 doubles, and 130 runs scored really worth?

Few baseball men were used to such bargaining finesse. Wagner, like many others, wanted to deal directly with the player. Katz agreed to let them meet alone.

In Tampa, Wagner heard: "I don't want to be traded, Mr. Wagner, and I'm sure loyal to the Reds. But if you're not going to pay me, maybe you ought to see what you can get for me in the trading market right now."

"Do you *want* to be traded?"

"I don't want to be traded. I want to be paid."

Wagner looked uncomfortable. He said his present offer, about $200,000, was pretty darn good.

"Then don't tell me I'm getting old," Rose said. He would soon turn thirty-six. "There's no way you can tell me you don't think I'll get 200 hits and score 100 runs this season. That's why you're making the offer you are." (Rose would get 204 hits and score 95 runs.) "Some people tell me, Mr. Wagner, that I oughta be the highest-paid player in the game."

"Have you considered this, Pete? You may be getting advice from too many sources."

Afterward Wagner announced that he was renewing Rose's contract at the 1976 figure of $188,000. Without thinking everything through, he had sounded the blast of war and now Cincinnati began to choose up sides, the ball *player* or the ball *club*. Passions made bubbles in the blood and it is said that Procter actually had an argument with Gamble.

Rose: "If I ended up having to play for the $188,000, when

other players were making triple that, I guarantee, I was not going to sulk.

"I mean go sulk and hit .220. Who does that hurt? The team, of course, and the fans who root for you, but most of all you hurt yourself.

"If I was gonna have to negotiate with other clubs as a free agent, I wanted to do it after a good year. That's simple, isn't it? Pay me $188,000, when Reggie's up at $580,000, and you only make me more determined to go for .320 and 220 hits. You only make me more determined to go for $600,000.

"Something else. I had the fans with me. Not all but most. I think the Reds were hoping I'd go to the writers and tell them I was disgusted and that I demanded a trade.

"That was the last thing I was gonna say. I *wanted* to stay in Cincinnati. Besides, if I came on demanding to be traded away from my hometown, I sure as hell could have lost the fans."

Spring training began. It has begun in every spring that I remember. Rose had a contract and within the contract a money war. He did push-ups, wind sprints, practiced bunting in Tampa, Florida. None of this was nearly as interesting to fans as the money war; fiscal follies fascinate, and so did the chance that the Reds would lose Rose after the season. A populist movement rooted itself in fertile Ohio soil.

William S. Maxwell, a freshman at Xavier University, took $37.50 of school lunch money and bought an advertisement in the *Cincinnati Post.*

WE WANT
PETE ROSE
IN
CINCINNATI

Write the Reds, asking them to give Pete Rose a fair contract. He has given Cincy fans baseball at its best for 14 years. His

statistics speak for themselves. His leadership has enabled the
Reds to win two World Series 2 straight years. Remember,
he's a money-maker for the Reds.

Write: Dick Wagner
         Cincinnati Reds
         Riverfront Stadium
         Cincinnati, Ohio 45202.

The Richter and Phillips Jewelry Store announced a Pete
Rose sale at its branch on Delhi Pike. Ten percent of all sales
would be placed in an escrow account called the "Let's Get
Pete Signed Fund," because "we want Pete to stay here in
Cincinnati."

Les Thomes, assistant general manager of the Contact
Lens Laboratories in Ft. Mitchell, Kentucky, abandoned
work and spent three days in Fountain Square collecting
signatures on a petition that said, "Sign Pete." Thomes told
the *Enquirer,* "I got eight hundred and almost no refusals. I
would have gotten more, if the weather was better and more
people had been standing around."

Bob Howsam put management's case on a radio program called "Redsline." Howsam cited salaries of less than
$250,000 for Willie Stargell and Carl Yastrzemski.

"Those two are going downhill," said a fan calling in to the
radio program. "Pete has shown no indication he's going
downhill, has he?"

Howsam: "We think Pete with fourteen years is in the
same category with them."

Another caller asked if Joe Morgan, as the press had reported, was making $400,000, Rose's salary goal.

Howsam: "It's our policy not to divulge player salaries."

Caller: "But you've mentioned what Stargell is making."

Howsam: "We don't give out *Reds* salary figures."

Caller: "Until we know what Morgan is making then we

can't understand the full story. You aren't giving us the full story."

In describing the program, the Cincinnati newspapers reported that Howsam's effort had "backfired." "It looks like the entire future of the Reds is in jeopardy," the *Post* announced on page one.

No one, not even Rose or Katz, had anticipated such a shuddering groundswell. Not even Rose or Katz; certainly not Howsam or Wagner. From the point of view of the front office, the public had to be directed to shape up. There is so much of that in baseball; the men who run franchises like to tell the press and the townspeople what to feel and how to think.

On April 3, the Reds purchased three-column advertisements in the *Cincinnati Enquirer* and the *Dayton Daily News,* which ran under this boldface heading:

A SPECIAL MESSAGE TO CINCINNATI REDS FANS

There has been much talk and many stories written about our ball club's salary negotiations. We have said little, believing that such matters are traditionally one of confidence between ball club and player, employer and employee.

But some newspaper stories have tended to state the half-truth and misrepresent our endeavors. . . . YOU, the fan, are the most important consideration in our doing business. A newspaper without readers goes out of business. An airline without passengers folds. There's nothing so special about a baseball club that guarantees its survival. . . . A baseball club . . . must be *financially responsible* to exist in the long term. If not, there will be no baseball—just as there is no American Basketball Association and no World Football League. Contrary to what some persons might like to think, the world can survive without baseball. Thus, there must be sound opera-

tion, and we are disappointed that some other clubs don't
agree.

So where does this all lead? It leads to our present situation
with Pete Rose. We have great respect for his ability. But we'd
like our fans to remember that it was the ball club which
recognized Pete's talents and signed him to his first contract.
It is the ball club which hires people to train him and coach
him, and which surrounds him with other talented players to
enhance his performance. . . .

Our ball club has worked hard to sign Pete Rose. We began
last September when we sought to make Pete our first regular
to sign. We offered $200,000 for 1977 and $225,000 for 1978.
Pete and his agent countered with $450,000 for two years. We
later agreed, but were told the price had gone up. His agent
asked for more and we refused.

We have offered a salary increase of $135,000. Placed in
more understandable terms, we have offered a total salary of
almost $2,000 per game. Or put another way, the value to the
ball club of 1,717 reserved-seat season tickets.

We have made many attempts to work out that fair arrange-
ment. We have moved from $200,000 to $325,000. Pete, on
the other hand, started at $225,000; upped the asking price
to $400,000; and has shown no signs of compromise. A ball
club is a lot like a family. . . . We simply cannot permit one
player to jeopardize all this. . . .

Still, we are hopeful that we will reach agreement with Pete
Rose.

Rose: "That was some spring-training surprise. They got
some figures wrong. They say I'm jeopardizing the Reds. *Me?*
The Reds were going to have to deal with free agency, just
like everybody else, all the other clubs. And to their credit,
the Reds did. In 1989, there were four players on the roster
earning more than $1 million.

"That's now. This was then.

"Family. A ball club is a lot like a family. On the field and in the clubhouse, sure. But a contract negotiation isn't family business.

"The Reds and I were thousands and thousands of dollars apart. What did they want the people to believe? That I was a little kid? That I was asking for a raise in my allowance?"

Three days later, under an enormous headline proclaiming ROSE SIGNS, Earl Lawson wrote on the front page of the *Cincinnati Post:*

> Pete Rose, signed to a two year contract for a figure estimated between $700,000 and the $800,000 he was seeking, will resume his quest for his 3000th career hit when the Reds open the 1977 season today at 2:30 P.M. at Riverfront Stadium against the San Diego Padres. The Reds' three-time National League batting champ, who'll enter the season 238 hits shy of the 3000 mark, agreed to terms within two hours after the chartered plane carrying the team from its Tampa, Fla., training camp landed at the Greater Cincinnati Airport last night. "It was a long day, but a good one," said a weary Dick Wagner, the Reds' general manager.

The actual figure for the two years was $752,000.

An aftershock passed through on Sunday. The *Cincinnati Enquirer* had undertaken "The Pete Rose Poll," and 6,973 people responded. The Cincinnati public supported Rose against the Cincinnati ball club, by a margin of roughly five to four. Most (54.3 percent) felt Rose's salary demands were *not* in excess of his value. Most (55 percent) felt Rose had been underpaid in the past. Most (51.6 percent) felt Rose should be the highest paid Red. Most (55.8 percent) felt that if Rose left Cincinnati, their regard for the ball club would be reduced.

"Without him," wrote Norbert and Mae Ertel, "the Reds can go fly a kite."

"Keep Pete at all costs," wrote Mr. and Mrs. Walter Geiger.

"There is nobody in the U.S.A.," wrote J. W. G. of Cincinnati, the loyal, initialed, disgruntled opposition, "who is worth $200,000 a year."

"I can't believe all the things that have happened to me, good and bad," Rose says, "and there have been plenty of both. I mean with everything going on in the world, war and peace, the biggest thing in the papers was what the hell the Reds were gonna pay *me*.

"You figure that one out."

The Cincinnati baseball season was anticlimax. Danny Driessen batted .300—he never would again—and Rose batted a basic Rose .311, playing in every game for the fourth consecutive year. The Dodgers won the National League West by ten games and moved through the playoffs into the World Series. That was the winey October of Reginald Martinez Jackson. The Yankees won the Series in six with Jackson batting .450. In the final game he hit three consecutive home runs, each off a different pitcher, each on the first pitch.

Question: What happened to the talk about overpaid ballplayers? Roaring cheers for Reggie drowned that out.

Nobody asked if Jackson was overpaid at $580,000. Indeed Bill Veeck, the great entrepreneur who was running the White Sox on two shoestrings and two credit cards, called Jackson "the biggest bargain in the game."

Someone asked Joe DiMaggio what he thought he could earn if he were playing for the Yankees in the late 1970s. "I can't give you an exact figure," DiMaggio said, "but for starters Steinbrenner would give me half the franchise."

"I heard about that," Pete Rose says.

*   *   *

In 1978, Rose would be in the final year of that ferociously negotiated contract. "I was not looking for half the franchise," Rose says, "but I wanted a competitive salary, taking into account what players were making not only in Cincinnati but everywhere. I was coming up on my thirty-seventh birthday and I was starting to think of long-term security for myself and the children. I was not looking to leave Cincinnati and maybe most of all I didn't want to go through one more of those contract fights that was a war. Reuven Katz said he would see what he could do."

In May, Katz called Wagner with an innovative idea. "We'd like to set up a career contract. We want to work toward something that provides that Pete plays out his major league career for the Reds."

Katz spun out advantages. Permanent peace between player and employer. Reinforcement of Wagner's position that a ball club was like a family. Positive press for both Rose and the Reds. Aside from that . . .

Hold on. Was Dick Wagner listening or was Katz consuming costly time by talking to the front-office equivalent of a dial tone?

"Reuven," Wagner said, "it's the Reds' policy *never* to negotiate a contract during the season."

Rose: "It is real important to me that this come out. I'm saying I never wanted to leave Cincinnati. I wanted the Reds to sign me up for life.

"Wagner says the Reds never negotiate and after that, during the season, he renegotiated with a backup outfielder, Mike Lum." Michael Ken-Wai Lum, out of Honolulu, an effective pinch hitter, was not a player close to Rose in skills. Over a fifteen-year major league career, Lum batted .247.

Rose: "I want to stay with the Reds and in the end I get brushed off and lied to."

Years later, Wagner insisted that Rose did not really want to stay in Cincinnati. "The truth is that his marriage was breaking up," Wagner said. "He was having serious woman trouble. Cincinnati was getting too hot for him. Rose wanted to leave town."

Rose knew I was going to talk to Wagner. Pete generally took an aloof approach to my conversations with others. He was Pete Rose, the feller with all the hits. It didn't matter up there on Olympus—actually Given Road in Cincinnati— what the mortals were muttering down below.

But after Wagner, Rose sought me out, dropped the studied cool, and asked what I had heard.

"He said you had woman trouble and you wanted to take off."

"That's not true. I've had trouble with women, same as a lot of ballplayers, same as you. But I wanted to stay."

"I'm just telling you what Dick Wagner said, Pete."

Rose accepted that with a small shrug. "Well, who you gonna believe, Wagner or me?"

"That depends on what we're doing here. Is it the Dick Wagner story or the life of Pete Rose?"

"There's more money in me." Rose grinned. "I can't tell you everything all the time because some people might get hurt. But whatever I do tell you, bank on this, is true."

When Wagner rejected a career contract for Rose out of hand, whatever the reasons, Katz and Rose had to look hard at how management felt about the team's most famous player.

In private conversation later, Katz remarked to Rose: "They don't want you, son."

That was reality. Rejection was reality. It also turned out to be one hell of a spur.

On June 5, 1978, Rose singled against Steve Rogers of Montreal. Now he had his 3,000th major league hit. Only fifteen men before had gotten 3,000, a pantheon including Aaron, Yastrzemski, Lajoie, Mays, Speaker, Clemente, and, of course, Cobb.

Rose slumped for a bit, and then on June 14 at Riverfront, he hit two singles against the Cubs. He was off on a batting streak that carried almost into August.

Consecutive-game batting streaks are unusual and unpredictable stories. There is no preliminary scene setting; the pennant races set up the league championship series, which in turn set up the World Series. But a batting streak just appears, link by link by link. A batter gets a hit or two on one day, a few more the next, a week, two weeks—voilà, le streak. The media assembles. Trumpets blast.

Rose: "I'm out there trying to get my hits, same as always. I'm not thinking streak. That doesn't make sense. I'm thinking, same as always, I've got to try for a hit every time I come up. But I read the box scores. I remember what I do. Five games. Ten games. Fifteen. Twenty. Twenty-five. Reporters from out of town start showing up. Reporters and reporters and reporters. Before it's over, I'm giving a press conference every day for more than fifty guys. Fine with me. I *like* to talk about my base hits. I was hitting and I was having fun."

He would bat safely in forty-four consecutive games. That tied the National League record of forty-four, set in 1897 by Wee Willie Keeler (to little press attention). It left Rose twelve games short of Joe DiMaggio's major league standard of fifty-six, which won enormous attention across the summer of '41, the summer before the United States was bombed into war.

Some argue that Rose's accomplishment of 1978 was even more difficult than DiMaggio's achievement. In the thirty-seven years between the two streaks, baseball had changed, to the detriment of batters. Few pitchers threw sliders in 1941. Most got by with a curve and a fastball. Behind in the count they almost always went with the fastball. A smart batter counted on that. Evidence argues that the general level of pitching had improved by the late 1970s. Further, relief pitching had developed to just about the point it has reached today. As compared to 1941, batters of 1978 were swinging against more pitches and more fresh arms. Overall batting averages dropped by more than twenty points in the thirty-seven years.

That idea, Rose over DiMaggio, outrages and outraged some. Newspapermen reported telephone calls during the Rose streak asking if he had hit safely. All July the answer was yes. One caller said, "I hope Rose breaks his leg. He's a banjo hitter. He can't touch DiMaggio." Someone else protested that Rose had an "unfair" advantage. He was a switch hitter. And someone complained that some of Rose's hits were bunts, as though bunt singles were subversive. (DiMaggio never bunted during his streak.)

Unique to Rose's accomplishment was his age: thirty-seven. Keeler set his record at twenty-five. DiMaggio was twenty-six. Ty Cobb hit in forty straight games in 1911 when he was twenty-four. Tommy Holmes set a modern National League record of thirty-seven games when he was twenty-eight.

Rose: "I told the writers I didn't want a car for the streak, or anything like that. Just give me a bottle of Geritol and a jar of Grecian Formula. I was havin' fun."

Fifteen times, between June 14 and August 1, Rose hit safely in the first inning. Six times, he extended his streak with hits in his final at-bat. Six hits were bunts; in four of the games bunts were his only hit. He batted .385 during his streak with eleven two-hit games, six three-hit games, and one four-hit game. About this time, Thomas Boswell of the *Washington Post* observed: "Pete Rose is a rabbit who wakes up every morning in a world full of lettuce."

The drama of a streak builds to an antiheroic climax. For the most dramatic of moments comes as the streak is stopped. DiMaggio was stopped in Cleveland on a night when the third baseman, Ken Keltner, made two fine plays. Joe was composed after the streak ended on a ground ball to

short. DiMaggio did not seem upset, but leaving the clubhouse he forgot to retrieve his wallet from the trunk in which
ballplayers' valuables were locked. DiMaggio walked toward
a hotel with his roommate, Vernon "Lefty" Gomez, and Phil
Rizzuto, then a rookie.

"I forgot my wallet," DiMaggio said to Rizzuto. "Lend me
twenty bucks, kid."

Rizzuto obliged, happy to help an idol. When DiMaggio
and Gomez turned into a bar, Rizzuto followed. "I said lend
me twenty bucks," DiMaggio snapped. "I didn't say drink
with us, kid." Having a streak stopped improves no hitter's
mood.

On the night of August 1, with Rose's streak forty-four games
long, the Reds were playing in Atlanta; the Braves would win
the game, 16–4. Twice Rose hit the ball hard. In the second
inning, he smacked a line drive up the middle that Larry
McWilliams, a rookie left-handed pitcher, speared. Rose was
out before he left the batter's box. When he realized that
McWilliams had made a fine catch, he dropped his bat and
applauded. In the seventh, Rose cracked a liner off relief
pitcher Gene Garber that Bob Horner grabbed at third base
and turned into a double play.

Now it was the ninth. Garber struck out the first two Reds.
Garber threw sidearm with modest velocity but outstanding
control. When Rose came to bat the Atlanta crowd, 31,105,
cheered him for almost a minute. Rose tried to bunt the first
pitch toward third, but fouled the ball back. Working low,
Garber snapped the ball into Rose's knees. Garber missed the
inside corner twice. The count was two balls and a strike.

Garber was a pitcher, not a thrower. He surprised Rose
with a change of pace. Rose fouled the ball into the dirt. Two
and two. Garber curled into his windup and threw another
change. Rose tipped the ball. Catcher Joe Nolan held it. The
streak was done.

"Damn," Rose said in the clubhouse. "He worked that last at-bat like he was pitching the seventh game of the World Series."

"Did you want him to lay one in?" a reporter said.

"No, I didn't want that. Don't write that I did. I just hope I get to see Garber again tomorrow and I hit a frozen rope up the middle."

Then more calmly. "Don't blame him. He was doing his job. If I had any guts, I would have bunted that two-strike change. He fooled me, but it was low, a good pitch to bunt."

On the other side Garber was stylish. "There was one thing on my mind," he said, "and that was to throw strikes. The last thing in the world I wanted to do was walk him and have the streak come to an end that way. I mean I wanted the streak to go on. It's been a fantastic contribution to interest in baseball. But I wanted to get him out. That's what I'm paid to do."

"Did you work extra hard against Pete?" a reporter asked.

"I pitched as hard as I could that whole inning. Just ask the other batters how I pitched them in the ninth."

(Rose, long afterwards: "Is that what Garber says? When he got the other two guys it was routine. When he struck me out he jumped three feet into the air, great for a white guy. He knew I had to be going for a hit. I honestly think in that last at-bat Garber didn't throw me a single strike.")

Rose: "People still ask for my exact thoughts when the streak ended, when I struck out. And the answer is, I don't remember any more. I know I wasn't thinking, 'Good going, Garber.'

"My exact thoughts? They're coming back. I was angry. That was my exact thought. Anger. Not lay the ball down the middle, Garber. Hit the corners. Do what you want. But fight me man to man. Don't walk me.

"It was a long time ago, but I remember the next game fine.

"The next night I went 4-for-6."

*   *   *

The House of Representatives celebrated Rose that September. Cincinnati Congressmen Thomas A. Luken and Willis D. Gradison introduced a resolution praising his "gutty, enthusiastic, unselfish play, his irrepressible spirit and rare sportsmanship." Afterward congressmen lined up for autographs. Tip O'Neill, the Speaker of the House, said he had heard that Carl Yastrzemski was thinking of running for Congress.

"Why would Yaz wanna take a pay cut?" said Peter the Irrepressible.

Silvio Conte, a senior Republican from western Massachusetts, asked Rose to run for Congress himself.

"He lives in my district," Luken said. "Don't go giving him ideas."

Conte gave Rose a twinkly look. "The jump from baseball to Congress could be too much, Pete. You're used to catching foul balls, not sending them to the floor for a vote. You hit screwballs. You don't vote for their bills."

A fair portion of the Congress of the United States arrayed itself in an uncommonly orderly line to get autographs.

At the White House, Jimmy Carter said: "That batting streak got the whole country excited. It lifted everybody's spirits. The whole country is proud of you."

Pete nodded, moved, not wanting to get emotional. He gave the president an official Pete Rose wristwatch for Carter's daughter, Amy. "This is *special*," Carter said. "I think I'll give it to my mother, Miss Lillian."

Pete drifted on Freudian seas, but only briefly. "I guess I shoulda brought two watches," said Ol' Doc Rose to the president of the United States, shouldering guilt in the Oval Office.

He was a national hero now, beloved beyond his secret boyhood dreams, born on rocky infields where he hurled himself

into ball games in summer dust. He was exalted beyond the
seeming boundaries of his background, his education. He was
a hero everywhere, except, perhaps, at 100 Riverfront Stadium, Cincinnati, 45202, the home office of the Reds.

On September 28, 1978, Katz wrote Wagner: "Pete and I
expect to make every reasonable good faith effort to enter
into a contract . . . for next year and the years after. I understand you will contact us after the season is over."

On October 1, the Reds fired off a press release. "The Reds
today offered Pete Rose the largest salary in Reds history.
'We had a good meeting with Pete,' said Reds president Dick
Wagner. 'We'll be leaving for Japan soon [on a barnstorming
tour] and we think it best for all to conclude this matter
quickly.' "

Katz issued a counterstatement on October 10.

> The Reds management has made a business decision to
> make a final offer to Pete Rose on October 1, 1978, on a basis
> that would make Pete no better than the second or third
> highest paid player on the Reds. Not the highest paid player
> as previously reported, but, and I repeat, no better than the
> second or third highest paid on the Reds. It is also manage-
> ment's business decision to insist that Pete give his answer
> quickly and now. These are the words used in the Reds press
> release of October 1, 1978.

> Pete probably does become the first player in the history of
> baseball who was asked to make a decision for next year even
> before this year's World Series was over. Pete today declined
> the Reds offer. Further negotiations at this time would be
> futile. Unless a miracle occurs, Pete will participate in the free
> agent draft next month.

The late Ray Fitzgerald of the *Boston Globe* described
what happened next as the Greening of the Rose. Fitzgerald
didn't care for the process. Rose, he wrote, "became a barker

at his own carnival show." It's marvelous how certain journalists instruct the rest of us in the maintenance of our lives, our
fortune, and our sacred honor.

Rose: "I remember just where I was at the end of the '78
season. At the top of my profession. The Reds offer would
have left me down about fifteen from the top in salary.

"Fifteenth? Did that make sense?

"Did Dick Wagner *think* that made sense?

"Or did Wagner figure he'd just put up some numbers that
he could use in a press release?

"Everybody knows in *The Godfather,* how they make an
offer you can't refuse.

"Dick Wagner was no Godfather. He worked the other
way. He made me an offer he knew I couldn't accept."

The marketer (Katz) and the red-dot special (Rose) em-
barked onto seas that could be perilous. Sparky Anderson
told Katz, "Reuven, you know I love Pete Rose. Be careful
out there now. He doesn't have the bat speed he used to. I'm
not sure he can hit any more." Rose popped fifty-one doubles
in 1978, the most in the major leagues by a fair margin and
the highest total in his career. Well, we all know that leading
the major league in two-base hits is an indisputable sign of
slowed bat speed. There are only two surer signs: leading the
majors in triples and leading the majors in home runs.

Rose's bat speed had *not* slowed. (He would lead the
league in doubles again in 1980 and bat .325 in 1981.) What
we are dealing with here is a perception. Anderson, concerned for a player who had given him so much, perceived
a developing flaw that evidence suggests was not there. What
concerned Katz was that Anderson's baseball perceptions
were correct most of the time. Katz says, "It made me nervous."

Rose: "I wanted to figure a way where we could cut the
bidders down to teams I really felt I could work with. Assum-

ing there would be a lot of bidders, which we hoped, but
didn't know. I wanted something like four or five serious
bidders in place when I got back from the Japanese trip.

"I wanted to know just how I figured in each team's plans.
What position they'd have me play, as much as they could
tell me.

"I wanted a decision by December 5, the date of the major
league winter meetings, which is when plans for the next
year really firm up.

"Finally, I wanted to do this thing with a little style. Like
if you're calling to discuss a million-dollar offer, don't make
the damn call collect."

Rose issued a press release, listing alphabetically eight
teams "I would be willing to play for" (Boston Red Sox, California Angels, Kansas City Royals, Los Angeles Dodgers, New
York Yankees, Philadelphia Phillies, San Diego Padres, Texas
Rangers). Letters over Rose's signature went out to the executives at the chosen eight. That left sixteen clubs on the
reject list. More letters. Rejected executives were assured of
Rose's respect. If this operation was 93 percent marketing, it
was also 7 percent public relations.

By the time Rose returned from Japan, negotiations had
narrowed. The contending clubs were the Philadelphia Phillies, the Pittsburgh Pirates, Ted Turner's Atlanta Braves, and
the St. Louis Cardinals, the last three added starters. Rose
chartered a Learjet, spending his own money, and he and
Katz planned a tour that Katz promised "will be the most
exciting week of your life."

Rose felt guarded. "How much are we gonna get?"

Among others, Turner was offering $1 million a year for
three seasons and $100,000 a year for the rest of Rose's life.
"I guess we'll be all right," Rose said.

The Rosejet took off for Atlanta. Katz had prepared a
twenty-minute videotape. Rose at the White House; Rose on
the Phil Donahue show; Rose cruising through an ABC-TV

"20/20" interview; Rose selling a soft drink; and, oh yes, a few shots of Peter playing baseball. Stress Rose off the field. "You know more about Pete's skills on the field than I," Katz said to the baseball people. That was a soft toss. Katz was playing hardball, multimillion-dollar hardball, and opening the game with a soft toss. "The idea of the tape is to show you the excitement Pete creates even when he's not actually playing. I don't have to tell you how this will pay off in ticket sales."

Flamboyant, mustached Ted Turner loved the tape and repeated his offer of millions. "All I want to do is keep you here for a few years," Turner said, "until the Reds get rid of Wagner and you can go back to Cincinnati where you belong."

Thank you, Ted. Beautiful down here in Atlanta. Beautiful city. Don't know why Sherman would have burned it. Crazy Northern bastard. We'll get back to you, skipper, and thanks.

In Kansas City, Ewing Kauffman, who owned the Royals and had made his fortune from Marion Laboratories, a pharmaceutical firm, offered a four-year playing contract, with additional option seasons. The base was lower than Turner's, but various fringes would have made the final figure about the same. As a bonus, Kauffman offered Rose a share of oil investments. "I've done some research," Kauffman said. "I know your dad played football till he was past forty. We all know you have a shot at breaking Ty Cobb's record. I'd like to see you do that in Kansas City."

Gussie Busch, who owned the Cardinals, lay in a hospital suite, preparing for hernia surgery. He watched the videotape from his bed. He offered a lesser baseball salary than Turner or Kauffman but threw in an ancillary position as "a spokesman for Anheuser-Busch," the brewery that owned the Cardinals.

We were wondering about long-term security, Mr. Busch.

"Of course you were. When Pete is through playing we'll

see that he is given an important Budweiser distributorship."

Everybody wished Busch good luck with his surgery.

John Galbreath, who owned the Pirates, was a multimillionaire horseman who also ran the vastly successful Darby Dan Farm, outside Columbus. The Pirates situation was problematic, Galbreath said, when the Rose-Katz videotape ran down. The fans were not as solidly behind the team as he would like. Galbreath said he'd like Rose to take on an energetic speaking schedule around the Pittsburgh area to get the Pennsylvanians to rally round his team.

Pirate economics didn't enable him to match other offers, Galbreath said. But he knew Rose liked horses. So in addition to paying a baseball salary of about $400,000 a year, which would, of course, make Rose the highest-paid Pirate, Galbreath would set him up as a horse breeder. He would give Rose two of his finest brood mares, plus the stud service of Darby Dan Farm's crack stallions.

Rose wanted to be a horse breeder even then. "That offer could have been the best of all," he says, "but I couldn't know for sure. The blood lines were excellent. I could have ended up owning a string of very valuable horses. But that wasn't guaranteed. . . ."

Rose liked the Phillies. The team was contending and aggressive. It was a team he thought he could turn into a winner. The Phillies were so confident they would sign Rose that owner Ruly Carpenter sent a private jet belonging to his cousin, Hugh Sharp, to ferry Rose east from Cincinnati.

"The Phillies paid for the jet," Katz says. "They took us to the Carpenter estate at Montchanin, Delaware. Ruly Carpenter's wife, Stephanie, served Welsh rarebit. It was the most delicious Welsh rarebit I've ever had. No one enjoyed it." A sour negotiation supervened.

The videotape excited Ruly Carpenter. "That's great, Pete. What offers have you fellers had?"

"To give you some idea," Katz said, "we have some that run to seven figures a year."

"My God," Carpenter said. "That's a million dollars. We can't make an offer like that."

"Talk to us, Mr. Carpenter," Katz said. "Money isn't everything."

Carpenter would offer about $700,000 a season for three years, no perks, no long-term security.

Rose: "I felt sick. I wanted to play for the Phillies. But their package was worth millions less than Atlanta and Kansas City. I'd play for less, but not that much less. I felt sick."

Finally Carpenter said, "I'm afraid there won't be a signing. I've got all the press assembled at Veterans' Stadium, and there won't be a signing."

Katz said, "Pete. You've got to talk to them."

"What'll I say?"

"You'll think of something."

"Can we take the private jet back to Cincinnati?" Rose asked.

"You can if you pay for it," Carpenter said.

Rose: "I've done happier press conferences, but we got through it."

Riding to the airport, Bill Giles, a Cincinnati native who was the general manager of the Phillies, pointed out something Rose already knew. "You're third and fourth in a lot of all-time categories for the National League. If you go to Kansas City, you'll never break 'em. Wouldn't it be nice for your kids and your grandchildren to see your name on the top of those lists?"

"Not bad for me, either," Rose said.

"Would you really take less money to play in Philadelphia?" Giles asked.

"Yes, I really would."

"Bill," Katz said. "We're not through yet. Play around with the figures and see what you can do."

Giles went back to work. Television station WPHL had signed a contract with the Phillies specifying that the team and the station would share advertising revenue once a certain base figure was passed.

"Is Pete on our roster gonna pull in extra advertising?" Giles mused to an aide. "Is that William Penn up there on top of City Hall?"

Carpenter was intractable. WPHL was not. Giles convinced the station to increase its guarantee by $600,000 if the Phils signed Rose. That is $600,000 per year. The deal was in the black. Ruly and Stephanie Carpenter would not run out of Welsh rarebit.

On December 5, at the baseball winter meetings in Orlando, the episode concluded. Joseph Durso wrote in *The New York Times:*

> The wildest auction in baseball history ended today when Pete Rose signed a four-year contract with the Philadelphia Phillies for $800,000 a year [actually $810,000] and became the highest-paid player in the game. . . .
>
> Rose told a jammed news conference, "You could stack the money up and a show dog couldn't jump over it."

A most unusual wild auction. Rose accepted the *lowest* of all the finalists' offers to play where he thought he would be happiest.

"Rose made a lot of money for us," Bill Giles says. "We picked up the extra $600,000 from TV. Our ratings went up 20 percent, which I attribute pretty much entirely to Pete.

"We sold an extra 5,000 season tickets. That translates to

about $2 million a year. We paid him $810,000 and increased our revenues by at least $2.6 million.

"Pete was making money for himself and we were making money on Pete."

In Cincinnati, 1979, the Reds attendance dropped a quarter of a million.

9

Almost a Centerfold

POINTS EAST, PATERNITY, PEP PILLS,
AND *PLAYBOY,* 1979–1984

"In 1979, if you go by records in *The Baseball Encyclopedia,*
I had a year somebody might call good enough to dream. I
was out of Cincinnati, after sixteen straight big-league seasons where I grew up. Not exactly all of a sudden, but pretty
quick, I was a Philadelphia Phillie. Philadelphia? Who is that?
Ben Franklin and some last-place teams.

"I played 163 games for the Phils in 1979 and I batted .331.
I remember that real good. Someone in the Cincinnati office,
who was trying to explain away trading me, said my bat
speed had slowed down. Slowed down all the way to .331.
Plus I hit forty doubles for Philadelphia and, getting a couple
gray hairs away from forty years old, I stole twenty bases. In
all those 163 games, I struck out only thirty-two times.

"Except that I don't bet baseball, I'd bet you a lot of players
today would settle for a season like that. A lot? I mean damn
near all.

"So like we ballplayers say, between the lines it went very,
very good. But you don't get to live your whole life between
the lines.

"My marriage was going a little rocky. My fault. One hundred percent my fault. Still it was rocky.

"One day Karolyn says, 'You know what I'm gonna do, Pete. I'm gonna write a book about you.'

" 'How you gonna do that? There's a lot of things you can do, Karolyn, but one thing you sure as hell can't do is write a book by yourself.'

" 'Well, maybe I can and maybe I can't and maybe I'll need an assistant, but one thing I guarantee you, Pete. When I get the book finished, you're gonna read every word.'

"That gets your attention, am I right? Your wife is going to write a book about *you*. We got a free press, good thing, but maybe sometimes the press can be a little too free.

"Karolyn printed some stuff. It ran in *The Sporting News*. That was in March.

"Then, in September, *Playboy* ran an eleven-page interview with me. I say I'm good with the press, because I *am* good with the press, as a couple hundred reporters could tell you. But who was it who said, long time ago, even Babe Ruth strikes out. That also went for Ty Cobb. And it sure has gone for me. Maybe the *Playboy* interview wasn't a strikeout. There's some good baseball stuff in there. More like a pop to short, with one out, close game, and a man on third.

"I'll tell you when I was good and I'll tell you when I was bad.

"*Playboy* made me lose my cool. So there it is. I was bad."

The memoir of Karolyn Rose, composed with one Fred D. Cavinder of the *Indianapolis Star News,* appeared in *The Sporting News* of March 3, 1979. The headline speaks volumes:

Life With Pete Not Always a Bed of Roses

The Sporting News, founded by Charles and Alfred Henry Spink in March 1886 at North Eighth Street in St. Louis, for

many years advertised itself as "Baseball's Bible." It was an
independent weekly, run out of the Mississippi Valley for
decades by J. G. Taylor Spink and his heirs until 1977 when
the conglomerate craze reached North Lindbergh Boule-
vard in St. Louis and the paper surrendered to that huge
publishing combine called the Times Mirror Company. This
California company owns eight newspapers, sixteen maga-
zines, and four television stations.

But even in its independent day, *The Sporting News* was
not antiestablishment. *The Sporting News* provided box
scores of every major league game, standings in all the minor
leagues, and features and columns composed by sportswriters who took on the work, generally puffery, as a supplement
to their full-time jobs, covering a team for a daily newspaper.

I remember being asked to write a story by the late J. G.
Taylor Spink himself in 1954 when the Cardinals traded an
extraordinary outfielder named Enos "Country" Slaughter to
the New York Yankees. (Four minor-league players moved to
New York. One, Bill Virdon, would later manage the Yankees.) Slaughter played a bit like Rose. Enos Hustle.

On being told of the deal, Slaughter wept into a huge white
handkerchief, and the photo of rugged Country Slaughter in
tears won exceptional prominence. His place in the Cardinal
outfield was taken by Wally Moon, another simply splendid
ballplayer, who was fourteen years younger.

"I want you to follow them both," J. G. Taylor Spink directed me by phone. "Very closely now for the next two
weeks. Who gets a hit? When? Who doesn't get a hit? Then
let me have a thousand words comparing how they made
out."

Spink paused, before adding in a fairly long breath, that
this was a major assignment and he consequently would pay
me ten dollars.

That was and to an extent still is the generic *Sporting News*
story. Stay on the field. Write the ball games. That's what

people want to know. Work for what we offer and every baseball fan in the country will see your name.

Some recent *Sporting News* columns have been snippish and some have tried for humor, without threatening or even amusing the shade of Walter "Red" Smith. The governing premise of the sheet remains that it is Baseball's Bible, if you can suffer that hyperbole, which many cannot.

In 1946, *The Sporting News* attacked Branch Rickey for hiring Jackie Robinson. Integrating baseball, an editorial rang down halls of hollow, "would be too much for the boy." During the 1950s, the great pitcher Early Wynn began writing a column for a Cleveland paper. He wrote them himself in longhand; I remember because I typed a few. Wynn urged, as any pitcher might, a larger strike zone and demanded in those long-ago times higher salaries for ballplayers. Spink snapped back with a nasty editorial headline: Wynn Mill Pumps Muddy Water.

So this is not exactly a new-left paper, nor even *Hustler* magazine. Which made it all the more startling to see a *Sporting News* story appear with a provocative, semierotic, and ungrammatical opening.

"One night me and my husband Pete Rose the baseball player were doing three things which are very common in our life at home. We were in bed, watching late television, and munching junk food.

"The telephone rang and when I answered a female voice purred:

" 'I love Pete Rose.'

" 'Tell him yourself,' I said. 'He's right here beside me in bed.' I handed the phone to Pete.

"That tells you several things. . . ." Indeed it does.

The caption under the opening picture, in which the first Mrs. Rose seems lusting to pucker, presents Karolyn as a perfect baseball wife. She has, reports *The Sporting News,* "time for all members of the family at the start of a typical day, checking the morning papers with hubby Pete, some woman talk with daughter Fawn, and a note for son Petey's teacher.

"I'm careful who I give [our home telephone] number to," Karolyn writes, "but Pete gives it out, too. Pretty soon all kinds of strange types are calling and we have to change it again. . . .

"Groupies or Baseball Annies are part of the game, whether we like it or not—and I don't."

Rose sits years afterwards in the lime cement-block office, trying to decide how to get the Reds to play harder, better. He doesn't know. He knows how he played. Can he become the first truly great baseball player to become truly a great baseball manager? That has yet to be determined.

"You saw that Karolyn stuff?"

"I sure did."

"Hey, Rog, she's been a terrific woman. I wouldn'ta married her if she wasn't a terrific woman. I even went to a Catholic church to marry her and I'm not Catholic. But we had trouble." The face sets hard. "You know about that. You know we had trouble."

"It made the newspapers, Peter."

"And that was *then*, am I right? Now she's got a little heavier than she used to be. Why do they do that after a divorce? They get heavier. Ever happen to you?"

"Maybe it did."

"Hey, Rog. I know about you. Reuven Katz told me you been through a divorce. Or more than one."

Outside a few black players in street clothing are going into a version of jive talk. Rose gets up and kicks shut the door.

"I read a paper by a psychologist once . . ."

"Hey, how much do those guys really know?"

"Enough to charge $150 an hour."

"We both do better than that. I've made more money than $150 an hour grounding out."

"The paper says that when a woman gets heavy after divorce she may be saying something. She may be hungry, but she may be saying more than that. Like this: I don't want involvement with another man. So before an involvement happens, *I'll* put on some pounds and no other man will want to get involved with me."

"How the hell do they know that?"

"They don't *know*, Pete. These are theories."

A mote of a second. Nolan Ryan's fastball. Pete said, "So this means Karolyn is still too hung up with me, and I wasn't that great a husband, to want another guy?"

"Probably," I said, with more authority than I had any right to express.

"Well, let me ask you this," said Pete Rose, the great gamesman. "If you're so intelligent, how come you've had as much trouble with women as me?"

Beyond the office door, the players continued their wordplay. "Who pitches tomorrow, Pete?" I said.

Karolyn Rose's *Sporting News* story is agitated, angry, incomplete. Most of all, perhaps, it is sad. She writes with concern about "Baseball Annies," groupies, those women who materialize around major league ball teams and thrust themselves at the ballplayers. She seems proud of her family lifestyle, and a little embarrassed at its luxury as well. She has been a hard-working housewife, hustling laundry, ironing shirts, rearing children, and she muses about becoming a talk-show hostess. Beyond those understandable ambivalences, Karolyn sounds very proud of her man, hurt by her man as well, without being able to realize that by 1979, Pete Rose wasn't her man any more.

She wore a thin blue dress. She remembers that and he

does, also. "I had on a blue dress," she writes. "Very short! They were wearing them long, but I was wearing them short. I had my foot up on the rail. It was comfortable."

According to Karolyn the date was July 6, 1963, during Rose's fine tumultuous rookie season with the Reds. The place was River Downs racetrack, hard by the Ohio. Pete grabbed his binoculars during a race. "Who's got the lead?" someone asked.

"I ain't got time for that," Rose said. "I got something better in my binocs."

That "something better" was Karolyn Engelhardt of the West End in Cincinnati, dark haired, full of fun, only eighteen years old. The courtship was swift—neither is a patient person—and the wedding at St. William's Roman Catholic Church was attended by hundreds. Karolyn wore white and appeared radiant. Pete in a tuxedo looked like someone who would be more comfortable in warm-up clothes. Pete's father was best man.

Karolyn was surprised to find that the honeymoon suite came with twin beds. She describes herself as a bedroom "rookie." She has Pete shove the twin beds together and rip off the top sheet. Here, mercifully, Karolyn lets a curtain drop, as silently as a pair of bikini underpants.

Karolyn and Pete traveled to Venezuela for winter baseball after Rose's sophomore season, 1964, which was flat. Karolyn reports that the playing field was pebbly. Whatever, her husband made a few errors. People in the crowd started whistling. Karolyn joined them, whistling as loud as she could.

It was some time afterward that she learned that whistling at Venezuelan ball games is like booing at ball games in Cincinnati. Karolyn was booing her own husband, her sole means of support.

Dear Diary, was she ever embarrassed.

*   *   *

The Rose family liked throwing Halloween parties. Everyone was urged to come in costume. The pitcher Rawley Eastwick, actually Rawlins Jackson Eastwick, out of an upperclass Eastern background, arrived dressed as a farmer. Glenda and Russ Nixon (he was a coach who later managed the Reds) entered disguised as giant eyeballs. Karolyn skated in, dressed in the flouncy fluff of a roller-derby queen.

Scenes from a marriage, bright, bland, touched with silliness and joy. How wonderful to be young and in the major leagues. But other elements of Karolyn's tale resound less cheerily.

She remembers one Halloween when Rose put on costume and mask so that nobody knew him. Thus disguised, Rose went about tapping women on the fanny. One guest complained to Karolyn. The tone of Karolyn's prose here is not cheerful or forgiving. In the manner of wives whose husbands misbehave at parties, she seems just plain mad. Fair enough. But to put a piece in *The Sporting News* attacking your husband as the Great Gooser! Well, if that's liberation, here's to chauvinism.

"Karolyn originally wanted to try the book with me," says Big Bill Staubitz. "I just didn't think there was a book there. Karolyn had a few stories, but only a few. I sat for seven hours with tapes and I'd say, 'But, Karolyn, we've been over this before.' Someone told Karolyn Pete had stolen second. She wanted to know if he'd put second base in the trunk of the car. That sort of thing, five or ten times.

"Then she wanted to tell a whole lot of stories about Pete as a bed partner . . . I just walked away."

Fred D. Cavinder, who did not walk away, drew from Karolyn a litany of complaints probably best left within a marriage or taken to a therapist.

She complains about groupies handing Rose notes on

which their telephone numbers appeared. She goes over to one groupie and threatens her with a violent assault.

She reports that Rose sleeps in short bursts and gets up at intervals to raid the refrigerator. She adds, Holy Privacy, that Rose sleeps best with a pillow between his legs.

Anger develops over Karolyn's pages, finally exploding at the end. With an author's respect for freedom of expression, I could still support a constitutional amendment making it a felony for one party in a crumbling marriage or divorce to publish anything about the other party until fifty years after the final decree, by which time, probably, nobody would remember or care.

Karolyn was starting a radio interview program for a Cincinnati area radio station. She writes cheerily about interviewing several Indianapolis race-car drivers, and Muhammad Ali. (She doesn't mention a problem or two, like her allusion to "puck-off" time.)

"One day," she writes, "I decided I would question Pete Rose.

"We sat down at the kitchen table and I got the tape recorder going. 'Today my special guest is Pete Rose. How's it going?'

"He said, 'No, Karolyn. You don't interview that way.'

"He kept it up and I finally said, 'To hell with you.'

"He retorted, 'You stink, Karolyn.'

"Next day I returned to the kitchen and turned on the tape and there was Pete's taunting voice saying, 'You'll never interview me, Karolyn.' And I never have."

Except perhaps through attorneys at examination before trial.

The idea of Karolyn's book, Rose believes, "was more or less to crucify me. Put in a lot of bad stuff. Hurt my reputation. Maybe make me lose some of the commercials that I was doing. That way Karolyn's lawyers figured they could squeeze a bigger chunk out of my wallet.

"Now here's a funny thing. Funny and maybe sad. Karolyn herself wasn't looking at things the way the lawyers were. She told my lawyer, Reuven Katz, that she wanted a lot of money because she'd keep it real safe so that when I came back to her we'd be set.

"Come back to her! I wasn't thinking of coming back to her.

"Anyways, she got taken care of real fairly, I think, and the rest of that book that was supposed to crucify me never got written, far as I know."

Playboy magazine's interview with Rose appeared in the issue of September 1979, while Pete was on his way to smoking out 208 hits in his first season as a Philadelphia Phillie. "That damn paternity suit," Pete says. "One day I went to play in San Francisco and a guy hung a sign all the way across right field. Huge sign across the outfield stands where nobody was sitting at Candlestick Park and the damn sign says: 'Pete Rose Leads League in Paternity Suits.'

"I would say that got me a little mad.

"Most of the time when a fan gets on you, it's no big deal.

"I've got one special way to handle individuals who get really rough, Rose you are a no good s.o.b. And like that. I get myself real close to the character and I smile and then I throw him a baseball. With a soft toss. Now the no good s.o.b., me, has just given away a free major league ball and given it to the same guy who was abusing me. Man, does that get them embarrassed.

"Sometimes I just don't bother. When a fan starts shouting that I'm a bum, obviously he has never seen my personal financial statement.

"If a fan shouts, the way a few used to, 'Hey, Rose, you can't hit,' obviously the fan is an imbecile. I got 2,000, 3,000, 4,000

hits. *I can't hit?* The fan is worse than an imbecile. Pardon me. A fucking imbecile.
"But paternity suit signs are different. I am not the only guy in the history of the world, even the history of baseball, who got named in a paternity suit.
"I don't need no paternity suit signs. None. Zip. Zero, zero, zero, zero."

The *Playboy* interview is an innovative and somewhat dangerous subspecies of new journalism that dates from 1963 when the magazine sent a persistent Hollywood columnist to stalk Frank Sinatra with a tape recorder. In traditional journalism, the reporter interviews, of course, but the interview folds into the fabric of the story. The *Playboy* interview is bare question and answer, including bloopers verbatim and obscenities in naked color.

Bloopers and obscenities are as common in *Playboy* interviews as lilies in a summer field. One might even suspect that *Playboy* people listen for both with immoderate lust. When Ed Koch was running for governor of New York he said into a *Playboy* tape: "The suburbs are sterile . . . upstate New York is full of hicks and rubes." Suburbanites, hicks, and rubes vote. Mario Cuomo became governor of New York.

Running for president, Jimmy Carter discussed his own morality and burbled: "I try not to commit deliberate sin. But I've committed adultery in my heart many times." Voters forgave him the burble (if not his presidency).

James Earl Ray, the assassin of Martin Luther King, agreed to take a lie detector test for a *Playboy* interview. Ray wanted to establish his alleged innocence. He flunked the test. A feller signing on for a *Playboy* interview has to be careful.

If Pete Rose were careful, he could not have been the ballplayer that he was. He played with great knowledge of

how to win a game, but he also played with courageous aban-
don. No one can play baseball the way Pete Rose played and
be cautious.

This carries over, as it must, into moments beyond the
white lines. One of Rose's good Cincinnati friends remarked:
"Perhaps the shortest possible human measure of time is that
space between when an idea pops into Pete's head and when
it is sounded on his tongue."

Today Rose feels *Playboy* sandbagged him in its interview.
The operative *Playboy* reporter, Samantha Stevenson, then
a comely blond and now a comely redhead, feels Pete was
not suitably cognizant of her degree from the University of
Missouri School of Journalism.

Whatever. The cover of that magazine appeared promising photographs of a naked "Phi Beta Kappa Playmate." In
larger type, the cover carried this headline:

PETE ROSE SLAMS
FANS, MANAGEMENT,
MEDIA, PLUGS SELF

Stevenson, who now lives in California, remembers 1979
as "the height of the *Playboy* interview." She had worked in
television broadcasting, done some writing, and filled in fal-
low periods as a cocktail waitress. The idea of women sports
reporters then had a certain sexy novelty—women were still
suing to get into sports locker rooms—and Stevenson
remembers calling a *Playboy* editor and saying, "I'm a great
interviewer. You should have me work for you." She says she
always took time with people and listened carefully, gazed a
bit, and so got them to talk. She believes that many male
reporters resented her "because they were protecting their
turf.

"I had to work very hard and I had to be very creative to
get my stories," Stevenson says. "And then when I got a good

one, some of the men would say that the only reason I'd gotten stories about sports people was that I slept with them." Indignation lifts her tone from kittenish to leonine. "That's followed me for my whole career because I look good and interview well and I get good stories. It was always, 'She slept with them.' "

The published interview begins like this:
> *Playboy:* "Who's the best player in major league baseball?"
> Pete Rose: "I am."
> *Playboy:* "How do you figure that? Are you a better hitter than Rod Carew? [As a matter of fact, in 1979, Rose outhit Carew, .331 to .318.] A better slugger than Dave Parker? A better all-around player than Cesar Cedeño?" [Cesar Cedeño? Yes, Pete Rose was a better all-around player than Cesar on Cedeño's most magnificent day.]
> Rose: "It's not that simple. If you're talking about everything included—selling the game of baseball, public relations, popularity off the field as well as on the field, versatility playing more than one position, hitting the baseball from both sides, I'm number one. That's why I make the most money."

Now came a moment when Playboy wanted to push Rose into confessing that he had taken amphetamine pills, called greenies in the inventive chatter of ballplayers.

Greenies are "uppers," pep pills. In a popular story, one outfielder chasing a fly stumbled and seemed to lose all foot speed. From one dugout came the comment, "His greenie ran out."

Scores, probably hundreds of ballplayers swallowed greenies, as a way of staying intense through the long, demanding, relentless days that are a major league season. In this era, when fine ballplayers have been sent to prison for using heroin and cocaine, a greenie seems about as lethal as a vanilla milk shake. But in 1979, before the raging plague of illegal drugs was fully recognized, greenies were the stuff of scandal.

An amphetamine is a legal stimulant, available only by prescription. In addition to providing a certain lift, amphetamines are used as appetite depressors in some weight-reduction programs.

Stevenson, groping toward headlines, asked Rose if he had taken an upper.

Rose: "I might have last week. I mean if a doctor gives me a prescription of thirty diet pills so I can lose five pounds before I go to spring training, is that bad?"

Playboy: "Would you use [the pills] for anything other than dieting?"

Rose: "There might be some day when you played a double-header the night before and you go to the ballpark for a Sunday game and you just want to take a diet pill, just to mentally think you are up."

Playboy: "You keep saying you *might* take a greenie. *Would* you? *Have* you?"

Rose: "Yeah I'd do it. I've done it."

Having extracted this miniconfession, the *Playboy* interviewers next asked Rose about homosexuality among major league baseball players. Rose said he had never heard anything mentioned about any homosexuals in the major leagues.

Now *Playboy* went for all that was visible of the jugular of Peter Edward Rose. "There's just one more topic to talk about and that's the paternity suit filed against you by Terryl Rubio, the young woman in Tampa who says she had your baby."

Rose will have more to say about that presently. At the time of the *Playboy* interview, he was under instructions from his attorney to say nothing at all.

"You're wasting your time even asking me," he told Stevenson.

"Why won't you talk about it?"

"It's nobody's business. It's private."

"Private? It's been on national television. Do you deny the allegation now?"

"Look, you can say anything you want, 'cause you ain't gonna get nothing from me."

"Then let's go finish the interview."

"It's finished," Rose said. "I don't want to talk to fuckin' reporters any more. I know what you're gonna ask me and I ain't gonna talk about that shit."

"So the interview's over?"

"Fuckin' right it is."

The interviewers and the editors of *Playboy* were annoyed. Introducing Rose, *Playboy* wrote that "as a technician, he can't be ranked up there with the Dave Parkers and the Jim Rices." This is simply wrong. Rose did not have the batting power of Parker or Rice—physical size is significant here— but as a technician with the bat, he was better than either.

"Rose has one very important thing going for him," *Playboy* suggested. "He has become perhaps the most famous white sports star in the world."

The magazine is now 0-for-2. Rose could walk down the Champs Elysées in Paris or the Via Veneto in Rome without drawing a look, except from a visiting American tourist. Ballplayers are known in the United States, Japan, and around the rim of the Caribbean Sea. But nowhere else. Baseball is not a significant international game. Rose may have been the most famous white sports star in America. Chris Evert was more famous around the world.

Finally *Playboy*'s editors wrote: "In 1976 Rose led his team to a world-series *[sic]* sweep over the Yankees."

That's 0-for-3, if you're scoring. The Reds did sweep the 1976 Series from the Yankees, four games to none. Rose batted .188. Johnny Bench hit .533. So there is not much doubt about who led the Big Red Machine for those few, and quite memorable, ball games in October.

Rose: "I lost my cool with that paternity stuff. I guess I shouldn't have let that happen. It was a mistake. But if you look at the record, *Playboy* made some mistakes, too.

"I guess the best thing about that magazine is the pictures, if you care to look at that sort of thing."

The marriage of Karolyn and Pete Rose lasted for about seventeen years, from their wedding date, January 25, 1964, until December 29, 1980, when a final separation agreement was reached four days after the first Christmas of a new decade. By this time, the Cincinnati City Planning Commission had declared Rose "a listed property," essentially a municipal landmark protected by ordinance against "displacement or demolition."

Rose: "Protected against demolition? If I'm not mistaken, big-time divorce is Demolition Derby."

Karolyn Rose has said, says, and may say for the rest of her days, that Pete is the love of her life. In mellow moods, she still speaks of his kindness, generosity, sense of fun. She has even said that she fantasizes a day when Pete reappears at the door, comes back to her, the marriage to Carol, the other children Tyler and Cara, washed away by the fantastic currents of imagination. Nobody is hurt. Magically, everything becomes again as it was. Imagination.

The Giamatti-Dowd investigation created, among other things, open season on Rose. Some—Dowd himself and a few journalists—dropped hints or came out directly and said Rose was a womanizer.

Rose: "I'm not good at saying 'no comment,' but I'm trying to learn. I mean if I answer every charge against me that's appeared in every newspaper, maybe a charge made by somebody who doesn't even know me, that could be a full-time job, am I right?"

Karolyn says that she came to accept the fact that ballplayers sleep around. Rose, she says, forced her toward divorce by being blatant about episodes with other women.

Rose: "This is very good practice time for me. Practice at saying no comment."

A notorious magazine article in the spring of 1989 portrayed Karolyn as a loving earth mother. (Rose: "Anybody can write what they want.") Pete came across as an amoral tramp.

Actually the facts of the divorce, as far as they can be ascertained, indicated that *Rose v. Rose* was a divorce case like most others.

Karolyn came out charging behind a legal phalanx and asserted that she was Mrs. Peter Edward Rose, mother of two, and unemployed. She asked that she be awarded 60 percent of the family's net worth.

In calculating Rose's net worth, Karolyn's lawyers included his baseball pension rights. In the sour argot of divorce court, Karolyn was "taking a run."

Negotiations raged through the summer of 1980—Rose would hit 42 doubles for the Phillies, leading the National League—and the settlement probably disappointed Karolyn and her attorneys.

Karolyn was awarded one house, one 1978 Rolls Royce, one 1978 Jeep. Pete would pay her a lump sum and yearly alimony payments for eleven-plus years. Child support would be $600 a month, plus all educational costs.

Pete got to keep another house and a 1979 Porsche.

The Phillies won the pennant in 1980 and Pete wanted to take young Pete to the World Series. Karolyn objected and Rose had to obtain a court order for his own son to watch him play in the Series. (The Phillies defeated Kansas City, four games to two.)

A court order to take your kid to watch you play? In the World Series?

Crazy time. Contested divorce is crazy time.

It was a damn bad period for the principals and the children, and it ill becomes anyone to gloat.

One Terryl Rubio of Tampa asserted in the Court of Common Pleas, Hamilton County, Ohio, that she was unmarried, delivered of an illegitimate child on March 24, 1978, and that Peter Edward Rose was "father of said child, a girl."

Rose: "When you're a public figure and you get hit with a paternity suit, you've got problems."

Rubio's lawyers talked about subpoenaing other ballplayers who would be asked whether they had seen Rose and the woman together. Rose: "We could end up with who was going with who. Girls. Guys. Husbands. Wives. A whole lot of marriages threatened. This was gonna be a mess."

The expedient solution was to make a settlement. Get the story out of the papers. Embarrass nobody further. Hope the commercials thus saved would cover the settlement costs. Which is what was done. Monthly payments and a lump sum on the child's eighteenth birthday to secure her education.

The child's name will not appear in this book. Her first name is, however, the last name of another famous ballplayer who starred for the Cincinnati Reds through the 1970s.

The Philadelphia Rose lifted a fine contending team to championships. He hit .331 in 1979. The Phillies won the World Series for the first time since the dawn of Doubleday in 1980, defeating the Kansas City Royals, four games to two. They reached the Series again in 1983, but lost to the Baltimore Orioles, four games to one.

Two stories particularly light Rose's Philadelphia years. In 1981, he singled off Mark Littell of the Cardinals and broke Stan Musial's record for National League hits. (Rose's number here was 3,631.)

After accepting Musial's congratulations, Rose went to a

telephone, there to hear words of praise from President Ronald Reagan. The conversation was wired over loudspeakers so that a large press gathering and a television audience could hear chatter between the ballplayer and the president.

"Mr. Peter Rose," a male White House operator spoke in a commanding tone.

"Yes."

"Hold on, please, for the president of the United States." The next sound was a dial tone.

Rose hung up. The phone rang again. The White House. But again, as Reagan was about to come on, the parties were cut off.

Rose looked up at the rows of journalists. "It's a good thing," he said, "there are no missiles on the way."

Rose was joining a Phillies team peopled with solid ballplayers: Larry Bowa, Manny Trillo, and at least two superstars, Silencio Steve Carlton and Mike Schmidt.

Rose: "People say Lefty [Carlton] wouldn't talk to the writers. That's not true.

"He wouldn't talk to the writers about *baseball*. But he loved wine. Ask him about the French red wine crop of 1978, Rog, and he'll talk to you all night. He'll talk to you, till *you* want to get away."

"But not about sliders."

"You're right there. Lefty wouldn't talk to writers about sliders."

Mike Schmidt is among the ten most productive home run hitters in major league history.

Rose: "But he was human. He slumped like anybody else. One time he was slumping pretty bad and I thought he was carrying that onto the field, not giving 100 percent at third base." Rose offered Schmidt a theory brought with him from the great days in Cincinnati. "When you're not hitting, that's the time to work extra hard on fielding. You're doing r with the bat, but you can still contribute with tl

When Schmidt won a Most Valuable Player award in 1980, he first thanked God. (Now we know God is not a pitcher.) Then Schmidt thanked his mother. Then he thanked Pete Rose.

Rose: "A good moment for him. A great moment for me."

In 1983, in the last year of the Philadelphia contract, Rose batted .245. The Phillies did not renew. Rose moved on to Montreal, where he languished until August 16, 1984. Then he came back to the Reds as player-manager in a wonderful enactment of the return of the native.

In Philadelphia, the word once again was Rose's bat speed was gone. That echoed in Montreal. But from August 16, 1984, until the end of the season in Cincinnati, Rose batted .365.

They surely must have thrown him a lot of change-ups.

Pete had fallen in love with blond Carol Woliung, once the hostess at a defunct Cincinnati pub called Sleep-Out Louie's. Rose heard certain scouting reports about Carol.

Rose: "You can write it. I heard she had the prettiest bottom in Ohio. Some scouting reports you check out personally."

Carol: "He came in for late breakfast. Of course I knew who he was. He was very polite. Very nice. Not, you know, aggressive, coming on too strong. Nothing like that. He was a gentleman."

Rose: "I can move this along. We got married when Montreal had a game scheduled at Riverfront. We married in the morning of April 11, 1984. I didn't need another big wedding. We got married at Reuven Katz's house. There were more waiters than guests. We tried to get married in Riverfront, at home plate, but they said batting practice was more important."

*   *   *

In each full season of managing, Rose brought the Reds home second. I remember the spring of 1987, in Tampa, when a familiar figure waved and I waved back toward the bearded, smiling face of Bart Giamatti.

We had met at an evening panel discussion at Yale, for which we each drew a generous fee. Sports in American Society. We joked later that it must surely be the most glorious form of larceny to be paid for speaking on sports. We talked poetry and power also, Frost and Dante.

"I've enjoyed this evening," Giamatti said.

"Plus the audience didn't stone us, Bart."

Now, 1,200 miles from Yale stood Giamatti, newly inaugurated president of the National League, twinkly under a broad-brimmed hat in the Florida sun. "I have never," he said in quiet tones of amazement, "been to spring training before in my life."

"Never?"

"Never. I've read *you* about spring training, of course, and enjoyed that immensely." To be stroked by Bart Giamatti was to know a master's touch.

Rose was picking up baseballs near the batting cage. "Isn't he marvelous?" Giamatti said.

"I'm working on a book about him."

"I know," Giamatti said.

"Back in New York, Bart, let's have lunch."

He turned *extraordinarily* twinkly. "I'd love to," Giamatti said, "but shouldn't you be writing?"

It surprised me when Giamatti fined Rose $10,000 and suspended him for thirty days, after a nasty incident with an umpire named David Pallone. In a tie game, Mookie Wilson, then with the Mets, hit a bounder to shortstop Barry Larkin with Howard Johnson on second. Larkin's throw may have pulled Nick Esasky off first base. Pallone delayed, then called

Wilson safe. Johnson kept running and scored the tie-break-
ing run.

Rose rushed onto the field and put his face up against
Pallone. The umpire gesticulated and one of his fingernails
nicked Rose under an eye. Rose bumped Pallone and was
ejected. Thirty days.

The suspension was the toughest in memory for an on-field
incident. Giamatti drew mixed reviews. He not only suspended Rose, he summoned broadcasters Joe Nuxhall and
Marty Brennaman, whose reporting of the play Giamatti
called "inflammatory, completely irresponsible, and un-
professional." He could chastise them because they were
employed by the Reds. Some saw in such chastisement a
disregard for independent reporting.

Then it was done. The thirty days passed. Rose went back
to work. Giamatti defended his own conduct. Some said he'd
never been much of a civil liberties feller, anyway.

Privately, I wondered how much Giamatti really knew
about pro ball. An umpire, after a close call, is supposed to
walk away from challenge. Turn your back. Leave the scene.
Avoid confrontation.

Pallone stood his ground. He was confrontational. He was
provocative. Rose was out of line and so was the umpire.
Thirty days? Try three.

Again I wondered how much Giamatti knew about pro
ball. Not the beau ideal, but the reality.

10

The Gambler

It became a point of pride, across three years of work and play, that neither Rose nor I was late for an appointment. We joked about his statement to players, during the managing years, "Give a hundred percent and be on time," but that statement was serious. We both recognized lateness as a galling form of discourtesy.

Now, in the most tormented summer of Rose's life (and in the last week of existence left to baseball commissioner Angelo Bartlett Giamatti) I found myself having trouble with an aircraft. Rose and I were going to talk yet once more. He was going to tell "his side" of the sordid gambling scandal that had placed on collision course the juggernaut careers of Pete Rose and Bart Giamatti. If I ever meant to be prompt, it was today.

But here was a pilot saying that we were fifteenth in line for takeoff—fifteenth!—and, soon after, that the crew of the plane behind us had detected a loose door flapping in the belly of our beast. Delay heaped upon delay. The loose door was inspected and certified as nonlethal. As we cruised over West Virginia in a sky full of cumulus clouds, the pilot

came on the loudspeakers and said that a violent thunder-
storm sat over Cincinnati. We could not fly into it. We would
have to circle and wait, circle and wait. Six miles above the
earth, Superhawk made oval sweeps across three states.

I was four minutes late for my appointment.

"Don't worry about it," Rose said. He wore white tennis
warm-ups and white sneakers. He looked better than he had
five days earlier when he had difficulty commenting on his
banishment for network television.

"Hey," Rose said, "if the plane can't get down, you can't
get down."

Rose was suspended from baseball on August 24, 1989. The
term of the suspension is permanent, with the right to apply
for reinstatement after one year. The reason was not delin-
eated in the brief agreement Rose and Giamatti signed,
which did, however, specifically state that there was no formal finding on the subject of Rose's betting on baseball.

Rose had admitted heavy betting on football and basketball through bookmakers and associating with felons. He denies, with great passion, that he ever, even once, bet on
baseball. But in the last press conference of his life, A. Bartlett Giamatti said it was his personal opinion that Rose had
indeed bet on baseball.

Some on Rose's side said a baseball commissioner, an impe-
rial power, could not have a personal opinion. "A king has no
opinions. A king can only be just." Surely Giamatti, the Yale
professor, understood that concept.

Such legal and historical argument is not the stuff of headlines. A widely held public perception exists that Rose was
banished for betting on baseball. It is not my particular purpose here to change minds. It is not a purpose here to offer
Rose as Saint Peter. Rather it is to give him a chance for a fair
hearing, knowing all the while, as Rose concedes, that he has
indeed bet through bookmakers and associated with felons.

(The principal victim of these offenses is Peter Edward Rose.) It seems appropriate to point out that most journalists who pillory Rose for betting through bookmakers are employed by newspapers and television stations that provide betting lines to facilitate their customers' betting with bookmakers. In a saying of New Englanders, sated with Puritan sermons, "When the fox preaches, look to your geese."

Some feel that across the summer of 1989 Rose and his advisors put together a public-relations disaster. Certainly by Labor Day, Rose, the storied ballplayer, had been eclipsed. Instead Rose was an embodiment of cautionary tales, a whipping boy for media moralists, and an object of ridicule for standup comics. At least one New York journalist warned me that if I wrote too ardently on Rose's behalf my own credibility would be suspect until the end of time.

I would say, in the balance, that Rose and his advisors were victims of and participants in the public-relations disaster in the summer of '89. The press responded to their mistakes with orgasmic glee.

Rose and two of his lawyers met in New York on February 20 with Commissioner Peter Ueberroth, and Commissioner-elect Bart Giamatti. A day later somebody in the office of Ueberroth or Giamatti disclosed the meeting to Murray Chass, a baseball writer with *The New York Times*. The *Times* quoted Ueberroth as saying "We asked [Rose] to do it. We didn't order him. There's nothing ominous and there won't be any follow through."

Shortly thereafter, Ronald Peters of Franklin, Ohio, thirty miles north of Cincinnati, a bookmaker who had branched out into selling cocaine, approached *Sports Illustrated* through a lawyer. Peters wanted to sell a story about Rose's gambling, which would include charges that Rose bet on baseball. According to sources at the magazine, a decision was made not to *purchase* Peters's story. No one, not even

John Dowd, the Inspector Javert of *Les Cincinnati Miséra-bles,* has found a check issued from *Sports Illustrated* to Peters. Peters did give *Sports Illustrated* highly charged information apparently for free.

The *Sports Illustrated* people then sought interviews with others, including players Rose had traded. Word that the magazine was undertaking a gambling investigation spread through baseball. Commissioner Ueberroth and Commissioner-elect Giamatti now had a problem. Was *Sports Illustrated* to be permitted to present itself as baseball's cop?

On March 20 a statement from the commissioner's office declared that John Dowd, a Washington lawyer who had prosecuted some hoodlums for the U.S. Department of Justice, was heading an inquiry "into serious allegations against Rose." *Sports Illustrated* was not to be permitted to police baseball. Baseball was policing itself.

On March 21, the magazine published a story that charged Rose with betting on baseball. Once that was done, the magazine hewed to the line that Rose had bet on baseball, justifying itself and publishing a certain amount of tripe. One story quoted the *New York Post* quoting anonymous sources as saying that Rose owed hundreds of thousands of dollars to—surprise!—Mafia bookmakers.

Sports Illustrated, going for a story, going for glory, became part of a prosecution team. Week after week, the magazine ran photos in which Rose looked haggard, angry, depressed, guilty as Nixon. Week after week, debris from his imperfect life became news. Rose tried to bring cash home from Japan without declaring it, and he got caught. The dirty bounder. Say, how many times has he been tagged for speeding?

"Nightline," the ABC-TV news-interview program, focused on Rose August 23, the evening when word of the imminent exile broke loose. One participant was Jill Lieber,

Sports Illustrated's resident Rose expert. In time, Jeff Greenfield, the moderator, asked a pair of questions in a single breath. Was Lieber eligible to vote for candidates for the baseball Hall of Fame and did she believe Rose deserved to be elected? Lieber avoided the first question, to which the answer is no. She is not eligible for a variety of reasons, one of which would be that she has not covered a sufficient number of major league games to make the requisite baseball judgments. Lieber sat hard-faced before a network camera and did not discuss her ineligibility. But she lectured millions of us on Rose's moral shortcomings. No, Lieber said, Rose did not belong in the hall.

Through the long investigation, *The New York Times* served, perhaps unwittingly, as a mouthpiece for Giamatti's office. Giamatti and his staff offered up various news items, an exclusive interview with this most eloquent of baseball commissioners. The *Times* was getting interesting material. Giamatti was getting his viewpoints printed. ("The *Times*," James Reston has pointed out, "has an extraordinary multiplier effect. What appears in the *Times* often appears later in a hundred other newspapers.")

The preeminent sports magazine aligned itself with the prosecution—in essence, John Dowd. The preeminent newspaper aligned itself with the man paying the prosecutor, Bart Giamatti. A properly long and detailed look at the press, the networks, and the Rose affair goes beyond the purview of this book. But it is in order.

How that suggestion is reviewed by *Sports Illustrated* and the *Times*, we will have to see.

Now here are fair questions: If Peters, about to become a convicted felon, could feed materials to *Sports Illustrated*, why couldn't Rose counterpunch and flatten his enterprising and whiney accuser? If Giamatti could grant a wide-ranging exclusive interview to the *Times*, why couldn't Rose shake down the rolling thunder of his career and add the trumpeting of a defense?

Those are excellent questions; no simple answers exist.

Rose confronted at least three problems. He *had* associated with questionable characters, in itself grounds for suspension from major league baseball. He had bet football and basketball through bookmakers, also in itself grounds for suspension. Finally, the advice he was hearing came from lawyers. Their perceptions were colored by the fact that they were lawyers, not publicists, and that they lived in Ohio, not Beverly Hills or New York.

The first strategy was to make no comment. Rose did tell reporters that he had not "flashed scores to gamblers" from the Reds dugout when a Riverfront Stadium scoreboard was being repaired. This led nowhere. All right, he hadn't flashed scores. But didn't he know those gamblers in the stands?

"No comment."

Had Rose *himself* bet baseball?

"No comment."

Pleading the Fifth Amendment is not an admission of guilt in a courtroom. Rose was not in a courtroom. He was in an office in Riverfront Stadium talking to the press and, through the press, the public.

Johnny Bench spoke for many when he said, a little irritably, "If Pete hasn't bet on baseball, why doesn't he just come out and say it?"

Why indeed? Rose's lawyers, who say they were cooperating fully with the commissioner's request for a confidential investigation, counseled *no* public discussion of gambling. Zero.

Over weeks Rose's silence—his refusal to discuss gambling, his refusal to deny that he had bet on baseball—played poorly in the press. Abysmally is not too strong a word.

By the time Rose did say he never bet baseball, months of no comment had eroded his credibility. One is innocent until proven guilty, except when one declines to protest one's innocence. Then legal concepts fade and blur and extralegal concepts materialize. "Where there's smoke there's fire." Or, as Johnny Bench asked, "Why can't he just say he hasn't bet on baseball?"

A journalist from the *Washington Post* told me, "I guess you're going to write a three-part book:
"Pete Rose: The Baseball Years
"Pete Rose: The Gambling Years
"Pete Rose: The Years in Prison."

Rose and I touched base on several occasions during the investigation and I think his deportment with me is significant. He mentioned in March that *Sports Illustrated* was digging into his gambling, asking questions of people who might have grudges against him: players he traded, his former wife. "Were there vultures like that in the press," he wanted to know, "when you started out?"

We talked about that for a bit and I asked what he intended to say in his own defense, if matters came to that.

"I don't want to talk about gambling. Besides, the biggest bet I made all year was $2,000 on the Super Bowl. For a guy with my income a $2,000 bet isn't *serious* gambling."

Opening Day at Riverfront Stadium brought armies of the press, producers from the three major networks, and something like a two-hour nonstop press conference. Rose tried to keep the focus on baseball. The reporters tried to laser in on gambling.

He was brusque when I greeted him, probably uncomfortable with the thought of being alone and, perhaps, being grilled. It was no day for a grilling. When I finally got Rose alone toward twilight, I said, "If you get exonerated,

I'll set down a helluva chapter called 'The Vultures of the Press.' "

Rose shook his head. He seemed both touched and stricken. "Be careful, Rog. This is heavy." Then he rushed off.

On a third occasion, breakfast at the Grand Hyatt Hotel in New York City, he met my eyes and said he had not bet on baseball. "It's ridiculous. It would be funny if it wasn't so serious.

"I know they are going to have to give me something for gambling and the association thing. I didn't hang out with [bookmaker Ron] Peters, but I did hang out with Paul Janszen. That makes me a lousy picker of friends. Worse than lousy. Horseshit. So I'll get something. Maybe six months. Maybe I deserve six months.

"But I never bet baseball. Never. Like I never stashed cocaine in my bats and I never threatened to break the legs of the kid of some bookie who was bothering me. I never did those things. None of them."

Finally I was studying the Dowd report and accompanying testimony in Reuven Katz's office one day in July—actually Katz's offices occupy several floors of the Tri-State Building in downtown Cincinnati—and emerged from a room with the report in one hand. Rose was passing in a corridor, wearing jeans and a T-shirt, oddly informal among the offices of necktied attorneys.

"You read that thing?" he said, pointing to Dowd's report, bound in black. "Now you believe I'm guilty, too. Now you believe I bet baseball, that I'm guilty as hell."

Once again, I saw the oddly stricken look. I meant to say no, I didn't think he was guilty as hell. I had found a very disturbing discrepancy in John Dowd's report. A discrepancy that raised serious questions. A discrepancy that, in short, smelled.

I didn't get that out. Rose recovered his poise and again was rushing somewhere.

In none of these episodes did Rose's manner appear to be that of a man who was trying to mislead me when he said he never bet on baseball.

What is the disturbing discrepancy? It leaps off page 223 of the report. It leaps and screams.

Dowd writes: "The testimony of Peters, Janszen and [Rose accuser Michael] Fry has been voluntary and forthright. Each has stood before the bar of justice and engaged in the most painful act of integrity—the admission of illegal acts. Each is now paying the debt society imposed for his acts against society. *None of them has anything to gain for his voluntary act of cooperation with this investigation.*" (Italics added.)

Blowing smoke past *Sports Illustrated* and the others, Dowd says a guilty plea is "a painful act of integrity."

Not when you've been caught dead to rights, Mr. Prosecutor. Not when you're plea bargaining, sir. Putting the names of Peters and Janszen in the same paragraph as the word integrity, Mr. Dowd, strikes some of us nonlawyers, who value words, as obscenity.

Peters had nothing to gain? Dowd cut a deal. If Peters talked, Dowd would write a letter to the judge who would be sentencing Peters for felony charges of drug dealing and tax evasion. Dowd would write the judge that Peters was "candid, forthright, and truthful." Probably the sentence would be lightened.

But who the hell was Dowd? Not nearly as influential as his employer. Dowd would write the letter and get the distinguished commissioner of baseball, Dr. A. Bartlett Giamatti, to sign it.

That was done. And after that was done, Dowd wrote, in his confidential report to Giamatti, that Peters had nothing to gain.

You can dress up a cheap suit by putting a fancy label on

it. But once you start pulling on the first loose string, it begins to unravel strand by strand.

One would think, hope, that the press is capable of learning. Before publishing the results of any investigation, investigate the investigator. Journalism 101. That lesson was taught by the foul career of Joseph R. McCarthy, the late senator from Wisconsin. And apparently forgotten.

What does the press tell us about John Dowd? *Sports Illustrated* informs us that he is "convincing." Others describe him as a "tall ex-Marine." What most press accounts leave out is that Dowd is a figure of controversy and fierce ambition.

A beefy-faced native of Brockton, Massachusetts, the blue-collar town that was the birthplace of Rocky Marciano, Dowd earned a law degree from Emory University in Atlanta in 1965, when he was twenty-four. He spent about ten years in the U.S. Department of Justice where, at the age of thirty-three, he became chief of the melodramatically named Organized Crime Strike Force 18. Strike Force dates from 1967; it is a superteam, bringing together investigators and attorneys from various government departments. Strike Force 18 reviewed cases of racketeering and corruption brought under the so-called RICO statute.

The strongest criticism of Dowd was overzealousness, a charge he denies. In 1979, the *Wall Street Journal* published a story suggesting that Dowd, trying to force testimony out of a convict, enlisted other convicts to beat the man until he did Dowd's bidding. Dowd sued the *Journal* and collected $400,000, which *The New York Times* called "the largest reported settlement in a libel suit that did not go to trial."

But an undeniable reality is that prosecutors and their incomes advance by means of convictions. Dowd's training is largely along prosecutorial lines.

In private practice he has become a full partner in the Washington firm of Heron, Burchette, where his estimated

income is half a million dollars a year. Dowd is, reports a
prominent Washington attorney, "one very heavy hitter."

Dowd had an awkward time with one client, Robert Reckmeyer, who sued, claiming Dowd had demanded that he
break some laws to get the money for Dowd's $500,000 fee.
Reckmeyer had already broken other laws. He was convicted
of distributing drugs in northern Virginia. Defended in federal court by a well-known Washington attorney, Plato Cach-
eris, Dowd defeated his former client.

John Dowd's investigation of Pete Rose took the form of an
"administrative procedure," as outlined in the bylaws of
baseball. The rules of a U.S. courtroom would not apply.
Dowd could also refuse to let Rose's attorneys be present
when he interrogated Rose's accusers; they were not present.
While Dowd was telling all reporters who would listen that
he was committed to fairness, in effect, he denied Rose the
right of cross-examination and the right to confront his accusers.

Of course, cross-examination could be a nuisance. Dowd
had these warbling felons, whom he would later praise, sing-
ing in harmony. Cross-examination is disharmonious. A good
cross-examination might tear apart the felon's credibility.
Then Dowd would have to confess that he failed to develop
hard evidence that Rose bet on baseball.

Perhaps the most pressing question about the entire situation is this: Why have Rose's attorneys not presented their
case until now? Their answer is simple. They believe that the
commissioner had already concluded, as evidenced by his
letter to Judge Carl Rubin, that Rose had gambled on baseball.

"We offered many times to present Pete's case before an
unbiased decision maker," says Reuven Katz. "We were refused. Giamatti insisted on being the decision maker himself."

And so, Dowd's case stood unanswered.

That case—John Dowd's unanswered-until-now case—cites various expert witnesses who testify to the existence of betting slips, bookmaking records, and of baseball bets Rose is said to have made. It cites a handwriting expert and a fingerprint specialist. It cites tape recordings as further evidence, including one in which Rose actually makes a bet on baseball. But when a close examination of this "physical" evidence is begun, a great deal of the "rock-solid" case starts to unravel. Like that cheap suit.

Paul Janszen, weight-lifter and professional gofer, has been accused of hatching a clever blackmailing and extortion scheme to obtain money from Rose. Indeed, another figure, one Scott Estes, has provided a sworn statement that he personally heard Michael Fry, a convicted felon and former Janszen associate, state that he and Janszen conspired to frame Pete Rose. Estes served time with Fry at the federal penitentiary at Terre Haute, Indiana. Estes, like Janszen and Peters, is a felon. But unlike those two, Estes had nothing to gain for this admission—no plea bargaining, and no payment for the magazine rights to his statement.

According to Estes, Fry was angry at Rose because Fry wanted Rose to finance him in a weight-lifting gym in Kentucky. Rose backed out of the deal. Janszen was angry at Rose because Pete refused to continue to associate with him, and had failed to pay him an alleged debt.

As this scheme emerged, in 1988, long before either *Sports Illustrated* or the commissioner's office showed any interest in Rose's associations, Rose engaged Roger Makley of Dayton, a tough former federal prosecutor and U.S. magistrate, to advise on criminal aspects of Janszen's threats. Makley's job eventually expanded, courtesy of John Dowd and associates, and Makley found some experts of his own.

These experts are part of the story that Rose never told.

They offer testimony that would certainly give any jury food for thought. These experts show the Dowd report to be about as airtight and waterproof as a cobweb.

[Note: It is not possible in this biography to present a complete and detailed rebuttal to the Dowd report. That is, perhaps, a separate book, 500 pages long. What we present here are selected examples of the opinions of certain experts who examined the report and its supporting documentation.]

Dana Martino, out of Syracuse, New York, is a Dartmouth graduate. A practicing attorney in Ohio, Martino is a former professional gambler who used to work in Las Vegas. He claims a comprehensive knowledge of both the practical and theoretical aspects of gambling. Martino has reviewed all of the material in the Dowd report, and in particular, three betting sheets that supposedly link Rose to gambling on baseball. His conclusion? "What Dowd calls betting sheets are not real betting sheets."

To recognize why they are not, one has to be a gambler. Not the office-pool variety of gambler, or the friendly-wager-down-at-the-tavern variety of gambler, but a regular, heavy gambler. People have agreed on very little regarding Pete Rose in recent months, but about one thing there is no serious dispute: Pete is a real gambler. Paul Janszen is not.

As Martino explains it, a real gambler is aware of the way betting sheets are used. Gamblers use them to record their wagers at the beginning of the betting day or week, and their winnings (or losses) at the end. To do that requires a personalized system, unique to the bettor and consistently followed. Some bettors record the teams on which they have bet on the right side of the sheet, with the teams they have bet against on the left. Some use a top-and-bottom approach. Some circle "their" teams. But all bettors do *something* consistently, otherwise they would never remember which teams they picked.

According to Martino, none of the betting sheets that Janszen produced show any system at all. The teams that Rose putatively bet on occur almost randomly on the page— some on the right, some on the left. It is the kind of mistake no real gambler could afford to make. Martino would have testified to this, and is adamant about his conclusions.

Martino also points to the discrepancies on the betting sheets Dowd put forth for baseball games. It's apparent that one of the alleged games (Los Angeles at St. Louis) could never have taken place because both teams were not scheduled on the day in question. And the game involving the Reds and the Montreal Expos had the teams playing in Cincinnati; in reality, they were scheduled to play in Montreal.

Would a man like Pete Rose, who's practically memorized every at-bat in *The Baseball Encyclopedia,* make those kinds of mistakes?

Or is it the handiwork of a non-gambler who was trying to shake down serious money?

Expert witness number two is Robert Massie, a handwriting analyst who resides in Dayton. Massie worked for many years with the Montgomery County, Ohio, Sheriff's Department. He is currently a consultant to the Miami Valley Regional Crime Laboratory and also serves as a consultant to private organizations and to various governmental investigative agencies, including the FBI and the Secret Service.

Massie examined the originals of three sheets of paper (two white and one yellow) that the government had previously obtained from Janszen. They are described in the Dowd report as "betting sheets" allegedly prepared by Rose according to Janszen. Massie was able to examine these three sheets of paper for a handwriting analysis only after they had been exposed to treatment by ninhydrin, a chemical used in fingerprint analysis. This treatment caused the ink impressions on the three sheets of paper to bleed so much that the line quality of the handwriting could not be completely distinguished. Since the distinguishing of line quality is essential in determining the genuineness of a handwritten document, Massie was not able to make any finding of any kind on the authorship of the documents.

Massie states: "I can't explain how any expert in handwriting analysis would ever come up with any finding as to whose handwriting appears on those three sheets of paper. It's impossible." John Dowd's handwriting expert argues that the writing on these three sheets of paper is Rose's. But he neglects to mention that he too examined these same sheets only after they had been treated with ninhydrin and the line quality distorted. Keep in mind that the writing on the sheets is also printed—not in script—making positive identification even more unlikely.

It is these same three sheets of paper that, the media reported, contained the fingerprints of Pete Rose. From this, the media concluded that the sheets were of Rose's unquestioned authorship and constituted damning circumstantial evidence that he bet on baseball. But expert witness number three, Ralph Nickoson, a veteran fingerprint analyst also from Dayton, comes to some very different conclusions. Nickoson was employed by the Dayton Police Department for twenty-four years, the last fifteen as a fingerprint examiner in the identification section. He is a Certified Latent Print Examiner and has appeared as an expert witness in court on many occasions.

Nickoson examined the three pieces of paper comprising the so-called "betting sheets." His examination included an analysis of special photographs taken of these three sheets in order to determine what fingerprint and handprint impressions could be found. He observed that the sheets were suspiciously lacking in what he described as smudges, ridge detail, or other indications of being handled. He explains that when someone writes on a piece of paper or otherwise handles a paper for any purpose, chances are he is going to touch and handle it in such a way that any number of fingerprint and handprint impressions, identifiable and otherwise, will remain.

In fact, as Nickoson's analysis discloses, there are a total of only three prints of any kind on the three sheets. Only one is clearly identifiable as the right index finger of Pete Rose. The other two prints do not show enough points of identification to enable a fingerprint analyst to conclude that they are in fact the prints of Rose. One of the prints, a right thumb print, Nickoson says, lacks sufficient ridge detail for a positive identification.

But how is it possible that these three sheets of paper have a total of only three prints on them? And how do you explain Rose's identifiable fingerprint being on only one of the sheets?

One possible theory is that Pete may have held that particular sheet for a moment, as though someone gave it to him to look at, and then either put it down or gave it back to another person. Janszen, by his own admission, routinely handled a great deal of Pete's autograph business. Thus Janszen in the ordinary course of business would have Rose handle paper after paper, many times without Pete paying any particular attention to what he was doing. Isn't it plausible that Janszen might have had Pete deliberately touch one or more of these sheets of paper in order to get a fingerprint? Thereafter, Pete's writing could be forged on those sheets of paper to reflect betting activity and the sheets used as circumstantial evidence to prove he bet on baseball.

On September 5, 1989, long after the August 24 press conference and long after the Dowd report was filed, the *Cincin-*

nati Post reported that one of Dowd's own polygraph experts, William Robertson, concluded that Janszen lied when he said that Rose had bet on baseball. Dowd told *Cincinnati Post* reporter Al Salvato that "this makes no difference. *The independent evidence* [the questionable betting sheets] *is most important."* (Italics added.)

Think about it. The most important evidence in John Dowd's indictment of Pete Rose is three alleged betting sheets on which the handwriting is unidentifiable, on which the fingerprints are smudged, and which do not, in the words of a gambling expert, resemble real betting sheets. And all of this key evidence is supplied by a convicted felon who John Dowd's own polygraph expert claims lied.

And why hadn't Dowd turned over that damaging information on Janszen to Rose's lawyers in the interest of fairness?

Dowd: "They changed the whole posture of the situation. They come to court and concoct a defense that I'm unfair. So I'm not playing their game anymore."

But still the search for a smoking gun continues. Ron Peters claimed, in the Dowd report, that he made and played back to Pete Rose a tape recording of Pete on the phone placing bets on baseball games, including a bet on the Cincinnati Reds. Peters kept this tape, he explained, just in case he needed insurance someday to get back monies Rose might owe him.

Peters said that this tape was in a mover's box, and told Dowd that the box was in the possession of his ex-wife. But that's where the Dowd report leaves off. Dowd's people did visit the former Mrs. Peters, who let them search her home for the box with the tape. The box described by Peters was found. There was no sign of any tape.

Mrs. Peters, in an affidavit made after the Dowd report was

prepared, said, "It's my opinion that this entire mysterious tape business is without any foundation whatsoever and simply the product of my ex-husband's fantasy and imagination."

What does one conclude from all this? Such spooky stuff prompted Samuel Dash, counsel to the Senate Select Committee on Watergate and employed as an expert witness by the Rose defense team, to assert in open court that if Dowd had submitted the Rose report to him, he, Sam Dash, would have fired John Dowd.

We trudge into a conference room in the offices of Hamilton Projects, the marketing agency that represents Rose. (The building also houses the *Cincinnati Enquirer*.) Rose looks more relaxed than he did during the legal maneuvering that so dominated his life and the sports pages. But the old teasing humor is gone. Humor must await another day, another year, another verdict. Rose is a man with a serious, indeed agonizing, story to tell.

"Some say things began to come apart for you when you had to retire."

"Who says?"

"A lot of people, Pete. Just because I mention something doesn't mean I endorse it."

"I know that and if you have any tough questions, ask them. I'm here to answer tough questions."

"You looked bad striking out on August 17, 1986, against Goose Gossage. Then you never played again. You never announced your retirement. I asked if you didn't want to say goodbye around the league and you said, 'I don't need that stuff.' Then you said, 'The fucking writers were on me for staying in the lineup. Now they're on me for not being in the lineup.' "

"Rog, are there going to be a lot of 'fucks' in this book? I use the word around the dugout. I don't much like to see it in print."

We talked a bit about how a writer wants to set down the way a character speaks but tries not to be excessive. You don't use every expletive, every belch.

Rose listened hard, but he was still considering the question about his retirement.

"What happened to me about retiring is I went 3-for-4, 5-for-5, 0-for-4. People seem to forget that. Two days later I struck out against [Lance] McCullers. Three days later I struck out against Gossage. Three-for-4, 5-for-5, 0-for-4, and 0-for-2, how much is that?"

While the tape ran, I took a few notes on the back of an envelope. Journalism 201. An envelope is fine. Lincoln wrote the Gettysburg Address on the back of one.

I added. "Eight-for-15."

Rose: "The last three games I started I got eight hits."

"Then why didn't you play any more that year?"

Rose: "It's simple. I'm glad you asked. Because my buddy Tony Perez shared first base with me. Tony was in his last year. He had announced his retirement. He was a couple of home runs behind Orlando Cepeda as the most productive home run hitter of all the Latin players.

"He did end up tying that record. As a matter of fact, in the last week of the season Tony played and he was player of the week in the National League. I let him play the whole month of September instead of me because he was swinging the bat good and I wanted him to get the record."

"But, Pete, wouldn't you have liked to say to all the world, 'I'm retiring'? Then go around the National League and say goodbye to all the ballplayers, all the fans, even the umpires?"

Rose: "If I knew what was going to happen to me, I would have done that. But I didn't know and I had my philosophy.

"You see, play or manage, I was going to the ballpark every day. I was putting my uniform on. It was not like I was going to be away from it.

"This is important. I never looked at myself as a circus performer.

"I've been a ballplayer. Run a 'Pete Rose Night' now at Riverfront, I honestly believe, Rog, that you couldn't get in everyone who wanted to support me.

"Back in '86 I felt and I still feel that I've been honored in every ballpark in the National League just by having had the opportunity to play in them.

"I've had great days in New York. I've had good days in Los Angeles. I tied Ty Cobb's record in Chicago. I got my 4,000th hit in Montreal and they stood for five minutes. I can't think of a ballpark where I haven't gotten a standing ovation.

"Retiring as a player, I was still going to be in uniform. I was in charge. So the idea, if this is what you're getting at, that I gambled more because I was unhappy retiring doesn't work out. At least not the way I see it."

The psychobiographical theory that retirement drove Rose into patterns of self-destructive behavior may never finally be laid to rest. But at least it has been addressed.

The more obvious question, the one everybody asks, is why Rose accepted banishment after fighting Dowd and Giamatti for six months.

Rose: "The litigation in the last months was about whether the commissioner was biased or not biased. He convinced me and some pretty good minds around me that he was biased when he sent the letter to Judge Rubin, who was going to be sentencing Peters. Giamatti says Peters had been truthful. That would mean that the commissioner was already convinced that when I said I never bet baseball I was lying.

"Why should I, a ballplayer, go to New York to a hearing knowing that the guy already made up his mind? The guillotine is already starting down and he wants me to put my neck under it.

"Reuven Katz, Bob Pitcairn, Roger Makley, and all of us

were trying to do something I did for my whole career. Play on a level field.

"What happened, if I'm not mistaken, is that the commissioner put all his trust and all his marbles in John Dowd's corner. You read the report. You have to know that I believe that Dowd was and is biased and he convinced the commissioner to believe what he believed.

"The press calls it a report. I call it a prosecutor's brief. John Dowd might be one of the best in the country at doing a prosecutor's brief.

"I'm in the middle of this. Sure there's something there. They get claims and they have to investigate.

"Dowd does a 225-page report on me and comes up with two paragraphs favorable to me. Come on.

"He does 225 pages and doesn't talk to Bernie Stowe, the clubhouse man for the Reds. Hey, if I was doing baseball gambling in the clubhouse, Bernie Stowe would be a big witness.

"He doesn't talk to Marty Brennaman, who spent time with me in my office every day.

"Why didn't he talk to Reuven Katz, who's been tuned into my finances for twenty years? I'm going to tell you why I settled. I didn't forget the question. I've never ducked a question from you, 'cuz I know you'll give me an even field. But I'm making a point first why I was fighting. First I was fighting, second I settled.

"I was fighting to keep my head from getting chopped. I never bet baseball. I swear I never bet baseball and the commissioner believes I did bet baseball and he's the judge, the jury, and the executioner. I'm not trying to change the rules of baseball. I'm just trying to keep my head on my shoulders. So I feel I have to fight against a commissioner who doesn't believe *me* and writes a letter to a judge asking leniency for a drug dealer."

No one got up from the table. No one walked about the room. Rose sat forward in his chair. Around the drab conference table intensity held us in thrall.

"Then why did you cut a deal?"

Rose: "I was fighting all summer to keep my head, right. I was fighting for something else. For no finding from the baseball commissioner that I bet on baseball. That's the important words in this agreement. I mean, the way it's been reported, it's like the most important words aren't there.

"If the commissioner insists that he make a finding that I bet baseball I don't sign any agreement."

"In our book, Pete, there are a lot of allusions to gambling."

Rose: "There are no allusions to betting on baseball.

"I gave John Dowd every one of my telephone records.

"I gave John Dowd all of my checking account records.

"I admitted I bet other sports through a bookmaker.

"Does that sound like a guy who was lying?

"They originally wanted to throw me out and make me agree to wait seven years for reinstatement.

"They came down six years, so I can apply after one year.

"Giamatti and Dowd didn't want to go to court anymore. Believe me, they didn't want to go to court. They would have lost. We think their evidence is hearsay. So why did I settle? That's what you want to know."

"Yes, Pete, that's what I want to know."

"I met with all four of my attorneys, Roger Makley, Bob Stachler, Bob Pitcairn, and Reuven. They told me that based upon everything they knew, even if we established that I didn't bet on baseball, the commissioner would put me on the permanent ineligibility list for the things that I had admitted, like betting through bookies and my associations. To stay in court for months and months with a chance that the commissioner would hear the case on betting on baseball—and you know how we feel my chances were there—would prove nothing.

"If I could get an agreement that made *no* finding that I bet on baseball, and that allowed me to reapply in one year [with a personal assurance from Commissioner Giamatti to Reuven Katz that he had an open mind on reinstatement and that he was not committed to a minimum of seven years or five years or anything like that] and that allowed me to continue to deny I bet on baseball, I would have gotten almost everything that I could get if I won or lost the lawsuit and maybe going to two or three more courts and going through the hearing. To me, it just wasn't worth it.

"I mean, the agreement came down to this: that the commissioner would make no finding about betting on baseball and that I could reapply for reinstatement after one year. Rog, even if I had eventually won in court—and I'm sure I would have—I still would have been banned for that associating with gamblers stuff. So the way I saw it, the agreement was okay.

"For the good of my family, myself, for baseball and even the commissioner himself, the settlement was the right thing to do. We gave in on some things, they gave in on some things, and we did the right thing. I have no regrets. I did some bad and stupid things. I deserve to be punished. Making this settlement was the right thing for me to do."

"The commissioner told the press that he believed you did bet on baseball."

Rose: "In some other life I'm going to talk to him about that."

"There is a public perception that you bet on baseball."

Rose: "A lot of this is the media. I can't blame all those people. This is a pretty complicated story. But they haven't gotten it out just right. Let me tell you what happened here.

"About six months ago they [the baseball brass] called me in."

"Did they say they were going to investigate your gambling in general?"

Rose, loudly: "No! No! No! You get a 'no' on that three times. When I went there in February Fay Vincent was there. Giamatti was there. Ueberroth was there. Katz was there. [Katz's partner Robert] Pitcairn was there. I was there.

"They asked me: 'Do you bet on baseball?'

"I said, 'No, sir. I didn't bet on baseball.'

"They said, 'You bet on anything?'

"I said, 'The last bet I made was the [1989] Super Bowl. I might have bet on the wrong team.'

"Ueberroth says, 'I don't want to hear about football. I'm not concerned with that. I'm concerned whether you bet on baseball or not.'

"I said to Ueberroth, 'Sir, I do not bet on baseball.'

"And that was the end of it. That was the end of it. *So that was the end of it.*"

As it developed that was the end of nothing.

Rose: "Let me tell you something else about how that whole deal in February turns out to crucify me. You're right, that wasn't the end of it. I *thought* it was the end of it.

"Somebody in that meeting asked me about a Pik Six," a betting parlay that Rose had hit at the Turfway racetrack.

"I didn't think it was any of their damn business whether I bet on a Pik Six or not. Racetrack betting is legal and I just didn't want to get into all this.

"I was also trying to protect a friend of mine, Jerry Carroll, the owner of the track. I've been around tracks. I know the way it is. It's okay for the owner of the track to bet but when the owner of the track wins big, people think there's some funny business.

"So Jerry Carroll sort of gave me the Pik Six there at Turfway. Two races had already been won and he still let me in on the ticket. So in trying to protect Jerry Carroll, I actually said I had nothing to do with the winning Pik Six.

"I call that a white lie, a fib. Now a lot of the media says if I lied about the Pik Six, I must be lying when I say I don't bet baseball.

"I say, wait a minute, wait a minute. Slow down here.

"When I got ready to leave that meeting in February I looked at the commissioner and I said, 'Commissioner, I want you gentlemen to help me.'

"And they said, 'What do you mean?'

"I said, 'Because I'm missing spring training today, I *know* as soon as I get back with the Reds it's going to leak that I was here. It's not going to leak from Mr. Katz. It's not going to leak from Mr. Pitcairn. I'm sure not going to tell anybody.

" 'I want to know, gentlemen, what to tell the media tomorrow down in Plant City.'

"Ueberroth said, 'Well, you tell the media that you came to New York because we wanted your advice on some baseball matters.' We're talking about truth and lying. The man who ran baseball tells me to go back to the national media and fib about why I was in New York. That seems to be okay. But I can't fib about the Pik Six?"

"What actually happened when you got back to spring training?"

Rose: "Reporters asked what I was doing in New York, after the story leaked out. I said—as the outgoing commissioner and the incoming commissioner had asked me to say— that they wanted my advice on some baseball matters.

"The reporters said, 'Why did they have you come all the way to New York?'

"I said, 'You'll have to ask the two commissioners for an answer to that one.' "

Rose was sitting forward on the edge of his chair. He was animated, and clearly anxious to tell his story. I don't think I had ever before seen him sit for so long in one place.

"I want to ask you about Paul Janszen and I want to tell you that most of the press seems to believe him."

Rose: "I can't help that."

"Maybe you can. Tell me why the hell you hung around with characters like Peters and Janszen when you could have been hanging around with decent people like me and Reuven Katz."

Rose did not smile. He said, "I didn't hang around with Peters. I hung around with Janszen. He helped me with my weight lifting, staying in shape."

"I read he was a barrel salesman before he met you. Not highly educated. Never got a college degree. Now he's made at least $50,000 from *Penthouse* magazine for telling a story. For a retired barrel salesman, he seems like a pretty smart character."

Rose: "Well, we'll see, we'll see.

"We haven't put everything together. Maybe we never will. But I honestly can't believe that baseball went to Paul Janszen.

"Way back in January [of 1989], Janszen told friends of my wife he was going to go to the commissioner and blackmail me that I bet on baseball."

"Which friends of your wife?"

Rose: "One of my wife's best friends. He called up this girl, and she told us he said he was going to kill my wife, Carol, and going to do real bad stuff to my kids if I didn't pay him $50,000.

"So here's what this guy is going to do. Blackmail me that I bet on baseball, which I never did. He said he was going to wait on that until spring training when all the press was there and all the press was doing baseball. So he planned this out. I mean, he planned this out."

"Tell me how well this fellow Janszen knew you."

Rose: "He hung around with me for a year. Just the summer of '87. I got along with him because he was real good in the lifting and he seemed like he was a nice guy.

"I didn't have any clue that he was involved in drugs. I should have been more suspicious. Do I have to say that? I guess I do. All right, I should have been more suspicious.

"I hear stories that Janszen was in the drug business before he met me. I figure, making a mistake, it doesn't matter what he used to do long as he doesn't try any crazy drug stuff in front of me.

"I begin to get a picture. Janszen has a lot of drug money that he can't spend. He told me one time, 'Pete, I've got to get rid of my Corvette. I've got to take off my Rolex. I've got to get rid of my ostrich shoes. I've got to get inconspicuous.'

"I said, 'If you worked hard and saved your money, why do you want to be inconspicuous?' That's how naive I was.

"How can a guy like me who's supposed to be street smart make a mistake like that? I'm tuned in to a lot of things but I'm sure not tuned in to heroin or cocaine."

"So you really had no clue Janszen was involved in drugs?"

Rose: "No. No. I found out during spring training of 1988. Janszen asked me, he asked Reuven Katz actually, could he borrow $30,000.

"Reuven told me in spring training. He said, 'Paul Janszen wants you to lend him $30,000.'

"I said, '$30,000? For what?'

"Katz said, 'Janszen said he needed to hire a lawyer. Janszen is going to get prosecuted for drugs. He says you're his only hope.'

"I said, 'Reuv, I can't lend anybody $30,000. That's just too much to lend. Maybe we'll loan him ten, if he pays me back.'

"So we loan him ten. That's what the $10,000 check to Janszen was for.

"I thought, 'I got to get away from this guy. He's in the drug business.'

"Janszen made some road trips with me. He must have felt he was very close. But I'm thinking, 'Janszen, take a hike.

Janszen, I don't need problems with drug agents and stuff. Janszen, I got to fire you as a friend.' "

"Did you tell Janszen that directly?"

"No. I was in Florida. He was in Cincinnati. I just ducked him."

"Pete, at the time of the $10,000 check, did Reuven Katz say, 'Watch it. This Janszen could be dangerous'?"

Rose: "I don't remember exactly what Reuven said, but he wrote on the bottom of the check that it was a loan. Reuven does civil practice. You know. Contracts. Estates. Pension plans. He and Bob Pitcairn brought in Roger Makley from Dayton, who has real criminal experience, and after Makley spent some time going over the situation, he was the guy who blew the whistle.

"He said, 'Don't fall for that loan stuff. This may be blackmail or obstruction of justice or extortion. Don't pay anybody another dime.'

"After that the threats began. Janszen spread the word he was going to kill my wife, Carol. He was going to do terrible stuff to my kids, unless I pay him $50,000."

"How about going to the cops, Pete? Cincinnati police? The FBI?"

Rose: "I talked with my lawyers. This is a mess. Janszen knows I've been betting through bookies. If that goes public I maybe get suspended from baseball. I want my situation with Janszen settled quietly. I want Janszen out of my life. I don't think he will hurt my family. He's already in trouble with the Feds. But if I go to the cops, stuff about my betting through bookies can come out and get into the media. I'm trying to get Janszen out of my life *and* stay in baseball."

I took a beat. I took a breath. And many more. To appreciate how convincing Rose is one-on-one you have to see the fire in his eye, the set of his shoulders, the pain on the Mount Rushmore face. One-on-one, he is a most convincing witness.

Caught in the moment, I blurted: "Pete, this is the most amazing thing. The greatest ballplayer of our time put out of the baseball business by some fucking bum."

Pete, who does not like to see expletives in print, corrected me. Pete said, "Some lying bum."

I remembered how Pete called down the visage of his dead father in describing triumphs of his life. "I have a hard question, Pete. About your father. Suppose Mr. Rose were with us today?"

Rose: "That's not hard. My dad would be real angry at me. He'd be even more angry at Paul Janszen.

"Dad was a no-nonsense person, but he liked fun. He took me to a racetrack when I was eight years old. My father liked to go to the track on weekends. He wasn't a big bettor. Never bet the grocery money, anything like that. He just liked the entertainment of the racetrack, same as I do."

"Would your dad be most upset about the punishment you've gotten? Or would he be more upset about the fact you bet with bookies?"

Rose: "Ah, I don't know. I think he'd probably understand that I love sports and like to watch them and like to root and that a bet sharpens that up for me. He would probably say that as a pro ballplayer or manager, I shouldn't bet through bookies. Just the way he preferred that I didn't smoke or drink. And I don't smoke or drink."

We were now approaching the question of addictive behavior.

"*Time* magazine put you on a cover as America's premiere addictive gambler. The editors of *Time* have diagnosed you as America's number-one addictive gambler."

Rose: "I don't believe I am a compulsive gambler."

"Did Giamatti or his people ever ask you to undergo therapy or counseling for gambling?"

"No. In fact they said that was not their concern. It was strictly my business. But I'm willing to meet with a counselor. I don't think there would be very many meetings, but if there have to be, I'll do what I have to do so I can solve this problem.

"In 1989 I got to spring training on February 1, the earliest I ever went to spring training. I left April 3. The only gambling I could do down there was bet on dogs. I went to the dog track three Saturdays in two months.

"I told that to Jill Lieber, the writer from *Sports Illustrated.*

"She said, 'Yes, but you sent your money every night.'

"I told her I'm not the sending money type of guy. If I'm going to make a bet it will be on something I can watch. If I bet on an event, I want to watch the event.

"I'm not the type of guy that's going to be on the baseball field managing a game when he's sent his money to see the Kentucky Derby. I'll bet the Derby if I can watch the Derby."

"Did Lieber or anybody else from *Sports Illustrated* print that?"

"I never saw it. I guess they figured they had a better story if they made it sound like I'm a compulsive gambler."

"How do you react in your gut when you read stories that you *are* a compulsive gambler?"

Rose: "I don't know how to react. I don't know what a compulsive gambler is.

"If I go to some counselor and he tells me that I'm a compulsive gambler and he's qualified and that's his diagnosis, I accept that. But I want you and the readers and everybody else and even John Dowd to understand that if the counselor says I am *not* a compulsive gambler, then be fair. Really be fair. Accept that, even if it means *Time* magazine has to admit that it was wrong.

"Personally, if it comes to it, I don't think the counselor is going to find that I have a problem. I have no idea what he would ask me. I would be as honest with him as I could. I think once he talked with me for an hour he would understand why I gamble."

"Why do you gamble, Pete?"

Rose: "Why do I gamble? Why do I gamble? As a baseball man, I have a hell of a lot of free time. Begin there. What's that story about the umpire, they asked him long ago, did he like umpiring? The fans got on him. The ballplayers got on him. The umpire said—and he was talking about the baseball life—'Yeah, but you can't beat the hours.'

"Gambling is enjoyment for me. It fills free time. I go to the racetrack and I sit with the owner of the track. I like that. I like the company of people with money and I'm competitive. I like to win on the ballfield. No, I didn't have the most natural ability in the world, but there's nobody who ever wanted to win baseball games more than I did. More than I do.

"I like to win my bets. When I win, a lot of the time I give the money to my wife, Carol. You know Carol. You know how beautiful she is. Well, there's one other thing Carol is world-class in. That's shopping. I get some pleasure setting her loose in a mall.

"If I lose my bets, hell, I lose. I never went to the track and lost all my bets and on the way home wanted to kill the cab driver. I never even didn't tip him.

"You like classical music, Rog. You say it's good for the soul. Probably you couldn't tell me why. Gambling gives me a charge. What is it they say, different strokes for different folks?

"Here's another thing. I played for the Phillies. The last two years I was playing for the Phillies I lived forty minutes from Atlantic City.

"In those two years I went to Atlantic City three times.
"Twice I went with my wife over to the Bunny Club. The
other time I went to work. Do a baseball card show.

"I don't play baccarat. I never shot dice in my life. I play
blackjack very sparingly. I mean, does that sound like a compulsive gambler, a man who lives forty minutes from a casino
and goes there three times in two years?"

"But hasn't your gambling increased over the years?"

Rose: "It has in dollars. When I'm making more than
$100,000 a month, a $10 bet doesn't give me a kick.

"People read Janszen's lies. I'm not talking about that here.
I'm talking about something that's true. In a bad stretch I
dropped $34,000 in three months. My income for those three
months was what, $400,000? So I'm saying I never lost money
that hurt me or my family to lose.

"The guy who makes $200 a week—and I know guys like
that, 'cuz I didn't start out rich—the guy who makes $200 a
week doesn't understand, you can't expect him to understand, that me losing $34,000 in three months isn't going to
eat me up. I don't like it, but it isn't going to eat me up. I can
come up with the $34,000.

"I don't know that much psychology but I believe that a
compulsive gambler who's getting close to fifty years old,
which I am, is supposed to have financial problems. I don't
have financial problems."

"Let me put something to you, Pete. Do you want to say,
as a supposed compulsive gambler, getting toward fifty,
you've got a lot of money? Do you have a lot of money?"

"Rog, I'm well fixed. As far as the money goes, I wouldn't
have to work another day for the rest of my life."

"Do you want to tell me what you have?"

Rose: "It's nobody's business what I have."

"Is it maybe the business, Pete, of the American people
who've read you're a compulsive gambler? Pete, get serious.
Half the country believes you're tapped out."

Rose: "Okay. I own two homes."

"You own a home in Indian Hills on four acres, am I right?"

Rose: "Five."

"You have five acres. You have quarter horses on the five acres."

Rose: "Right now I have riding horses. They're worth about $15,000."

"You have more cars than horses."

Rose: "I have two Porsches, two Mercedes, and a Rolls Royce."

"Plus a new house in Plant City, am I right?"

Rose: "A beautiful house on Polo Place, which is in the most elite part of town."

"You have a tennis court in Plant City?"

"Sure."

"That's the court you didn't invite me to play on this spring."

"It wasn't finished until after you left Florida."

"Am I missing something? Investments, whatever?"

Rose: "I've got to go back to saying what I believe, it's nobody's business what I have."

"Pete, everybody thinks you're in despair and downright broke."

Rose: "They're wrong on both counts."

Street lore says gamblers die broke. Rose does not fit the street-lore profile of a gambler.

But technical literature is more complex and enveloping. Addictive gamblers are described as being emotionally dependent on gambling, needing the pleasure of gambling. A short-term withdrawal, such as the one Rose describes in spring training, is regarded by clinicians as inconclusive.

A second aspect of addiction is the need always to bet bigger and bigger sums to get a so-called "gambling high." Rose denies betting more, except in relation to increases in his income. He sees a bigger bet as something like a more expensive car. He can afford it. Nobody is telling him to join Auto-owners Anonymous.

Finally, the betting of addictive gamblers by definition interferes with their lives. Betting certainly left Rose vulnerable to the people he calls "scabs." That he admits.

He is ready now to submit to a full clinical evaluation. Curiously, the commissioner's office, compassionate to ballplayers caught with cocaine, has not shown the slightest interest in an informed, impartial professional look at Rose's gambling. Instead there is righteous prattle about the sanctified authority of the commissioner of baseball.

"You went on something called Cable Value Network and you sold signed balls and what we Eastern elite types call bric-a-brac. The day you did that, people said, 'My God, the guy must be so bankrupt he has to go on this cheap cable network and sell some bats and balls. Some bats and balls, maybe his own.

"There's a pretty good writer, Frank Deford, who told Sam Donaldson, Diane Sawyer, and thirty million Americans that you selling stuff on Cable Value Network looked like a wino selling his blood. Pete, how could you do that for $10,000?"

Rose: "Rog, you think I did that for $10,000?"

"People tell me that you did."

Rose: "You believe them, you don't believe me?"

"You got more than $10,000?"

Rose: "Let me ask you a question. Let me ask a question of everybody who thought what I did was tacky.

"Rog, would you do what I did for $100,000? That's what I got paid. A few hours' work for $100,000. Tacky? How could anybody that knows me think I would go up to Minneapolis and do all that selling for $10,000?"

"That's been printed, Pete. It's been stated on television. People believe it."

Rose: "Four hours of work for $100,000, what do you call
that?"

"A fair day's work for a fair day's pay."

Rose: "Do you think Frank Deford would work four hours
for $100,000?

"I went up to Minneapolis and my goal was to beat the
Cable Value Network record. That's not Cobb. That's not
Ruth. But I'm a compulsive breaker of records.

"The old record up there was set by Reggie Jackson. He
did this CVN show for five hours and did $980,000 business.
Sold $980,000 worth of stuff.

"I did the same show for four hours—after I'm banned
from baseball—and I did $1.2 million. That's products sold.

"Reggie did the show. Willie Mays did it for two weeks.
Henry Aaron did it. Duke Snider worked the show. What a
bunch of blood-selling winos.

"How come I'm the only one who gets criticized?"

"Well, the published criticism was tougher than just that.
Carol has a baby. You miss managing a game. The baby is
born and—in the public perception—while Carol is suffering
in labor, you're out selling secondhand baseballs marked
Pete Rose."

Rose: "Listen: I signed this cable agreement in June. I'm
going to work this thing in August. I'm getting $100,000
for four hours, and my wife is going to have a baby in September.

"She happened to go into labor early. Now there's people,
I hear this too, who say that miserable Pete Rose left his
bleeding wife to go sell baseballs.

"Here's what happened. The Reds played a Monday night
game in Chicago. We won the ball game, 6–5.

"I got a call at the Westin Hotel in Chicago that my wife
was in labor. Carol's in early labor. Nothing urgent. Early
labor.

"I can't sleep. I get up at 4:00. I get out of bed and I catch a 5:30 A.M. plane to Cincinnati.

"At that hour there's no nonstop. I land at 7:30. I go straight to the hospital. I'm right by Carol's side.

"Carol has the baby at 1:45. A little girl, my second daughter. We named her Cara.

"I don't like to have to defend myself against garbage charges, but I'm telling you, Rog, I really participated in Cara's birth. After the baby was born, I cut the cord.

"There's something else I'll always remember. I don't want this to come out like I'm looking for sympathy. I'm not.

"But deep inside I was more worried about this birth than any of the others. I thought, this has been a terrible year for me and the Rose family generally. I was afraid all of a sudden the baby would be born deformed.

"After I cut the cord I counted all the baby's fingers and all of her toes. She was fine. I was sweating. That's how much I was *not* involved in the birth of my daughter.

"Now I guess we get to Minneapolis. My wife wanted to be alone after the birth because she was exhausted. So I go and fulfill my contract in Minneapolis to pick up the six-figure check.

"Tacky. This is tacky? I'm looking after my loved ones and making a living.

"This was the darkest day of my career. At 3:00 on August 23, I knew I was going to be unemployed the next day. I had signed the agreement with Giamatti.

"What do people want me to do, sit at home and cry about an agreement I had entered into?

"I have to go on with my life, don't I? Do I or don't I?"

"You do, Pete."

There is a certain perverse joy many get watching a hero fall. On a level beyond consciousness, many resent heroes. Millions, including members of the media, play the role of spellbound or even secretly gratified observer as a hero falls.

They may feel that a hero has let them down. Or, they may feel, when a hero falls: "I knew I was just as good as he was. In fact, I was better." Egalitarianism.

"Pete," I said, "a lot of Americans probably would have gotten satisfaction from a picture of you on television crying in a corner."

Rose: "I would have cried if this decision from Giamatti had been handed down to me. But I agreed to it. I signed an agreement. You don't cry when you agree to something, when you compromise. When you are sure you did the right thing.

"There is no written finding that I bet on baseball. I can apply for reinstatement next year. This is the best deal that I could get. I'm not crying."

"We're looking at tough questions, Pete."

Rose: "That's all right. Anyway, things like my dad, my money . . . hell, we'd rather be talking baseball . . . my stupid associations, they're not as tough for me as they would have been six months ago. Because if you've read what I've read the last six months, you'd have to believe I was one of the ten worst people in the world.

"So I *want* to get my side down. What seemed like tough stuff six months ago just bounces off me today.

"Like if you didn't know me and my family, Rog, you'd have to believe my children hate me.

"This writer, Pat Jordan, puts out a magazine story and he uses a quote that my daughter Fawn said when she was eleven years old. Fawn is twenty-three years old today.

"The quote is that I was the worst father in the world. Fawn said that when she was eleven. When I was getting divorced from my first wife I probably was the worst dad in the world in Fawn's eyes. But she's twenty-three now. We get along fine.

"She got a degree in psychology not so long ago. I was so proud of her because she is the first person in our family to

graduate from college. She wrote me a note saying she knew
I couldn't attend the graduation because the Reds were in St.
Louis. I surprised her by flying in Saturday morning, seeing
her graduate, then flying back Saturday night for our game.
Does that sound like a terrible relationship?

"You've been with me and young Pete, Rog. Does he act
like he doesn't like me? That's ridiculous."

"What has Petey been saying about the banishment?"

Rose: "He's a stud. He just says 'hang in there.' He's hitting
.295 [for Erie in the Class A New York–Penn League] and he
leads the league in almost everything except home runs. He's
had to put up with a lot of garbage this year. He's got to be
a stud to have gotten through that.

"Like Jordan writes there were times when Petey didn't
have my phone number. If he wanted to reach me he had to
get the number from Reuven Katz. You know when one of
those times is? Right now. I was getting so many nuisance
calls I had to change my number the other day.

"This has been going on for years. So I said to Petey, and
he understood, that when he wants me, and if, maybe, I
change my number, he can get the new number from
Reuven Katz, whose office is listed and whose home is listed
here in Cincinnati."

"Why wouldn't you just call over to Karolyn and give her
your new number?"

Rose: "It's hard. Every time I call Karolyn's house it's up-
setting. Sometimes she gives me a runaround. Sometimes she
gives me a lecture. I'm sorry about this but this is the truth.
I don't want to get caught in one of these long telephone
situations with her. So that's why Petey and I have the setup,
reach me through Reuven.

"Not like it comes out in the magazine that I'm such a big
deal my own son has to reach me through a lawyer's office."

*   *   *

Opinions and egos are the stuff of controversy. Fair enough. Poor reporting is something else: journalistic malpractice.

Rose: "Let me give you more stuff that is just plain wrong.

"There are stories that I sold one of my World Series rings to pay off gambling debts.

"There is a story that I gave a World Series ring to a bookie to settle a gambling debt.

"There is a story that I had to get a second mortgage on my house here to pay gambling debts.

"Every one of those stories is simply wrong. I helped a guy who I liked, Joe Cambria, to have a copy made of one of my Series rings. I gave him permission to order a ring which he paid for himself: $3,150. Isn't that a little different than paying off a bookie with a ring?

"A writer in spring training said: 'We understand you've taken out a second mortgage on your house to pay gambling debts.'

"I called Reuven Katz and I said, 'Do I have a second mortgage on my house?' Reuven said I did. When I won't be seeing him for a long period of time Reuven has me sign a lot of stuff. Reuven said, 'Remember those papers you signed last time? I told you one of them was for a second mortgage.'

"I didn't remember. I said, 'Where's the money?'

"Reuven said, 'The money is a line of credit, Pete. Your accountant wanted it available in case all of a sudden you needed cash. If you do, the interest is tax deductible.'

"We explained this to the media as clearly as we could. And what happens? There are more stories that I took out a second mortgage to pay a bookie.

"I've made my mistakes and I've accepted a pretty good hit for them. I've lost a job I loved."

"Now what's ahead?"

Rose: "I don't know what I'm going to do next year. I'm not interested in going to Japan. I might visit. I won't work there.

Two things I look forward to next year, if I'm still out of baseball, are watching the Indianapolis 500 and watching the Kentucky Derby. I've always been working on Derby day and on Indy day.

"Something else I'm going to do is watch Petey play ball. A lot.

"I've got so many things to sort out.

"I know about tomorrow. Tomorrow I'm taking [five-year-old] Tyler to the zoo."

It is extraordinary that my years with Rose should build to considerations of journalism, ethics, family ties, due process, just cause, and the life and death of a Renaissance scholar.

What the hell happened to second base?

It's still there, it always will be, the way we were one spring.

11

Fathers and Sons

PLANT CITY, FLORIDA, MARCH 1989

When Pete and I began voyaging together in what now seems so very long ago, we did not really know each other well. He recognized who I was, knew my Brooklyn roots and that some of my books had sold well. For myself, I had observed Rose, surely underestimated his measure in the early seasons, heard his chatter, seen his headfirst slides, and, like so many others, come to accept him as an American institution, but somewhat remote. We had not talked much one-on-one. We were no more than genial strangers. Then suddenly we found ourselves thrust into the intimacy of a collaboration which, to be worth our time or the time of readers, would have to go beyond such matters as pickoff plays and into sometimes painful details of Rose's extraordinary life.

So much has happened in these several years. Pete Rose stopped playing major league baseball. Pete Rose, Jr., began playing minor-league baseball. Pete has been suspended from the game.

As I started the book I had three children. Two survive. Whatever the adversity, one tries to prevail.

Now of Pete I remember lines composed by John Kieran

to help a great Yankee team say farewell to Lou Gehrig, who
was young and strong and dying:

> *We've been to the wars together,*
> *We took our luck as it came.*

Pete and I know each other well; I feel considerable admiration for him. He is indeed an American institution. On the
whole, he deserves to be one.

Rose's tough, competitive core is rough-hewn granite that
will always be, as today, the stuff of legend. Quite apart from
that, on a scale that may seem smaller but surely is no less
important, shines his compassion.

One day, during the 1986 season, Buddy Bell, who played
third base for the Reds before the arrival of young, fiery Chris
Sabo, knocked at the door of Rose's office. Bell is a soft-voiced
man, handsome, fair haired, and restrained. A year earlier
Bell's wife Gloria gave birth to their fifth child, a girl the Bells
named Traci. Traci Bell was born suffering from Down's
syndrome.

Bell mentioned that doctors had just discovered a dysfunc-
tion in the infant's heart. The next day Traci would undergo
open-heart surgery. Bell was asking if he could miss a game.
Would it be all right with the skipper if he took tomorrow off?

"Buddy," Pete said, "you don't have tomorrow off. You
have off for as long as you want. You look after your little girl.
I'll worry about the pennant race." Rose's look, not quite a
smile, was alive with concern. He reached across his desk and
patted Bell's arm.

Two days later Bell was back in the clubhouse. "The surgery went well," he said. "Traci's going to be all right."

"Long operation?" I asked.

"Five hours," Bell said. He puffed air through his cheeks.

"Gloria and I were out there waiting for five hours before we got word."

"Well, the doctors came through for you and Pete came through for you."

Pete had met my second son, Roger Laurence Kahn, in the spring of that year, 1986. Or Roger had met Pete Rose. Roger was a good high-school baseball player and a high-scoring lineman in hockey until he discovered Topanga Canyon and California girls. By 1986, he was a junior at UCLA.

The Reds were still training in Tampa and Roger followed me onto the field at Redsland, under a hot spring sky, wearing a sweatshirt that proclaimed: Prop. UCLA Athletic Department. Rose was chattering near the batting cage. "This your boy?" he said. "How you doing, son?" Rose poked a finger at Roger's stout chest and said, "UCLA. That's the University of California at Los Angeles, am I right?"

"Right," Roger said. He was twenty. His tone sounded patronizing.

"Miller, Jackson, Haley, Hatcher, and Richardson," Rose said. "If I'm not mistaken, that's the starting five, the UCLA basketball team."

He was dead right. Roger looked startled. He had underestimated Pete Rose. Later Roger said to his mother, in a youthful inversion, "I don't think he was too impressed with me."

In fact, Pete enjoyed bantering with Roger and asked me later what kind of athlete Roger was, what kind of student. I mentioned Roger's academic achievements and his hockey. Pete was indeed impressed. He wondered why anyone who liked playing hockey that much would move to southern California. I wondered the same thing myself.

Now, in August, the telephone rang at a small apartment I had taken in Cincinnati, and Roger began a confusing story. He was in Westwood Hospital for drug rehabilitation, he said.

I had not known Roger was using drugs. "Heroin," he said. "You know I sniff it. I play in this fast-pitch softball league and one of the Los Angeles Lakers turned me on."

"You sniff heroin?" Incredulity!

"Sure, but I'm in rehab. I turned in this pusher. He got away from the police. He's coming after me with a gun. And this hospital says that unless you give them $7,000 for me right now, they're throwing me out into the street. If that happens, I'm a dead man. If that happens, you have a dead son."

Some of what Roger said was so. The insurance company behind the UCLA health plan insisted that Roger's heroin use was a long-standing condition. Lone Star Insurance refused to meet his hospital bill. The story about the pusher was probably fiction. Whatever, Roger was in a dangerous situation and I had better fly to California to help him.

In the Reds locker room, I stopped for a moment to talk to Dave Parker, the 230-pound right fielder who had spent time himself in drug rehabilitation. "Can you actually sniff heroin?" I asked.

Parker took the question as an accusation and began blabbering in anger.

"Not to write, Dave. It's in my family."

"Oh, sorry," said this gigantic, wounded man. "Yeah, you can sniff that stuff. It's the worst there is. You get a quick high. It makes your nose go crazy. I got a T-shirt here. Dave Parker: Say no to drugs. Give it to the kid. But I'll be straight with you. Kicking heroin is tougher than kicking cocaine."

Into the lime-green office, closing the door behind me. Rose was making out a lineup card. "I have to leave you for a little while, Pete. Roger's in drug rehab. I better go to California."

Rose continued to work on the lineup. He did not look up

as he said, "Tell him to get off the pot and get high on your books."

"This seems serious, Pete. The kid has been messing with heroin."

Rose put down his pen and I saw the same sad, almost smiling look—concern, perhaps alarm—that had touched Buddy Bell.

"Sure," Pete said. "Go out there, then, and tell him I said hello, if that'll help. Fly well. You can handle this. You're strong. Whenever you get back here, I'll do everything I can to make the book easy for you."

And so Pete did.

Roger rallied through rehabilitation. "What's the prognosis?" I asked a young California psychiatrist named Greg Sawyer.

"I don't envy you the next two years."

Greg Sawyer, who was wearing sneakers and an open-collared shirt, was accurate as a sharpshooter's bullet.

On July 7, 1987, in the intensive-care room at Las Robles Hospital in Thousand Oaks, California, Roger died. He had these strong hockey player's hands, graced by a braiding of dark hair. Even as he died, the hands looked strong. Strong, well-remembered, motionless.

Roger felt he had been driven hopelessly into debt by heroin. He wrote me a farewell letter which began: "After twenty-two years in the amusement park, this roller coaster isn't fun any more, so I'm getting off the ride."

I don't believe I'd wept for thirty years. Lose a son and you discover your own tears. Poor Roger. Sweet bloody Roger. I had bought a coffin for my father. Now I would have to bury my tortured son.

The funeral service on Martha's Vineyard was presided over by a Roman Catholic priest. Roger's mother said the priest was wonderful with children and she would ask him to recite the Twenty-third Psalm.

The Lord is my shepherd;
I shall not want.
He maketh me to lie down in green pastures.

Those words start this towering psalm, as most of us have known it. I heard each word throughout the porches of my brain and thought, or fantasized, Good. Sufficient. Surely the blood of King David coursed through Roger when he was quick and warm.

The gentle priest recited:

Yahweh is my shepherd,
I lack nothing.
In grassy meadows
He lets me lie.

Indignation tore my heart. Who dares edit the King James version of a psalm of David? But the spirit, the spirit, that was what to take away. My boy was gone now. Soon he was laid in sandy soil, above a windblown wetland, to lie unmoving there, silent for eternity.

I flew home and the telephone rang at 12:30 that night. "Rog, this is Pete. I heard. I'm sorry. That the boy I met?"

"Yes. The boy you met in spring training."

"I'll tell you this. You haven't lost him. He's up there in the sky right now and he's playing catch with my dad."

Pete Rose's consolation overwhelmed me. I wept and then apologized for weeping.

"What are you apologizing for?" said gruff and mighty Peter Edward Rose. "When my dad died I sat in my room and I cried for three days."

There would be a memorial service in Manhattan at the meeting house of the Society of Friends. Roger's mother came from generations of Pennsylvania Quakers. "I'll be there," Rose said. "I don't know how I'll get there, but I'll come."

When Pete arrived at the meeting house, I explained a Quaker service. "Anybody here may speak. You just stand and say whatever is in your heart."

Pete wore a dark suit. He looked stricken. "I wouldn't know what to say." Rose can talk to presidents and all the swarming press. That is a special pride of his, like his bat speed. I had never before heard him suggest, much less come out and state, that he wouldn't know what to say at any time.

"You can talk about whatever you want. Youth. Drugs. Baseball. Anything."

Pete looked pained. "Is it all right if I just sit in the back and be quiet?"

A pianist played a poignant work by Schubert. Someone read the Twenty-third Psalm in the version we remember. Peter Malkin, the Israeli warrior who captured Adolf Eichmann, spoke Kaddish, the ancient Hebrew monotheistic prayer for the dead. Some others talked and then, since Roger was a child of the twentieth century, the pianist played a stirring work by Shostakovich.

Only two people from baseball came on that warm July morning to comfort our stricken family. One was Mrs. Jackie Robinson. The other was Peter Edward Rose.

Baseball's representatives were not numerous. But we had the very best.

Life renews itself if you can be patient and find, along with grief, the quality of courage within yourself. When the spring of 1989 came round, I flew to Florida for a few more days with Pete. The Reds had moved their spring training site from Tampa to a quiet village, some twenty-five miles inland, called Plant City. The team has a fine facility there, four diamonds, including a lovely new ballpark that seats 6,700 people. Plant City is a somnolent place, looking as Florida villages did forty years ago. Roadside stands sell baskets of strawberries, $1.50 a huge flat, large red strawberries, ambrosia to the tongue. The town is proud of an annual event called the Strawberry Festival and proud also to be the spring base of the Reds.

The team crackled with energy. On one field, Barry Larkin, Chris Sabo, Kal Daniels, and Eric Davis took batting practice, jockeying in baseball's immemorial manner. Larkin cracked some line drives and said, "I may hit third this year." This solid young shortstop batted .296 in 1988.

"In what," Eric Davis said, "an old-timers' game?"

Davis went into the cage. The cyclone fence behind the left center-field alley was almost 400 feet away. Some distance beyond the fence rose a tan metal building. Davis, who stands six-foot-three but weighs no more than 185 pounds, began cracking drives of phenomenal proportions. The ball climbed the sky, a golf shot, a rocket launch. The baseball rose and rose and carried and carried, very long home runs.

As the drives soared, Davis made small cries. "Roof," he said, "Roof." None of his wallops landed on the building roof. Five *cleared* the roof. Davis was hitting the baseball 500 feet.

Rose wandered from batters to pitchers, talking to players, to coaches, not so much a friendly sergeant as a friendly colonel, who knew he had a regiment of talent.

When we retired to his office, Rose said, "I don't know how you got through what you did, your boy taking his life. I don't think I'd have the strength myself."

"I pray you never have to have it."

Rose put an arm on my shoulder. The press was gathering and it was time to go to work. Pete Rose was ready.

"I just was figuring I got about a fortieth of my hits off the Niekros," he began. "About seventy off Phil and thirty off Joe. Damn, I wish Mrs. Niekro had had triplets."

Big Bill Staubitz, Associated Press reporter and sometime

bailiff, first saw Rose as a catcher playing for Western Hills High School during the 1950s.

"Big," Rose said to Staubitz, "if I give you any more quotes, are you gonna get 'em right?"

"I always get them right," Staubitz said.

"You never get 'em right. Got a tape recorder on you?"

Staubitz, huge, genial, baldheaded, opened his jacket. A recorder was tucked under his belt.

"That thing turned on?" Rose said.

"Sure it's turned on," Staubitz said.

"Got any batteries in it?" Rose said. The room sounded with laughter. Rose as Prince Hal. Staubitz as Falstaff.

"You know who made this game, who made baseball," Rose said. "Babe Ruth. He's the man who put the people in the ballparks. Thank God for Babe Ruth. If Babe Ruth had been a soccer player we wouldn't be here.

"I got a dog story for you," Rose said. "One time we went on a road trip and Pedro Borbon, who used to pitch for us, had this dog, a mutt. Borbon was thinking very hard. He was going to be away fourteen days. So he bought fourteen bags of dog food and took off and locked the door to his apartment. Can you imagine what the place looked like when Borbon got back? Damn dog not only ate the dog food, he ate the leather off the furniture, too. And you know what Borbon had been thinking. Fourteen bags of dog food. Fourteen days. The dog will eat one bag a day. Nobody told Borbon that the dog didn't know how to read a menu."

"Borbon helped you in that fight with Buddy Harrelson," someone said. "He got out there pretty quick."

"I know," Rose said. "I hear about it every spring. Borbon is always looking for a job in baseball and every year he calls and tells me I should hire him because he helped me in the fight.

"Here's a hair story. The Reds have this rule, no facial hair.

The players can't wear mustaches or beards. Hell, we're lucky they let us keep our eyebrows. In 1984, I said, 'It seems kind of strange to me that the best starter in the league, Rick Sutcliffe, 20-and-6, and the best reliever, Bruce Sutter, couldn't pitch for my team because they have beards.' Doesn't make sense to me. I often wonder what the Reds would do if every one of the players took the rule a little further and came to the ballpark one day, completely shaved, every last player, every one looking like Yul Brynner.

"The Reds went so far in '82 that they traded for Jim Kern, a pitcher with Cleveland. Kern had a beard and they put his picture in the yearbook, but not until the press guy painted out the beard. Painted the damn beard out of the damn yearbook. Then, of course, they made Kern shave it. He didn't win a game in Cincinnati.

"What the hell is wrong with wearing a beard? You want your players not to be maniacs. You want them to bust tail during the ball games. You want them to dress nice and comb their hair. But what the hell is wrong with a beard?

"Abe Lincoln wore a fucking beard.

"You getting the quotes right, Big, cleaning them up? How ya doing, Big? It looks like we got a pretty good team."

"Reds gonna win it?" someone said.

"That's a brilliant question. How do I know whether we're gonna win it? Five teams could win it. Who's gonna win it? That's what we play the season to find out."

Although Rose sometimes sleeps late after night games, his spring-training days begin almost at first light. He suggested breakfast the next day at a Plant City restaurant called Buddy Freddy's.

"Buddy Freddy's."

"That's it. This isn't New York. They soft-boil eggs very good."

During dinner in downtown Plant City, a perky, button-

nosed waitress, who said her name was Kelly, served with
good cheer. She had lived all her years in the Plant City area,
Kelly said. She was married and getting divorced. She had a
baby. Money was a problem. A waitress by night, she drove
an auto parts delivery truck starting up at 8:00 A.M., five days
a week.

None of this was said in a whining way. Kelly was a lively
woman of twenty, bearing up amid difficulty. She was
thrilled to report that she had served dinner to three or four
major league ballplayers.

"Have you met Pete Rose?" I said.

"No. I've seen him."

"If you'd like his autograph, come to Buddy Freddy's restaurant at 7:45. I'll see what I can do."

The next morning Kelly appeared, prompt and nervous. I
repeated some of her story to Rose. "See that Porsche outside?" Pete asked. "It isn't locked. There's a small box in the
back. Open it and take a baseball. I'll sign it for you."

When Kelly returned, her face aglow, Rose said, "It's very
important that you have a good lawyer."

"I go to legal aid," Kelly said.

"Get yourself the best lawyer you can afford," Rose said. "If
there's any violence, any threats of violence, remember, you
don't have to let him in the house."

In the trying days of the paternity suit and the divorce, late
in the 1970s, Rose had come under fire as a chauvinist. Anyone listening to his earnest counsel to the button-nosed Plant
City waitress named Kelly might have taken him for chair-
person of the Cincinnati chapter of NOW. Or, perhaps, as
Kelly's concerned uncle.

This cool March day would be Pete's last with his son for a
long time. Petey was going off to Sarasota to report at the
Baltimore Orioles' camp for minor leaguers. Petey is taller
than his father, almost six-foot-two, a good-looking boy and

suddenly very appealing. I say suddenly because at River-front Stadium, where Petey put in seven years as a batboy, mostly he was silent.

"We've had a good month," the father said. "He's been living down here with me. We've had a very good month."

"The best time we've ever had together," Petey said.

"I gave him batting clinics," Pete said.

"And good ones," Petey said.

Aside from Rose's managerial seat, there was only one other chair in the office, a large, badly frayed black leather swivel, that may well have been the property of the original Cincinnati Red Stockings. A young black sat in the swivel chair. His name was Arthur Rhodes and he was a pitcher. He would be Petey's roommate at the Orioles farm hands' spring motel.

Arthur had shown courage in taking the chair. The rest of us had either to stand or sit on the floor. But, in the presence of Pete Rose, Arthur was not up to making conversation. He sat in the chair, trying to wear his game face. Awe shone through.

"Remember, Petey," Rose said to his son, "when you hit the ball, grit your teeth."

"Dad, can I borrow your pen?"

Petey took a black pen and began lettering inside the bill of his baseball cap.

"Let's see that," I said.

Petey had printed: "Grit your teeth."

Then, with the faintest suggestion of a smile, Petey took his own bat and began to letter on the round top of the light wood. He lettered a magic number: 4,192. One more hit than Ty Cobb.

Father and son grinned at each other and Petey excused himself to go to a batting cage and try one hundred more swings, gritting his teeth.

"I thought working out with the Reds in early camp would help him," Rose said, "but, damn, baseball is a funny business. They told me that would be tampering so, can you believe it, I had to get special permission from the commissioner of baseball to have my own son work for a few weeks with my team.

"Petey was offered a baseball scholarship in California and he was thinking of taking it, but he had a great summer of American Legion ball. He hit .435 with seventeen homers for the Buddy Post in Cincinnati. His team won the national Legion championship at Middletown, Connecticut. Then the Orioles made an offer.

"I know some people here with the Reds were thinking of trying to sign Petey. But then they seemed to get the idea that it would put too much pressure on him and me, having another Pete Rose in the organization. Far as I know Petey can take pressure fine and the situation wouldn't have bothered me at all. I mean, if I was filling my roster and I had to pick between Petey and another kid, be sure Petey would have to be a whole hell of a lot better before he was the one I picked."

"That could be pressure then," I said, "on both of you."

"I'm just happy he's signed to play pro," Rose said. "I started pitching to him as soon as Petey could hold a bat. Never underhand. I didn't want the ball coming in on an arc. I always threw overhand. One day, I musta been a little wild. Petey was no more than two years old. I'm high. I'm low, I'm outside. Petey, two years old, yells at me, 'Hey, Dad, get that crap over the plate!' "

I had seldom seen and felt Rose more relaxed, which may say something about Pete, as the milestone of fifty nears, or say something about the two of us. Rex Bowen, a distinguished, white-haired senior scout for the Reds, goes back in baseball for more than half a century. "Pete is maturing as a manager and as a person," Bowen said. "It's remarkable how much he's matured over the last two years."

"You're having fun," I said to Rose at Plant City Stadium.

"And not only around the ballpark. You've seen all that stuff about Wade Boggs and the lady, Margo Adams. Wade's a fine, fine player, and he's a friend of mine, but Margo Adams hitting him with a palimony suit like that. Wade must have handled that wrong.

"So I got to do this banquet with Wade the other night and you know there are vultures around. So somebody says that Wade Boggs has really been hurt by this sex scandal.

"My turn. I tell them they have it wrong. Wade isn't hurt. He's just banged up.

"You just have to be so careful when you're a public figure. There's the one paternity suit that got my name in bad headlines. Somebody else tried. She never made the papers.

"I gave this woman a lift from Columbus to Cincinnati. Drove her in my car, dropped her off, that's all.

"Next thing, she gets herself pregnant, God knows with whom. Her lawyer calls Reuven Katz and says that I'm the father.

"I've had enough. I'll meet her at a hospital for blood tests.

"She never showed. They were just taking a run at me. Happens all the time.

"This woman says I got her pregnant and I never even slept with her.

"You know me, Rog. I'm not that lazy."

Don Buford was supervising the Orioles' minor-league training at Twin Lakes Park in Sarasota. He is white haired, well spoken, and small for an athlete, perhaps five-foot-seven, but in three World Series with Baltimore, Buford hit four home runs.

He mentioned that 125 minor-league players were in his

charge, from the best prospects, who would play Triple A baseball, to near novices, just out of high school, who would play in rookie leagues, if they played anywhere at all.

I mentioned that I had run a minor-league team, the Utica Blue Sox, in 1983, and that I'd had to keep reminding myself that the drill was baseball first and group therapy second.

Buford smiled. "Or maybe the other way around," he said.

Petey was on diamond three, fielding ground balls at third base. You could see he has sure hands. Batting practice was less than overwhelming. Many of the younger players are still adjusting from aluminum bats to wood. Major league batting practice pitchers are hired to throw strikes. The young minor-league pitchers were having trouble this early March day getting their fastballs over the plate.

Young Pete bats left-handed. He does not switch. He hit some hard line drives to right and right-center. Afterward we sat in a deserted section of the bleachers.

"I notice they gave you number 82," I said. "Would you like to wear number 14, like Dad?"

"I don't think so," Petey said. "I don't want to end up with 82, but I don't want 14 either. I love number 14, but I want my own identity."

"Do you get kidded about your name?"

"Not here," Petey said, "or anyway not yet. One time in Cincinnati I was playing for a team called Tyra Trucking. That day I was pitching. They really got on me, even from the batter's box. 'So this is the great Pete Rose. He's not so great.' Stuff like that.

"Dad was there. He heard what was going on. He said, 'Look, as soon as the batter starts blabbing at you, here's what to do. Quick-pitch him. His mouth will be working and the ball will be by him for a strike.' That worked out."

"What was the name of the loudmouth team?"

"I remember that very well," Petey said. "The other team was called Satisfying Concrete."

"There were some stories," I said, "where you seem to be criticizing number 14 as a father."

"That isn't what I mean," Petey said. "Dad knows what I mean. I mean that I missed him a lot.

"I don't remember much before 1979. There was a batting cage for me in the yard. A few things like that. Just sort of pictures. But from 1979, I really remember. Dad and Mom were getting divorced that year and Dad had to go to Philadelphia. The divorce hurt. It hurt a lot. And then count the years, 1979, 1980, 1981, 1982, 1983, Dad wasn't playing for the Reds. It was like I never saw him. Dad had disappeared."

"Were you lonely?"

"Mom did a good job. I wasn't lonely. I missed my dad."

Petey looks directly at you when he speaks, this handsome, rangy boy, an exemplar of sincerity.

"You know what I wish?" he said. "I wish that once, just once, I could have seen Mom and Dad sitting together watching me play ball. That never happened. I guess it never will.

"So that's what I really mean. Not that he's a bad dad."

"And he did spend time with you," I said. "I watched him pitch batting practice to you one day. You hit a line drive up the middle. Your dad turned and you caught him over a kidney."

A quick smile. "You were there," Petey said. "That's right. And then Dad threw at me."

"You were brushed back by your own father?"

"No. Not brushed back. Dad drilled me. In the ribs." A slower smile. "After he got back to Cincinnati, then we've had some good, fun times. I even asked the Orioles if I could live with Dad at Plant City and commute down here to Sarasota. It's not a bad drive, but they told me no.

"People ask, Did I want to play for the Reds? Look, if I'd

grown up in Kansas and there was a team the Kansas Tigers, then I'd want to be a Kansas Tiger. But this is fine being here. More than fine. Even with number 82. Just give me a uniform and a glove, and I'm pretty happy.

"Besides, a lot of people think I just got signed because of my name. Dad's name, that is. So it could be for the best I'm in another organization."

I mentioned the night of September 11, 1985, at Riverfront Stadium. "When all the people were cheering and Cobb's record was gone and you had an arm around your father, your own father was crying in your arms, weren't you close to crying yourself?"

"I mighta been. But I wasn't."

"Why not?"

"Dad always told me that crying was sissy."

The boy was growing up and his dad was growing up and, slight foreshadowing of dread, you had to hope that all of this was in time, and the father finding the son and the son at last finding the father in a place called Plant City in the spring of 1989 was not happening too late.

"You remember what your dad told you at the Reds' camp?"

"Want to see my Orioles cap?" Petey said. He took off the orange cap and turned it over so I could see the inside of the bill.

At the center Petey had inked P.R. "That's not my dad," he said. "That's me." On the left side, there appeared his father's counsel: "Grit Your Teeth." On the right side Petey had printed something of his own: "Hit the Shit Out of the Ball."

We laughed. A coach shouted, "Better get in with the other guys, Petey. You don't want to miss lunch."

"You got enough?" Petey asked.

"For now," I said. "We'll talk some more."

"I'd like that," Petey said.

He stood to his full height, six feet one and a half, and adjusted his hand-inked Baltimore cap and began jogging toward the mess hall, a young ballplayer, in a prime of youth and sinew, jogging through sunlight on spikes, gliding and soundless, cruising fresh-cut grass.

He stopped suddenly and turned. "Good luck with the book," Pete Rose, Jr., called. We waved and he returned to jogging; another Rose was making his way into baseball and the world.

"That's a boy to be proud of," I said to Pete, back with Eric Davis and the rest at Plant City. "He's doing fine."

"I wish we could say the same about your boy," Rose said. It runs so deep, this triad, baseball and fathers and sons. "After I lost Roger," I said to Rose, "whenever I'd see a good young athlete, I'd feel a knife of sadness. Nothing against the athlete. Just why did Roger have to play the end game with himself. With Petey, this is the first time since the death that I've been able to see a young athlete and just feel good, without the sadness."

"That's something for me to hear," Pete said.

"No matter how much you love somebody," I said, "you don't want to be carrying that so far that you feel you have to die because he died. We both loved our fathers. We've gone on."

Pete paused. We were not being glib. "I had a funny relationship with my own father," he said. "A lot of guys, when their dad passes away, they just try to forget about it, you know?

"I look at my dad's death like this: Sure, I miss him. He was a great guy, gave me everything I am, but I repaid Dad in some respects. He went to ten straight spring trainings and saw me there. He got to see me win the batting title in '68 and '69. He got to see me play in the World Series in 1970.

That's a part of the relationship I keep burned into my mind.

"You can't forget your dad passed away. You don't want to forget. And you can't spend the rest of your life crying. I'm going on. Petey's going on. I'm sorry about your boy but you're going on. Obviously."

Pete Rose's face was neither boyish now nor grim. It was the face of a grown man coming into sight of his fiftieth birthday.

"There's nothing really that special about me," Rose said. "All I am is my own father, going on with life in a different generation, and given more opportunity.

"Come on, Rog. Let's watch the ballplayers."

We walked out into the morning. It was one of those days that has a glow to it like love, one of those days when you want to live two hundred years.

Two hundred years.

Yes.

At the very least.

Index

Aaron, Hank, 109, 146, 194, 265
Allen, Lee, 50
Allen, Richie, 116
All-Star Games, 91, 119, 124;
  1970, 26, 133–135
Alou, Matty, 126, 127
American Association, 86
Anderson, Sparky, 12, 31, 35–36,
  44, 120, 130–132, 136,
  146–147, 156, 157, 169–170,
  171, 176, 201
Appalachian League, 66, 86
Arbitration, 167–169
Armbrister, Ed, 172
Atlanta Braves, 101, 197, 202

Backman, Wally, 55
Baltimore Orioles, 137–138, 182,
  226, 281, 282, 283, 284
Bando, Sal, 151
Barnett, Larry, 172
Barnicle, Mike, 172
Barrow, Ed, 143
Baseball Hall of Fame, 7, 48, 71,
  185, 235
Basketball, 47, 152, 232, 236
Batting championships: 1968,
  126–127; 1969, 127–128; 1973,
  155

Bell, Buddy, 272–273
Bench, Johnny, 115, 121, 125,
  133, 136, 138, 146, 148, 151,
  153, 155, 165, 171, 176, 177,
  181, 185, 225, 236
Bender, Chief, 5, 121, 132,
  142–145, 180
Bergesch, Bill, 40
Berra, Yogi, 158
Betting on baseball, 75–76;
  history of, 50–51; 1989
  gambling charges, 12, 224,
  231–270
Biles, Eddie, 82–83
Black, Joe, 115
Blacks in baseball, 7, 108–109,
  163, 212
Blanco, Damaso, 118
Blasingame, Don, 104–107
Bloebaum, Buddy, 82, 89, 93,
  116, 125
Blue, Vida, 151
Boggs, Wade, 284
Borbon, Pedro, 156, 279
Boston Braves, 95
Boston Globe, 170, 172, 200
Boston Red Sox, 30, 169–175,
  179, 202
Boswell, Thomas, 196

Bouton, Jim, 25
Bowa, Larry, 227
Bowen, Rex, 283–284
Boxing, 63–64, 72–73
Boyer, Ken, 116
Boyle, Buzz, 81
Brennaman, Marty, 230, 251
Brinkman, Chuck, 80
Brinkman, Eddie, 80, 81, 89
Bristol, Dave, 97, 99, 101–102,
   125, 127, 130
Brock, Lou, 116
Brooklyn Atlantics, 52, 53
Brooklyn Dodgers, 48, 52,
   95–96, 109, 122, 130, 168
Brown, Paul, 132, 170–171
Browning, Tom, 37
Buford, Don, 284–285
Burick, Si, 149
Busch, Gussie, 203–204

Cable Value Network, 264–265
California Angels, 202
Campanella, Roy, 29
Capra, Buzz, 156
Carbo, Bernie, 173
Carew, Rod, 221
Carey, Max, 17
Carlton, Steve, 36, 227
Carolina League, 86
Carpenter, Ruly, 204–206
Carroll, Jerry, 254
Cars and car racing, 3–4, 90, 99,
   270
Cepeda, Orlando, 249
Champion, Aaron B., 48, 50, 52
Chass, Murray, 233
Chicago Cubs, 48, 143, 195
Chicago White Sox, 106, 192
Cincinnati, Ohio, 3, 9, 17–18,
   45–46, 75, 111–112, 140
Cincinnati Bengals, 64, 132,
   170–171
Cincinnati Daily Gazette, 49,
   50, 51
Cincinnati Enquirer, 12, 17,
   149, 189, 191, 248

Cincinnati Post, 12, 132, 139,
   144, 183–184, 187, 189, 191,
   246–247
Cincinnati Reds, 45–46, 81, 101;
   championships of 1970s,
   145–146; farm system, 86–102;
   1963, 104–112, 215; 1964,
   114–117; 1965, 118–119; 1966,
   119–121, 124, 125; 1967, 125,
   128; 1968, 125, 126; 1969,
   130; 1970, 132–138; 1971,
   142–145; 1972, 148–152; 1973,
   155–160; 1974, 164; 1975, 30,
   169–175; 1976, 30–31, 53,
   176–177, 223–224; 1977, 183,
   187, 191–192; 1978, 193–200;
   1985, 34–38; 1987, 8; 1989,
   237, 260, 277–278, 280;
   opening day customs, 17;
   playing style, 30–31;
   purchased by Marge Schott,
   12; Rose comes from minors
   to, 102, 103; Rose first signs
   with, 81–82, 89; Rose
   manages, 8, 10–14, 55–56, 71,
   78, 213, 229, 272–284; Rose
   negotiates contracts with, 5,
   10, 27, 32–33, 121–124, 132,
   143–145, 153–154, 160,
   181–194, 200–201; Rose
   plays for, 9–10, 27, 30–38,
   53, 61, 102–201; Rose
   re-signs with, 32–34; Rose
   traded from, 9–10, 27–28,
   67, 204–207
Cincinnati Red Stockings, 17,
   47–53
Clemente, Roberto, 109,
   127–128, 133, 137, 146, 147,
   150, 194
Cleveland Browns, 42
Cline, Ty, 137
Cobb, Ty, 7, 17, 21–24, 32, 194,
   196, 250; Rose breaks hitting
   record of, 7, 10, 12, 24, 37–38,
   287; Rose on, 23–25, 26–27,
   35, 149

Commercials, 148, 154–155, 203
Concepcion, Dave, 148
Contracts. *See* Salaries and
    contract negotiations
Crosley Field, 128–129, 130

Dale, Francis L., 121
Daley, Arthur, 156
Daniels, Kal, 55–56, 278
Dash, Samuel, 248
Davis, Eric, 278
Dayton Daily News, 149, 189
DeBenedetti, Reno, 91, 92
Denny, John, 36
Dernier, Bob, 33
Desselle, Tommy, 149
Dietz, Dick, 133
DiMaggio, Joe, 27, 113, 123, 143,
    167, 179, 192, 195–197
Doubles, 97, 123, 164, 209, 225;
    career record, 29, 123, 201
Dowd, John, 234, 238–248, 250–
    252
Dowd Report, 238–248,
    251–252; discrepancies in,
    243–248
Driessen, Dan, 7, 180, 192
Drugs, 221–222, 257, 264, 274
Drysdale, Don, 109
Durocher, Leo, 96
Durso, Joseph, 206
Dyer, Duffy, 156

Eastern League, 86
Eastwick, Rawley, 216
Ellis, Dock, 137
Epstein, Mike, 151
Erardi, John, 135
Errors, 91, 93, 95, 120
Esasky, Nick, 229
Esquire magazine, 164
Estes, Scott, 242
Evans, Dwight, 171

Fastball, 195
Feeney, Chub, 157–158, 160
Ferguson, Jim, 130

Fielding, 91–92, 95, 96, 137,
    147, 164, 228
Fimrite, Ron, 175
Fingers, Rollie, 151
Finley, Charles, 150–151, 167
Fisher, Cherokee, 50
Fisk, Carlton, 172, 173
Fitzgerald, Ray, 200
Florida State League, 87, 96
Football, 14, 43, 64–65, 76,
    77–80, 140, 169, 170–171, 232,
    236–237, 254
Ford, Whitey, 9
Fosse, Ray, 26, 133–135, 137
Foster, George, 7, 146, 150, 169
Free agency, 32, 122, 143,
    146, 166–169, 180, 182–183,
    190
Friend, Bob, 24, 27, 124
Fry, Michael, 239, 242
Fryman, Woodie, 180
Furillo, Carl, 129

Gaharin, John, 167
Galbreath, John, 204
Gambling charges (1989), 12,
    224, 231–270; Dowd Report,
    238–248, 251–252; Rose on,
    248–270
Gammons, Peter, 170
Garber, Gene, 197–198
Garrett, Wayne, 156, 160
Garvey, Steve, 38
Gehrig, Lou, 179, 272
Geneva Red Legs, 89–95
Geronimo, Cesar, 146, 169, 171,
    172
Giamatti, A. Bartlett, 157,
    229–230, 231; and 1989
    gambling charges, 224,
    231–239, 241, 250–259, 266,
    267; and Rose's thirty-day
    suspension, 230
Gibson, Bob, 109, 116, 127
Giles, Bill, 28, 205–206
Giusti, Dave, 150
Gold Gloves, 146

Golf, 47, 161–162

Gooden, Dwight, 8

Gossage, Goose, 248, 249

Gould, Charlie, 48

Grant, M. Donald, 158

Griesser, Ralph, 79

Griffey, Ken, 169, 171

Grote, Jerry, 158

Gullickson, Bill, 35

Harmon, Pat, 139–140, 145

Harrelson, Bud, 26, 155–160, 163–164

Havlicek, John, 161–162

Heffner, Don, 119, 125

Helms, Tommy, 15, 38, 56, 97, 98–99, 120, 126, 128, 145

Hermanski, Gene, 122

Hershiser, Orel, 13, 14, 35, 58–59

Hertzel, Bob, 149

Hickman, Jim, 133

Hoard, Greg, 17

Holmes, Tommy, 196

Holtzman, Ken, 151

Hornsby, Rogers, 149

Horses and horse racing, 3, 18–19, 110–111, 204, 254–255, 270

Houston Astros, 13–14, 16, 35, 145

Howsam, Robert, 31–34, 128, 130, 142–145, 152–153, 158, 160, 180, 181, 188–189

Hoyt, Waite, 24–25, 136

Hunter, Catfish, 30, 133, 151, 167

Hutchinson, Fred, 43, 44, 102, 105–107, 110, 116–118

Jackson, Reggie, 151, 182, 192, 265

Jallow, Norm, 93

Janszen, Paul, 238, 239, 242–247, 255–259

Japan, 11, 269

Johnson, Howard, 229

Jordan, Pat, 267, 268

Kaline, Al, 137

Kansas City Royals, 202, 203, 225, 226

Katz, Reuven, 11, 12, 19, 27, 29–32, 43, 166, 167, 169, 181, 183, 185–186, 189, 193–194, 200–206, 238, 250, 257, 268

Kauffman, Ewing, 203

Keeler, Wee Willie, 195, 196

Kern, Jim, 280

Klemesrud, Judy, 164–165

Kluszewski, Ted, 156

Knothole Ball, 74

Kolb, Gary, 118

Koosman, Jerry, 155

Koufax, Sandy, 109, 116

Kuhn, Bowie, 168, 182

Lanier, Hal, 127

Larkin, Barry, 229, 278

Larsen, Don, 174

Lasorda, Tom, 35

Lawson, Earl, 107, 136, 144, 183–184, 191

Lee, Bill, 170–173

Lieber, Jill, 234–235, 260

Littell, Mark, 226

Los Angeles Dodgers, 14, 34, 35, 58–59, 115, 164, 167, 168, 181, 192, 202

Los Angeles Times, 135

Lum, Mike, 193

Lynn, Fred, 173

McCovey, Willie, 109, 118, 133

McDonald, Bill, 92

McEnaney, Will, 180

McNally, Dave, 167–168

Macon, Georgia, 97–101, 150

McVey, Calvin, 50, 52

Magekurth, George, 52

Mahaffey, Art, 80

Major League Baseball Players Association, 33

Makley, Roger, 242, 250, 258

Mantle, Mickey, 9, 25, 109, 116, 148

Marichal, Juan, 109

Maris, Roger, 25, 109
Martin, Billy, 176
Martino, Dana, 243–244
Marx, Jerry, 81–82
Massie, Robert, 244–245
Matlack, Jon, 149, 160
Mays, Willie, 109, 148, 149, 158, 194, 265
Messersmith, Andy, 167–168
Miller, Marvin, 166, 167, 182
Milner, Eddie, 37
Milner, John, 155
Milwaukee Braves, 109, 110
Milwaukee Brewers, 101
Minor leagues, 85–102
Montreal Expos, 28, 31, 35, 168, 180, 194, 244; Rose plays for, 28–30, 34, 228
Moose, Bob, 150
Moret, Roger, 172
Morgan, Joe, 131, 145, 146, 148–149, 150, 155, 172, 174, 188
Most Valuable Player: 1973 National League, 160; 1975 World Series, 120
Munson, Thurman, 30
Murray, Dale, 180
Murray, Jim, 135
Musial, Stan, 6, 105, 110, 115, 123, 149, 226

National League Championship Series, 145; 1970, 137; 1973, 155–160; 1975, 170; 1976, 176
National League Rookie of the Year (1963), 110
New York Haymakers, 50–51
New York Herald Tribune, 143
New York Mets, 26, 55–56, 93, 116, 149, 155–160, 230
New York Mutuals, 49, 51
New York–Penn League, 86, 89–90, 101, 268
New York Times, The, 156, 206; and 1989 gambling charges, 233–236

New York Yankees, 22, 30, 48, 53, 109, 116, 143, 167, 174, 176–177, 179–180, 182, 192, 202, 211, 223
Nickoson, Ralph, 245–246
Nixon, Richard, 113, 165
Nixon, Russ, 80, 216
Noeth, Laverne Rose (mother), 40, 44–45, 61–64, 70–74, 90, 92, 94, 102, 141
Nohr, Pappy, 80–81
Nuxhall, Joe, 230

Oakland Athletics, 150–152, 160
Odom, Blue Moon, 151
O'Malley, Walter Francis, 165
Otero, Reggie, 118
Otis, Amos, 133

Pallone, David, 230
Parker, Dave, 37, 223, 274
Parker, Harry, 159
Paternity suit, 19, 25, 218–219, 222–224, 226
Paul, Gabe, 81–82
Perez, Tony, 31, 91, 93, 124–125, 131, 136–137, 173, 174, 249; traded by Reds, 180–184
Perry, Gaylord, 126–127
Peters, Ronald, 233–234, 235, 238, 239, 242, 247–248, 256
Peterson, Fritz, 133
Philadelphia Phillies, 116, 130, 149, 202, 204–206; 1979, 209, 218, 226; 1980, 225–226; 1983, 228; Rose plays for, 209, 218, 225–228, 261–262, 286; Rose released from, 28, 228; Rose traded to, 9–10, 27–28, 31, 67, 103–104, 204–207
Piniella, Lou, 176
Pinson, Vada, 107, 108, 109, 115
Pitching, 12–13, 28, 49, 109–110, 146, 195–196
Pittsburgh Pirates, 27, 109, 116, 126, 130, 137, 150, 160, 170, 202, 204

Plant City, Florida, 277–278
Playboy interview, 210, 218–224
Press and press relations, 6, 28,
    35–37, 125–126, 135–136, 143,
    153, 164–165, 183–184,
    187–192, 202–203, 210–224;
    and 1989 gambling charges,
    233–270. *See also specific
    publications*
Profanity, 92, 93, 248–249
Professionalism, 47, 48
Purkey, Bob, 114

Rapp, Vern, 32
Records, 29; career doubles, 29,
    123, 201; five-for-five days,
    16–17; forty-four-game hitting
    streak, 7, 9, 27, 195–199; total
    hits, 7, 10, 12, 24, 37–38, 287
"Redsline" (radio show), 188–189
Reilly, Rick, 36
Reiser, Pete, 86
Relief pitching, 195–196
Reserve clause, 122, 167–168
Reston, James, 235
Rice, Jim, 223
Richardson, Bobby, 109
Rickey, Branch, 122, 212
Riverfront Stadium, 17–18, 28,
    129–130, 133
Rivers, John Milton, 30–31
Rizzuto, Phil, 197
Robertson, William, 247
Robinson, Brooks, 137–138
Robinson, Frank, 107, 108, 109
Robinson, Jackie, 6, 212
Rogers, Steve, 194
Rookie of the Year (1963), 110
Rose, Cara (daughter), 266
Rose, Carol (second wife), 16, 43,
    57, 224, 228, 256, 257, 261;
    marriage to Rose, 228, 265–
    266
Rose, Caryl (sister), 40, 64, 72
Rose, David (brother), 40, 45,
    66–70, 113
Rose, Fawn (daughter), 267–268

Rose, Harry Francis (father), 12,
    38, 43–44, 60–81, 139–142,
    215; death of, 44, 45, 141–142,
    276; relationship with Rose,
    43–44, 56–60, 71–81, 94–95,
    102, 110, 141–142, 259, 276,
    288–289
Rose, Jackie (sister), 40, 42–43,
    64
Rose, Karolyn (first wife), 10,
    163–164, 268; breakup and
    divorce from Rose, 10, 19, 25,
    104, 210–226, 286; marriage to
    Rose, 111–114, 215; *Sporting
    News* story by, 210, 212–218
Rose, Peter Edward: appearance
    of, 1, 2, 88, 94, 97, 104, 148, 165;
    birth of, 40–41, 64; breakup and
    divorce from first wife, 10, 19,
    25, 104, 210–226, 286; early life
    of, 42–44, 64–81; education of,
    2, 13, 73–81; ego of, 7, 71; as first
    baseman, 7, 119; first hit, 24;
    gambling charges (1989), 12,
    224, 231–270; as left fielder, 7,
    119, 120, 146–147; marriage to
    first wife, 111–114, 215;
    marriage to second wife, 228,
    265–266; named Charlie
    Hustle, 9; paternity suit, 19,
    25, 218–219, 222–224, 226;
    playing style, 26–27, 69, 135–
    136; relationship with his
    father, 43–44, 56–60, 71–81,
    94–95, 102, 110, 141–142, 259,
    276, 288–289; as right fielder,
    7, 119, 137, 146; as second
    baseman, 7, 61, 80, 91, 95, 96–
    97, 106–107, 117, 118–119,
    120; suspension from baseball,
    232, 252, 253, 267, 271; as
    third baseman, 7, 31, 119–120,
    169–170, 177; throwing arm,
    147–148. *See also specific
    awards; championships;
    players; positions; records;
    series; teams*

Rose, Pete, Jr. (son), 38, 225–226, 268, 270, 271, 281–283, 285–288
Rose, Tyler (son), 11, 16, 56–57, 59, 270
Rubin, Judge Carl, 241, 250
Rubio, Terryl, 222, 226
Rudi, Joe, 151
Runs scored, 102, 164
Ruth, Babe, 22, 25, 170, 179, 279
Ruthven, Dick, 33
Ryan, Bob, 170
Ryan, Nolan, 13–14
Ryba, Mike, 106

Sabo, Chris, 272, 278
Sadecki, Ray, 127
St. Louis Cardinals, 48, 82, 89, 105, 109, 116, 127, 130, 174, 202, 203, 211, 226
Salaries and contract negotiations, 5, 10, 27, 30, 32–33, 48, 82, 89–90, 109, 121–124, 132, 143–145, 152–154, 160, 193–194; and free agency, 166–169, 180, 182–183, 190; 1977, 181–192; 1978, 200–207
San Diego Padres, 18, 37–38, 202
San Francisco Examiner, 136
San Francisco Giants, 16, 101, 109, 126–127, 218
Scheele, Carl H., 71
Schmidt, Mike, 227–228
Schott, Marge, 10–12, 48, 121
Scott, Mike, 14
Scully, Vin, 58, 136
Seaver, Tom, 155
Seeberg, Tom, 131
Seghi, Phil, 81, 82, 96, 122–123
Seitz, Peter, 167, 168
Shamsky, Art, 93, 94, 97–101, 113–114
Show, Eric, 37
Simmons, Curt, 116

Sisler, Dick, 117, 119
Slaughter, Enos, 89, 211
Slumps, 92, 116, 177
Smith, Red, 168, 179, 212
Snider, Duke, 265
South Atlantic League, 86, 102
Southern League, 86
Spahn, Warren, 110, 124
Speaker, Tris, 123, 194
Speaking engagements, 162–164, 204
Spink, J. G. Taylor, 211
Sporting News, The, 47, 125, 136, 210–211; Karolyn Rose's story in, 210, 212–218
Sport magazine, 138, 174
Sports Illustrated, 36, 163, 175; and 1989 gambling charges, 233–240, 242, 260
Stargell, Willie, 150, 160, 188
Staubitz, Bill, 75, 77, 78–79, 216, 278–280
Steinbrenner, George, 30, 192
Stengel, Casey, 6, 130, 179
Stevenson, Samantha, 220–223
Stottlemyre, Mel, 133
Stowe, Bernie, 251
Stump, Al, 21–22
Sudol, Ed, 158
Sutcliffe, Rick, 280
Sutter, Bruce, 280

Tampa, Florida, 86, 96–97, 169, 187, 273
Templeton, Garry, 38
Tenace, Gene, 151–152
Tennis, 4–5, 47, 161
Tenzy, Steve, 79
Texas Rangers, 202
Tiant, Luis, 170, 173
Time magazine, 125–126, 169, 259
Tolan, Bobby, 137
Trillo, Manny, 227
Triples, 57–58, 97, 102, 130
Turner, Ted, 202, 203
Twombly, Wells, 136

Ueberroth, Peter, 233, 234, 254, 255
Umpires, 55–56

Valenzuela, Fernando, 14
Vander Meer, Johnny, 95–97
Veeck, Bill, 192
Vietnam War, 66–67, 112–113, 169
Virdon, Bill, 29, 150, 211
Vollmer, Clyde, 80

Wagner, Dick, 31, 103, 180–186, 189, 193–194, 200–201
Wagner, Honus, 22, 149
Wall Street Journal, 240
Waner, Paul, 149
Washington Post, 196, 237
Washington Senators, 107
Wehmeier, Herman, 80
Western Division Championships, 145
Western Hill Mustangs, 77–79
Weyer, Lee, 55, 56

Williams, Billy, 143
Williams, Dick, 151
Williams, Ted, 6, 115, 123, 149, 167
Wilson, Mookie, 229
Winter baseball, 117–118, 215
World Series, 146, 179, 195; 1911, 174; 1926, 174; 1952, 115; 1956, 174; 1961, 134; 1963, 109; 1964, 116; 1969, 93; 1970, 137–138; 1972, 150–152; 1973, 160; 1975, 30, 120, 169–175; 1976, 30–31, 53, 176–177, 223–224; 1977, 192; 1980, 9, 225–226; 1983, 9, 226
Wright, Clyde, 133
Wright, Harry, 48
Wynn, Early, 212

Yastrzemski, Carl, 188, 194
Young, Dick, 159

Zimmer, Don, 80

Photo Credits

Page 1: top left, Topps Baseball Card Collection; top right: courtesy of Jackie Schweir; bottom, courtesy of David Rose.

Page 2: top, courtesy of Jackie Schweir; center left, UPI/Bettmann Newsphotos; center right, courtesy of David Rose; bottom: courtesy of David Rose.

Page 3: top left, courtesy of David Rose; top right, UPI/Bettmann Newsphotos; center, courtesy of Jackie Schweir; bottom, UPI/Bettmann Newsphotos.

Page 4: top, Carl Wellinger, *Cincinnati Enquirer;* center, UPI/Bettmann Newsphotos; bottom, UPI/Bettmann Newsphotos.

Page 5: top, UPI/Bettmann Newsphotos; center, UPI/Bettmann Newsphotos; bottom, provided by David Rose.

Page 6: top, UPI/Bettmann Newsphotos; center, UPI/Bettmann Newsphotos; bottom, AP/Wide World Photos.

Page 7: top, UPI/Bettmann Newsphotos; center, UPI/Bettmann Newsphotos; bottom, AP/Wide World Photos.

Page 8: top, AP/Wide World Photos; center, UPI/Bettmann Newsphotos; bottom, AP/Wide World Photos.

Page 9: all, UPI/Bettmann Newsphotos.

Page 10: all, UPI/Bettmann Newsphotos.

Page 11: all, UPI/Bettmann Newsphotos.

Page 12: all, UPI/Bettmann Newsphotos.

Page 13: top, UPI/Bettmann Newsphotos; center, Dick Swain, *Cincinnati Enquirer;* bottom, UPI/Bettmann Newsphotos.

Page 14: top, Gerald McCauley; bottom, Michael Keating.

Page 15: all, AP/Wide World Photos.

Page 16: top, courtesy of Reuven Katz; center, courtesy of Reuven Katz; bottom, Susan M. Ogrocki/Photoreporters.